D1715955

Imre Nagy,
Martyr of the Nation

Imre Nagy, Martyr of the Nation

Contested History, Legitimacy, and Popular Memory in Hungary

Karl P. Benziger

LEXINGTON BOOKS

A DIVISION OF
ROWMAN & LITTLEFIELD PUBLISHERS, INC.
Lanham • Boulder • New York • Toronto • Plymouth, UK

LEXINGTON BOOKS

A division of Rowman & Littlefield Publishers, Inc.
A wholly owned subsidiary of The Rowman & Littlefield Publishing Group, Inc.
4501 Forbes Boulevard, Suite 200
Lanham, MD 20706

Estover Road
Plymouth PL6 7PY
United Kingdom

British Library Cataloguing in Publication Information Available

Library of Congress Cataloging-in-Publication Data

Benziger, Karl P., 1956-
  Imre Nagy, martyr of the nation : contested history, legitimacy, and popular memory in
Hungary / Karl P. Benziger.
      p. cm.
  Includes bibliographical references and index.
  ISBN-13: 978-0-7391-2330-0 (cloth : alk. paper)
  ISBN-10: 0-7391-2330-0 (pbk. : alk. paper)
  1. Nagy, Imre, 1896-1958. 2. Nagy, Imre, 1896-1958—Death and burial. 3.
  Collective memory—Hungary. 4. Hungary—History—Revolution, 1956. 5.
  Hungary—Politics and government—1989- 6. Memorialization—Hungary. I. Title.
  DB956.6.N33B46 2008
  943.905'2092—dc22   2008001515

Printed in the United States of America

Contents

Acknowledgments

The contested history of Imre Nagy fascinated me from my very first visit to Hungary, and on a subsequent stay I decided to try and get underneath the debate regarding Nagy and the various narratives forwarded by the different political parties vying for power. The story I ultimately found was that of a man very much shaped by his times, and with all the foibles that blessedly seem to inform most human beings. This makes his final stand against the Soviet backed government all the more remarkable.

The savage repression that followed in the wake of the failed Revolution was offset in part by a creeping liberalization not to be found in other parts of the Soviet sphere. Nagy and his confederates were at once cast into oblivion, only to be resurrected later by those within and outside the Hungarian Socialist Worker's Party in their bid to democratize Hungary. When the Republic was finally established, victims and perpetrators of the communist period were left living side by side. Political debates became entwined with Hungary's bitter history, and stories of collaboration with particular party strands were used to damn political opponents. The debate about Hungary's Cold War history and Nagy's place in it continues to this day, as most recently evidenced by the turbulent events that marked the fiftieth anniversary of the Hungarian Revolution of 1956.

Though writing is a solitary business this project could not have been completed without the generous assistance and guidance from the institutions and persons who have so graciously helped me along the way. I am grateful for the funding provided by the Rhode Island College Faculty Research Committee and for a sabbatical that helped fast-forward the research and writing of this book. I would be remiss not to acknowledge the impact of the Fulbright teacher exchange and a subsequent grant that fostered my interest in

Hungarian politics and history. It was a Civic Education Project grant from the Soros Foundation that allowed me to complete my dissertation centered on Nagy's memorialization. The librarians at the Széchenyi Library and the library at the University of Szeged were and remain extremely helpful as were the archivists at the Open Society Institute and the Pedagogical Archives in directing me through their vast array of resources. Interviews have been invaluable in my understanding of how texts and curriculum are understood and used in the classroom. Likewise my conversations with various political figures and historians have enlivened many parts of this story, I am indebted to the following for being so generous with their time: BenŒ Csapó, BenŒ Csapó, Sr., István Deák, Józsefné Kelemen , György Fábián, István Farkas, Éva Rostané Földényi, JenŒ Fónay, Tibor Glant, József Gréczi, Gábor Gyapay, Béla Jazimicky, RezsŒ Hidasi, Illés Kocsis, Andrea Kökény, Kálmán Kovács, Tamás Kovács, Imre Mécs, Éva Molnár, József Müller, Mihály Palinkás, Judit Pihurik, János M. Rainer, Ottó Sándorffy, Péter Szebenyi, Imre Szekeres, András Tóth, Miklós Vásárhelyi, Leo Zacharia, Béla Zárug, Péter Zoltán, and Anikó Zsolnai.

I met many wonderful people during my stay in 2006 and am especially grateful to the economist János Horváth, MP for our conversations and comments on several chapters. László Miklósi provided me with invaluable guidance regarding the problems of teaching the contested history of 1956 and the development of civil society. Likewise, László Horváth at the Pedagogical Archives provided excellent ideas and directed me to the many sources at his disposal.

My dear friends and colleagues, Huba Brückner, and Tamás Magyarics have read through many chapters and have offered encouragement and superb advice throughout my investigation. Robert Cvornyek and Anthony Carlino have remained steadfast throughout, reading through many drafts of this manuscript. In addition, I have valued the many theoretical conversations I have had with Richard Weiner and our mutual explorations of history and memory. I have had several careers before coming to the wonderful profession that I am now a part and want to thank my mentor Donald Johnson for his model of scholarly generosity and humanity and Matthew Mancini for his suggestions and guidance over the years. The photographer James Ulrich has always provided me with his expert advice regarding images and their interpretation. He graciously prepared the photos included in this book. Finally, I would like to thank my editors at Lexington Books, Julie Kirsch and Jessica Bradfield for all of their help in getting this book to print.

The most fortuitous happenstance of my life, however, was in Hungary when I met my wife Klára Benzigerné Gendur. In all of my work she has provided invaluable help with translation. Her knowledge of 19th and 20th century Hungarian literature and music was essential to my understanding of the subject. She accompanied me on all interviews and on my many visits to libraries and archives. Her desire to understand the history and politics of the post World War II period matches mine and together we have enjoyed this exploration. This book is dedicated to our two children Emese and George who will be the next generation to shape the interpretation of this bitter history and will hopefully learn lessons that will lead to a more peaceful and less vengeful world.

Chapter One

Introduction

On June 16, 1958, Imre Nagy the Prime Minister of Hungary during the ill-fated Revolution of 1956, was put to death by the Soviet-backed regime of János Kádár and buried in an unmarked grave. Thirty-three years later, in a spectacular reversal of fortune, the communist regime was de-legitimized by the public funeral and reburial of Imre Nagy, a ceremony attended by well over 300,000 Hungarians. In a forceful assertion of the collective will, the Hungarian people demonstrated their power to resist the tyranny of foreign occupation and made plain their desire for an autonomous state. A referendum held in November of that year underscored the Hungarian people's desire to strip the Communist Party of power. But with sovereignty assured, the seeming unity displayed at the funeral quickly disintegrated. A fierce dispute publicly emerged between the various political factions in regard to Nagy's place in Hungarian history; encapsulated by the 1996 parliamentary debate over a bill making him a martyr of the nation, a debate that persists to this day.

The Hungarian Revolution of 1956 was one of the most significant events within the Soviet sphere during the Cold War. Imre Nagy was a central figure in this drama whose memory continues to haunt the contemporary political landscape. *Imre Nagy Martyr of the Nation: Contested History, Legitimacy, and Public Memory in Hungary* is a study of the ways in which commemoration and mythmaking conditions the process of political socialization in contemporary Hungarian society. Politicized memory is seen in this present study as a critical contingency that must be factored into any comprehensive, scholarly discussion of the period. Though the political transition in Hungary was characterized by negotiation, the power of the opposition rested in the legitimacy accorded to it by a majority of the Hungarian people. The significance of popular interpretation is revealed in the *memorialization* of Nagy in

1989 and the subsequent debate over memory exemplified by the parliamentary debates that took place in 1996. This debate still continues to inhabit contemporary political discourse to this day. The story is compelling because it is one of transformation and redemption.

Nagy had been a co-founder of the Stalinist one-party state established in Hungary in 1948 and had remained passive in the wake of juridical murder unleashed by the state-sanctioned terror that followed. Infighting within the Hungarian Communist Party over issues of land reform and collectivization were subdued by the iron hand of Joseph Stalin's Hungarian disciple, Mátyás Rákosi. Nagy's confrontation with the Stalinist faction over agriculture and other economic reforms was facilitated by Nikita Khrushchev's critique of Stalin following Stalin's death in 1953. Nagy's demand for an ending of show trials and the rehabilitation of the victims was in line with Moscow's desire to stabilize Hungary in the wake of Rákosi's failed policies and can be seen as part of Nagy's attempt to undermine his opponents. Nagy's reforms were met with resistance by the Stalinist faction who ultimately engineered his ouster from power and the Hungarian Workers' Party (MDP). Yet his reforms for open discussion of economic and political policy continued within writer's circles and kept his reform agenda alive. The continued political instability led to his return to power. The Revolution that swept across Hungary on October 23, 1956, was accompanied by the demand from students and workers that Nagy return as Prime Minister. Interestingly, their demands for political change that included sovereignty and a democratic state had largely outpaced Nagy's earlier calls for reform in the context of a one-party state. Nagy, who remained committed to communism until the end of his life, was initially not in accord with the demands for a democratic republic and only slowly joined with the demands of the revolutionaries. His choice to join in the doomed quest to establish a democracy on October 30, ultimately led to the gibbet and his martyrdom. As a martyr of the Revolution, however, he signified a longing for a national identity tied to the spirit of democracy with roots going back to the Hungarian Revolution of 1848. In 1989 both reformers within the Communist Party and the various opposition parties made plain their association with Imre Nagy at the funeral in 1989. But after sovereignty was assured what was it that Nagy signified?

CONTESTED HISTORY AND THE UNSAVORY PAST

In 1992 I was the recipient of a Fulbright Teaching Scholarship to Hungary, which began my long-term relationship with the country and region. During my stay, the first of many, Hungary was in the process of re-evaluating its tortured twentieth-century past. Foremost was the relationship between the two communist regimes and the center right government dominated by the Hungarian Democratic Forum (MDF) and the more distant past encompassing Hungary's loss of two-thirds of its territory by the Treaty of Trianon from 1920 through World War II. What I found most fascinating during my stays was the variety of factional interpretations and their construction. What was left in and what was left out were all marked by furious responses from political parties excoriated in the context of these narratives. The staying power of the debate was underscored by the various political fights between the several governments following the second election in 1994 when the Socialist's center-left coalition took power. The infighting reminded me of my time as a social studies teacher in New York City and the controversy over what constituted national history. For example, a very different narrative can be constructed in the story of the American civil rights movement that includes or neglects figures such as Malcolm X or Ida Wells.[1] During the course of a debate over National History Standards in the United States Senate it was argued that narratives highlighting or including the radical stream in the political history of the United States tended to create a divisive rather than a unifying story of America.[2] Grand narratives are critical to the political process in both the United States and Hungary for their perceived legitimizing effects by political parties vying for power. They also represent an attempt at sealing off memory as the narratives selectively choose what is included or excluded from the story being told. This often leaves the trauma associated with an event such as the Hungarian Revolution and its demobilization unresolved.[3] The contrast between competing narratives is something that my students, both high school and college level, find both entertaining and interesting. The centrality of Imre Nagy to the construction of these various Hungarian grand narratives coupled with his controversial past captures the imagination and accounts for his durability as a national figure, though not without its own contestation.

Though subdued by issues of economy and transitioning into the European Union, the debate regarding Nagy and the Revolution continues to percolate beneath the surface of politics, and erupting in the course of elections and events commemorating the past. The competing grand narratives in Hungary almost assure that this will happen. How is it possible to write history in such circumstances where these stories are used for political ends? The Historian's Debate asked West Germans to "master the National Socialist past" in order to refocus on Germany's history in the long term. This attempt included an attempt to relativize the Holocaust. For example, the historian Joachim Fest argued for a moral equivalence in which the terror of Stalin is compared with that of the Holocaust, in which Hitler's obsession with extermination of the Jews is premised on the atrocities committed by the Soviet Union.[4]

The historian Martin Broszat asserted that memory is selective and often without nuance, and leads towards a tendency to the mythic. In this light, the emotional stories of the victims of the Holocaust create a block to an objective understanding of the period. Historicization, however, searches for complexity and nuance as a counter to mythologizing an event such as the Holocaust.[5] This separation between history and memory, however, was rejected by the historian Saul Friedlander who claimed, "When past and present remain interwoven, there is no clear dichotomy between history and memory." The demands for an objective history of the National Socialist period are naïve as they are informed by politically motivated agendas that create yet another narrative "dominated by the new agenda."[6] For example, in the context of the Cold War, German actions in the east at the end of World War II could be portrayed as an attempt to stymie the red tide from encroachment on the West, certainly suitable for those historians and politicians wishing to move beyond the stigma of the Nazi past, rather than an objective accounting.[7]

According to Friedlander, memory must play a role in the creation of historical narratives where the story of the past remains unresolved. On one hand, memory can easily be used to manipulate our understanding of the past as personal and political interests provide only selective accountings.[8] And yet, when taking this interestedness into account, perpetrators, victims, collaborators, and observers all have stories to tell that can provide valuable insights as to how events unfolded and how these varied interpretations were intended to be passed on to the next generation.[9] According to the historian Charles Maier ". . . it can be used not to confront the past, but to complicate it."[10] It is just these complications stemming from the memories of the participants that can serve to challenge widely held generalizations and interpretations.[11] The continuing debate over Nagy and the Revolution is indicative of a past not worked out. Intimations from various parties to master the past and move on further emphasize this unease.

Hungarian Prime Minister Ferenc Gyurcsány of the Socialist Party and President László Sólyom a founding member of MDF, though now unaffiliated claimed it was their intention to celebrate the fiftieth anniversary commemorations of the Revolution with the entire country. This seemingly echoed the desire of Jenő Fónay, a revolutionary and member of the *Emlékévet Elökészitö Bizottság* (Committee to Prepare for the Anniversary Year), that the central monument being constructed on the site of a monument to Joseph Stalin that was torn down in the early course of the Revolution, would bring new meaning and a renewed sense of solidarity among the Hungarian people. Underlying these assertions of unity, however, was a sense of bitterness that threatened to dilute the plans for a unified celebration. Mária Wittner, another revolutionary and a member of the leading opposition party

Young Democrats (FIDESZ), bitterly criticized what she claimed was a false sense of unity asserting that, "we are not going to assist in the preparation for the commemorations [in this context]." Raising the linkage between the Socialist Party and the former Communist Party she stated, "Those who suppressed or assisted in the suppression of the Revolution will have their celebration and those righteous people [revolutionaries and those who remained true to those ideals] will have their celebrations."[12]

Wittner's sentiments were verified in the context of the forty-eighth anniversary of Nagy's execution on June 16, 2006. Instead of a unified national memorial ceremony, various parties and factions memorialized Nagy separately. FIDESZ and the *Nagy Imre Alapítvány* (Imre Nagy Foundation) placed their wreathes at the grave site and later at the memorial of Imre Nagy in front of Parliament separately in the morning, ahead of the Socialists and the MDF who laid their wreathes in the afternoon. This is not a new issue. The inability to let go of the past for the sake of unity was first raised to me by both Imre Mécs, a former revolutionary and member of the Free Democrats (SZDSZ) and Miklós Vásárhelyi, who had been the government spokesman in the 1956 Nagy government and one of the founding members of the Historical Justice Committee that sought the rehabilitation of Imre Nagy and his confederates. Both men had been sentenced to prison for their roles in the Revolution. They claimed that the commemoration of Nagy and the Revolution in concert with the Socialists was not possible.[13] Working out of the trauma left in the wake of juridical murder, collaboration, and the corruption of the state, would be left to another generation to work through.

Political transition in Hungary was the result of many factors, including the reforms of Mikhail Gorbachev and the recognition that the overextension of the Soviet Union's empire had led to fiscal disaster. Hungary's financial woes led to a split within the Communist Party and coupled with Gorbachev's reforms of perestroika and glasnost provided an opening for a burgeoning opposition to negotiate change. But the question of political legitimacy loomed large over these problems and the opposition's use of the 1956 Revolution and Nagy's symbolic status underpinned their platforms and negotiations.

The story I wish to tell concerns one of contested history and the myth-making that accompanies the various politicized versions of the national spirit centered on Imre Nagy, beginning with his funeral and the ensuing discourse regarding his contested status as martyr of the nation, all the while looking back to the narrative strands that his memory conjures. A brief review of Nagy's life and crucial moments in recent Hungarian history reveals the contested meanings and contradictions surrounding Nagy and his legacy. The study concludes with the fiftieth anniversary commemorations of the 1956 Revolution and contemporary interpretations of Nagy's memory. The comprehensive and detailed description of Nagy's funeral in 1989 and the debate over his memory is informed by documents and interviews by many of the actors in this politicized drama. In order to bring the reader closer to this contested history I have included textual materials used in secondary and university education. My interviews with teachers further illuminate the pedagogical consequences of political socialization and debate in Hungary before and after 1989.

Are there lessons to be learned from this story? Perhaps so, as this story at once reviews the past and provides insight as to its influence and legitimizing effects in contemporary politics. The concept of the modern state exuded by either of the superpowers during the Cold War was ultimately conditioned by the distinct institutions and politics that inform Hungarian society, a lesson that might be applied to contemporary efforts at state shaping and nation building.

COMMEMORATION AND POLITICS IN HUNGARY

The funeral of Imre Nagy dramatically symbolized the legitimacy of the 1956 Revolution and its ability to sweep aside the thin veneer of legitimacy of the Soviet-backed regime. Hungary's tormented past provides fertile ground for contentious battles over memory and Nagy's commemoration provided the ideal setting with which to link 1848, 1956, and 1989 together in order to fortify the opposition's demand for a sovereign democratic state.

Hungary had been a powerful medieval kingdom until its defeat at the hands of Suleiman the Magnificent at the Battle of Mohács on August 29, 1526. From this time on except for brief intervals, the Hungarians have been under either direct occupation, or under the hegemony of another state—the Ottoman Empire, the Austrian Hapsburgs, Germany, and the Soviet Union. Occupation, warfare, and migration changed the nature of the Hungarian population over time. Hungary today is an ethnographic composite of Magyars, Jews, Germans, Serbs, and Slavs.[14] The appearance of a cohesive national culture is maintained primarily by language and Hungary's long history in Europe. But it is the very interpretation of this history that creates fault lines within the polity.

The interpretation of national symbols is intimately interwoven with power politics in Hungary and used as guideposts to specific points of memory utilized by all political parties in their bid for political legitimacy.[15] Political parties use this tradition to create historical narratives that legitimize their platforms and damn their opponents. The tumultuous history of the twentieth century ensures that the traps laid by various factions vying for power are particularly treacherous. Nagy as a communist presents problems for those espousing a liberal model of economic development. Charges of collaboration with Hungary's two communist regimes abound. In kind, politics that centered on anti-bolshevism and territorial revision of Hungary's interwar regime under Miklós Horthy, or Hungary's immediate post–World War II regime is freighted with linkages to the Axis powers and genocide. Political legitimacy in the newly founded Republic of Hungary pivoted on the reconciliation of factional and popular interpretations that either subdued or highlighted various aspects of Nagy's symbolic status and the events of 1956.

At a macro level, Nagy's relationship with either the Soviet Union or the United States in the context of the Cold War is not clear cut. His confrontation with the Stalinist faction inside Hungary at once seemed to be in accord with the official critique of Joseph Stalin by Nikita Khrushchev and Moscow. And yet, his political and economic reforms centered on light industry, slowing down of agricultural collectivization, and pluralism within the context of a one-party state ultimately placed him at odds with Moscow. His faithfulness to communism made him largely unpalatable to the United States. Sadly, only with the failure of the Revolution and his execution did Nagy become emblematic of the American desire to undermine communism in the satellite states of the Soviet Union.

This new examination of Nagy presents an opportunity to offer a more pragmatic approach to the politics of memory and contested history backed by a story mostly narrated by the actors themselves. In this study theory is not predictive, but is meant to provide a frame to examine and better understand the paradox of the seeming social solidarity presented at Nagy's funeral and the dissident narrative constructs that preceded and followed the event.

Funeral rituals are informed by the concept of *kegyelet*. *Kegyelet* is synonymous with Emile Durkheim's concept of piacular rites and is defined as duty towards the dead.[16] Though similar to memorial practice found in much of Central Europe, the historian István Rév explains that the "history of Hungary is one of battles lost, the normal public rituals are therefore funerals and burials rather than victory parades."[17] The political connection between personal funeral ritual and the state is made explicit in national public rituals that mimic the very personal remembrance that is the essence of *kegyeleti* ritual.

The manipulation of public memory is a function of power used by the political elite to forward their various political ends. Public memory links the present to the past and serves to underscore the legitimacy of the commemoration.[18] Not surprisingly, memorialization of national heroes has a long tradition in Hungarian politics. The establishment of the Dual Monarchy in 1867 enabled the Hungarians to re-imagine the glory of their past medieval kingdom. Though international affairs remained the provenance of Vienna, Emperor Franz Joseph was crowned with the crown of St. Steven, thus legitimizing him as a Hungarian King.[19] Outward manifestations of Hungary's "restored" glory could be found in the restoration of the Mátyás Templom that brought back to light the gothic features of the church and added neo-gothic touches to make it fit the nineteenth-century conception of what a gothic church should look like.[20] The present Hungarian Parliament building that has housed that legislative body since 1904 represented the modern state that Hungary wished to become and at the same time with its heraldry and architecture, linked Hungary to an older more powerful conception of the medieval state. Domestic affairs within the newly conceived kingdom was the concern of Hungarians, Hungarian became the official language in legal and academic institutions. According to the historian and diplomat Géza Jeszenszky, many Hungarians believed that economic growth and the process of forcing the various ethnic minorities within Hungary to assimilate into the dominant Hungarian culture, a process known as *Magyarization*, would be the formula that would lead to the rebirth of the Hungarian "empire of Mátyás Corvinus."[21]

Funerals in the wake of the failed 1848 Revolution served to fortify Hungarian nationalism. The return of the remains of the 1848 revolutionary Lajos Kossuth in 1894 from Turin, Italy, was marked by a funeral accompanied by three days of mourning.[22] According to historian Alice Freifeld the return and eventual interment of Ferenc Rákóczi II, leader of the failed Rákóczi Rebellion against the Hapsburgs, 1704–1711, was linked to the romanticized myth of the nation surrounding Kossuth and 1848. Public sentiment was such that Emperor Franz Joseph rescinded a law that had declared, "Rákóczi a traitor and [by extension] accepted the cult of an anti-Hapsburg rebel."[23]

The manipulation of symbols can take odd turns. Commemorations of the 1848 Revolution could not be stymied by the Hapsburgs. The ideals of national sovereignty and the demand for a democratic republic embodied in Sándor Petőfi's poem, *Nemzeti Dal* (National Verse) and the twelve student demands are fundamental to the March 15 commemoration of the day the Revolution began (see Appendix A). And yet, in the twentieth century the holiday was appropriated by the interwar regime of Miklós Horthy and the two communist regimes following World War II, both staunchly at odds with the liberal principles that marked the Hungarian Republic of 1848. During the interwar period the theme of national sacrifice was highlighted but the liberal aspirations of the Revolution were downplayed, whereas the communists played upon the theme of national liberation that emphasized the Soviet liberation of Hungary from fascism. In the communist portrayal it was Joseph Stalin who completed the work of the revolutionary Lajos Kossuth who became Governor of the Hungarian Republic in 1849.[24]

The appropriation of March 15 however, unintentionally set the Stalinist politics against the liberal principles set out in 1848 creating a counter narrative.[25] Not only was the holiday celebrated publicly, but these stirring poems and student demands could be found in secondary school textbooks used by students. It was no wonder then that the revolutionaries of 1956 were able to successfully link themselves to the spirit of 1848.

Now connected to the success of the Republic of Hungary, stories of national resistance in the face of failure continue in the contemporary period. For example, October 6, 1849, marked the day that Lajos Batthyány, Prime Minister during the Hungarian Republic 1848–1849 was executed by the Austrians in 1849 and reburied with honors in Pest in 1870.[26] On the same day Batthyány was executed 13 Hungarian generals met the same fate in the city of Arad (now in Romania). Hungarians use the term *vértanu* (blood witness) to describe martyrs of the nation. Their sacrifice is remembered by schoolchildren and political parties with flowers and candles at places of remembrance such as the Eternal Light Monument in Budapest that is dedicated to Batthyány's memory.[27]

The power of commemoration to stimulate controversy in contemporary Hungary is amply demonstrated on St. Steven's Day, a national holiday that celebrates the first king of Hungary on the twentieth of August. A *Búcsú* is the memorial day of a saint in the Roman Catholic calendar and has its origins in medieval times. Statues and plaques of Hungary's first king are highly decorated with the Hungarian tricolor (red, white, and green) flowers, wreathes, and ribbons, often from Hungary's leading political parties. According to legend, Steven founded the Hungarian kingdom in A.D. 996. The relic of St. Steven's hand is presented to the people at an outdoor mass held in front of St. Steven's Basilica in Budapest and is followed by a procession in the streets. The relic is given an official military honor guard and at the service in front of the basilica, Steven is invoked to intercede on behalf of the Hungarian nation for God's protection and guidance. The day mixes solemnity and celebration and is marked by fireworks and fairs heralding the end of summer.

The seeming political solidarity marked by large crowds at the basilica and at the fairs is betrayed by the procession itself, revealing one of the major fault lines in politics. One of the songs sung during the procession is known as the Székely Hymn. The Székelys were warriors given the task of protecting Hungary's eastern borders during the medieval period. The hymn was written by Kálmán Mihalik and György Csanád in 1921 one year after the Treaty of Trianon in which Hungary lost two-thirds of its territory and one-half of its inhabitants in consequence for Hungary's alliance with the Central Powers during World War I. Many nationalist factions in Hungary feel that the punishing terms of the treaty became reality as a result of Hungary's brief Communist Revolution of 1919. At the precession on August 20, 2006, the Miklós Horthy Society replete with a banner bearing Horthy's likeness, preceded a replica of St. Steven's Crown and at once resurrected memories of the National Christian platform that informed Horthy's ideology, which included policies promoting anti-Bolshevism, territorial revision, and anti-Semitism.

The dynamics of politicized commemoration can be potent. In the case of Nagy's funeral this process was powerful enough to signify what the sociologist János Kis calls the "moral ending" of the communist regime and is in part responsible for the success of the largest opposition party, MDF (Hungarian Democratic Forum), to win at the polls in 1990.[28]

Political scientist Katherine Verdery claims that Nagy's symbolic magnetism can be found in his power to legitimate a diverse number of platforms.[29] According to Verdery, Nagy has legitimating effects "not because everyone agrees on [his] meaning but because it compels interest despite divergent views of what [he signifies].[30] Because of this, Verdery claims that she is "not interested in the shared mentalities found in the conscience collective, but for conflict among groups over social meanings."[31]

This first level of meaning revealed by the funeral was a yearning for the democratic republic inspired by the martyred Nagy. It was largely unencumbered by the more complicated narratives that inform Hungarian twentieth-century history. Factional dissonance was present, but was temporarily subdued by this unity of purpose. The effervescent moment of unity was short lived, however, as evidenced by the ensuing debate over the nature of the state and Nagy's symbolic status. It is this contest that returns us to factional understandings that preceded the funeral. The establishment of the Republic served to enliven debate over Hungary's past and underlined the more complicated narratives in which various factions within the opposition and the Communist Party utilized Nagy's symbolic status both positively and negatively to legitimize their assorted agendas.

What was the meaning of Nagy's symbolic status in a country whose revolutionary spirit had been largely subdued and co-opted by the socialist "prosperity" that separated Hungary from other socialist countries under the Soviet thrall? In this guise, historical attachment needed to be found in the events leading up to the Revolution or prior to the ascension of the Stalinists in 1948. As we have seen, Nagy, who played a key role in the establishment of the Stalinist state, is problematic to the kind of heroic narrative used to legitimize various contemporary political factions, especially those that view the political transition of 1989 as the triumph of the capitalist model. Historical memory in this light is selective.

The politicized stories of Nagy and the Revolution that haunt the contemporary Hungarian political landscape are important because they anchor the various constructs of national identity and are critical to what Verdery refers to as "new meaning-creation."[32] The centrality of Nagy's role in the Revolution assures that he must be confronted in any discussion of 1956 and its relation to the Republic of Hungary after 1989 that is open to a continuing revision.[33]

This study begins with the funeral of Imre Nagy. The funeral begged the question as to what was the meaning of 1956 in 1989 and forcefully brought the contested interpretations of Nagy and the Revolution to the fore shortly after the funeral. The next several chapters return to 1956 and earlier points in Nagy's life, not to retell in full the story of the rise of the Stalinists or the Revolution, but to better understand the contested interpretations that emerged publicly after the funeral.

The potential volatility of state funerals can be exemplified by the funeral of László Rajk on October 6, 1956. Rajk had been the Minister of the Interior in the Stalinist regime of Mátyás Rákosi, and had the unfortunate privilege of being one of the first victims of Rákosi's show trials in 1949. His funeral can be viewed as one of the critical generators of radicalism prior to the 1956 Revolution. Both Rajk and Nagy were committed communists who actively worked to establish a Stalinist state within Hungary. They were not particularly interested in political pluralism. How was it that both men were transformed into symbols associated with national solidarity and the procedural republic demanded by the student and worker councils in October and November of 1956?

The brutality and scope of Rákosi's policies affected not only the political elite but a wide swath of the Hungarian population and a summary of these policies will help the reader understand the public groundswell of criticism against the Stalinist state prior to the Revolution. Further, memory of this period informs the contemporary politics of the right that includes an abiding mistrust of Nagy. Nagy's reform program and infighting within the Hungarian Workers' Party (MDP) are also reviewed in order to provide the reader with the necessary background to understand the significance of his actions during the Revolution. The summary ends with an examination of the demobilization put into action in the wake of the Revolution's failure and the paradox of many Hungarian's simultaneous sympathy with Kádárizmus and the Revolutionaries. Critical to this review of the Kádár regime is the role that schools and the attending curriculum centered on the "sorrowful October events [of 1956]" played in legitimizing the regime.

The final chapters of the book center on the contemporary debate over Nagy, the Revolution, and the politics of memory. Popular interpretation of Nagy helped set the terms of the debate between political factions vying for power during and after the transition from a communist to democratic state. The significance is borne out through an examination of parliamentary debates centered on Nagy and the 1956 Revolution that took place after the transition. Special attention is paid to the First Act of Parliament, 1990 and the Debate over the Imre Nagy Memory Bill, 1996. Political legitimacy in the newly founded republic pivoted on the reconciliation of factional and popular interpretations that either heightened or subdued various aspects of Nagy's symbolic status and the events of 1956.

My examination of the factional interpretation of Nagy and the Revolution continues with a close examination of secondary school texts, curricula, and practice. An examination of these materials is salient to understanding the process of political socialization, for it is in this context that the community and state meet and the public interpretation of symbols is discussed and reconciled. After 1989 texts and curricula reflect the contested memory of Nagy and the Revolution underlining continued unease with this historical period and the debate in the public arena.

The study concludes with an analysis of the debate over Nagy, the Revolution, and the bitter history of Hungary during the twentieth century set in the context of the fiftieth anniversary commemorations and in light of severe austerity measures and continued anxiety over integration into the European Union. What role does history and memory play in contemporary political debates that often seem disconnected to the daily struggles of the Hungarian people? Why should we pay attention to the Hungarian case? Perhaps the answer lies in part when we ask ourselves how we remember our own heroes. What is it that is worth remembering about us?

NOTES

1. The equalitarian playing field is a key value held dear by Americans and is reflected in social studies textbooks that portray the story of American development as one of continuous upward progress. The politics of confrontation regarding access to civil rights after the Civil War belies this story and the notion that the former slaves were ignorant of, or not yet competent to make use of fundamental legal principles such as equal access to the law. Further, narratives that include the confrontational politics of Ida Wells or Malcolm X, highlight the racism, violence, and denial of civil rights in contrast to the U.S. Constitution, thus providing a rationale for resistance and a reevaluation of radical politics generally not found in American high school texts through 1970. See: Seymour Martin Lipsett's discussion of "American Exceptionalism" in, *First New Nation* (New York: W. W. Norton and Company, 1960), 110–12, 203–4. An excellent overview of the Traditional vs. Revisionist debate was commissioned by the Executive Board of the Organization of American Historians entitled, "History, Democracy, and Citizenship: The Debate over History's Role in Teaching Citizenship and Patriotism" (2004) http://www.oah.org/reports/tradhist.html. Recent

scholarship locates the development of black radicalism in the immediate post–World War II period and before. For example: Peniel Joseph, "Waiting for the Midnight Hour: Reconceptualizing the Heroic Period of the Civil Rights Movement, 1954–1965," *Souls* (Spring, 2000): 8, Mary L. Dudziak, *Cold War Civil Rights: Race and the Image of American Democracy* (Princeton: Princeton University Press, 2000) and, Timothy B. Tyson *Radio Free Dixie: Robert F. Williams and the Roots of Black Power* (Chapel Hill: University of North Carolina Press, 1999).

2. The United States Senate voted in January 1995, 99–1 that the *National Standards for History* outlined by the National Center for History, that was initially strongly endorsed and funded by the U.S. government, not be certified and to allot no more monies for the production of standards by the Center. See: Gary B. Nash, Charlotte Crabtree, and Ross E. Dunn, *History on Trial: Culture Wars and the Teaching of the Past* (New York: Alfred K. Knopf, 1997), 231–35.

3. The historian Dominick La Capra addressing the problems of selective generalizations set out by various historians in the course of the *historikerstreit* (historian's debate) asserts, "Extreme or limit-events involving trauma pose especially severe problems for processes of coming to terms with the past." "Revisiting the Historian's Debate: Mourning and Genocide," *History and Memory*, 9, 1/2 (Fall, 1997): 84.

4. See: Charles S. Maier, "Immoral Equivalence: Revising the Nazi Past for the Kohl Era," *Reworking the Past: Hitler, the Holocaust, and the Historian's Debate*, Ed. Peter Baldwin (Boston: Beacon Press, 1990), 38–39, 42.

5. See "Martin Broszat and the Historicization of National Socialism," in Saul Friedlander, *Memory, History, and the Extermination of the Jews in Europe* (Bloomington: Indiana University Press, 1993), 95–96.

6. See: Saul Friedlander, "A Conflict of Memories? The New German Debates about the Final Solution," Leo Baeck Memorial Lecture 31 (Leo Baeck Institute: New York, 1988), 18.

7. Stories of forced marches made by the remaining concentration victims and the multitude of German sponsored atrocities are subdued in order to tell the story of the desperate struggle made by the German army to save the West. For the conservative Christian Democrat Helmut Kohl and allies this more heroic construction of history was useful in promoting a national story that emphasized West Germany's importance as an economic power and the integral role Germany had played standing against communism. See: Anson Rabinbach, "The Jewish Question in the German Question," in *Reworking the Past*, 61, 66 and Charles Maier, *The Unmasterable Past: History, Holocaust, and German National Identity* (Cambridge: Harvard University Press, 1988), 21–25.

8. Maier, *The Unmasterable Past*, 162.

9. James E. Young, "Between History and Memory: The Uncanny Voices of Historian and Survivor," *History and Memory*, 9, 1/2 (Fall, 1997): 50–51, 56–57.

10. Maier, *The Unmasterable Past*, 161.

11. For example, Saul Friedlander uses this technique as he debunks the myth of German ignorance of the Holocaust in *The Years of Extermination: Nazi Germany and the Jews, 1939–1945* (New York: Harper Collins Publishers, 2007), xxvi, 510–17.

12. Zsolt Gréczy, "Két ünnepre készül a jobboldal?" (Does the right wing prepare for two celebrations?), *Népszabadság*, Friday, June 16, 2006, 3.

13. Vásárhelyi was put on trial with Nagy. Miklós Vásárhelyi, interview by author, Budapest, Hungary, October 7, 1997. Imre Mécs, interview by author, Budapest, Hungary, November 7, 1997.

14. Péter Hanák, "A nemzeti identitás konstrukciója" (The structure of national identity), *Európai Szemle* 3 (October, 1997): 66–67.

15. I am referring here to the anthropologist Clifford Geertz and his extension of the sociologist Max Weber's concept of *verstehen* in his work *Local Knowledge* (New York: Basic Books Inc., 1983), 122–23, 142–46.

16. Emile Durkheim, *The Elementary Forms of the Religious Life*, trans. Joseph Ward Swain (New York, 1965), 446.

17. István Rév, "Parallel Autopsies," *Representations*, 49 (Winter, 1995): 31.

18. See John Bodnar's discussion of public memory in "Public Memory in an American City: Commemoration in Cleveland," in *Commemorations: The Politics of National Memory*, edited by John R. Gillis (Princeton: Princeton University Press, 1994), 75. See also Katherine Verdery's discussion of the use of dead bodies by the elite in post Socialist societies to create new meaning in *The Political Lives of Dead Bodies: Reburial and Post Socialist Change* (New York: Columbia University Press, 1999), 50–51 and Patrick H. Hutton, "Sigmund Freud and Maurice Halbwachs: The Problem of Memory in Historical Psychology," *The History Teacher*, 27, 2 (February, 1994): 150.

19. Benedict Anderson, *Imagined Communities: Reflections on the Origin and Spread of Nationalism* (New York: Verso, 1991), 82. See also: Éva Somogyi, "The Age of Neoabsolutism, 1849–1867," in *A History of Hungary*, ed. Peter F. Sugar, Péter Hanák, Tibor Frank (Bloomington: Indiana University Press, 1994), 251.

20. John Lukacs, *Budapest 1900* (New York: Grove Weidenfeld, 1988), 50.

21. Géza Jeszenszky, "Hungary through World War I and the End of the Dual Monarchy," *A History of Hungary*, 270. Mátyás Corvinus, 1458–1490 is known as Hungary's renaissance king who brought Hungary's power to an apex prior to the Ottoman incursion.

22. Lukacs, *Budapest 1900,* 120.

23. Alice Freifeld, *Nationalism and the Crowd in Liberal Hungary, 1848–1914* (Baltimore: The Johns Hopkins University Press, 2000), 288.

24. Alice Freifeld, "The Cult of March 15: Sustaining the Hungarian Myth of Revolution, 1849–1999," in *Staging the Past: The Politics of Commemoration in Hapsburg Central Europe, 1848 to the Present*, ed. Maria Bucur and Nancy M. Wingfield (West Lafayette, IN: Purdue University Press, 2001), 264–76.

25. Maria Burcur discusses this problem in her essay, "Birth of a Nation: Commemorations of December 1, 1918, and National Identity in Twentieth-Century Romania," in *Staging the Past*, 289.

26. Freifeld remarks that the "commemoration of the Revolution and monarchy could not be disentangled." As mentioned earlier the Compromise of 1867 provided for the crowning of Franz Joseph as the Hungarian monarch. In this guise many Hungarians could swear allegiance to the king and maintain a deep loyalty to the Revolu-

tion. Freifeld's chapter "The Celebration of Compromise," in *Nationalism and the Crowd in Liberal Hungary*, especially pages 220–23.

27. On October 6, 1997, I observed a class of schoolchildren with their teachers lighting candles at the monument. October 6, 2006, revealed a monument well remembered by the major political parties. The importance of sites of memory relating to the 1848 Hungarian Revolution and their interpretation in the twentieth century can also be found in John Mason's excellent article, "Hungary's Battle for Memory," *History Today*, 50, 3 (March, 2000): 28–34.

28. János Kis, "Between Reform and Revolution: Three Hypotheses about the Nature of the Regime Change," *Lawful Revolution in Hungary, 1989–94*, Béla K. Király and András Bozóki, ed., (New York: Columbia University Press, 1995), 41.

29. Clifford Geertz discusses the importance of charismatic figures in their ability to stimulate both negative and positive political dialogue in his seminal essay "Centers, Kings, and Charisma: Reflections on the Symbolics of Power," in *Local Knowledge: Further Essays in Interpretive Anthropology* (New York: Basic Books, 1983).

30. Verdery, *The Political Lives of Dead Bodies,* 31.

31. Verdery, *The Political Lives of Dead Bodies*, 36.

32. "Nationalism is a kind of ancestor worship . . . Given this view, the work of contesting national histories and repositioning temporal landmarks . . . challenges the whole national genealogy." From "Dead Bodies Animate the Study of Politics," in Verdery, *The Political Lives of Dead Bodies*, 41, 51.

33."Ghosts arise from unsettled graves—from deaths that trouble the living . . ." Charles Lemert, *Durkheim's Ghosts: Cultural Logics and Social Things* (Cambridge: Cambridge University Press, 2006), 26–27.

Chapter Two

The Funeral of Imre Nagy: The Meaning of 1956 in 1989

If you are without guilt, then those who sent you to the gallows are murderers. Let their punishment be the contempt of the nation . . .

—Tibor Méray[1]

The power of Imre Nagy's symbolic status was well understood by the Soviet-backed regime when it replaced Nagy's revolutionary government in the wake of the Revolution's failure. János Kádár had Nagy's body, as well as the bodies of his Minister of Defense Pál Maléter and Press Secretary Miklós Gimes, buried under a garbage heap near the site of their execution on June 16, 1958. It wasn't until February 1961 that the bodies were moved from Gyüjtőfogház Prison to Plot 301 in the Köztemető (Public Cemetery) and buried anonymously with other victims of Kádár's terror.[2]

Nagy was controversial in life. His national communist platform made him a difficult fit both for those within the Communist Party and for those who espoused the vision of a Hungarian Republic akin to the short-lived one of 1848. It was his decision to join with the revolutionaries demands and establish the Republic of October 30, 1956, a decision that ensured his status in death as a martyred Prime Minister, embodying both the trauma and hope of the Revolution. In death his body was abused in the same manner as the other revolutionaries executed by the regime and represented an extraordinary affront to a large majority of Hungarians. The funeral of Imre Nagy represented the culmination of a long-term strategy of protest in which the demand for a proper burial was linked to the legitimacy of the state. Hungary has a history of linking political legitimacy with memorial practices that dates back to the nineteenth century. The hope of national continuity is made manifest in the context of funereal rites. It is the politicized rites of memorial that include the

17

burial of the dead and the remembrance of symbolic figures that assist in linking Hungarian identity to the concept of community and nation.

The construction of national history in this guise is intimately interwoven with the symbols of national identity. Whether originating from the 1848 Hungarian Revolution or points from Hungary's distant past, what binds these diverse acts of memorial together are their focus on national sovereignty. The string of disasters that has befallen Hungary since the Battle of Mohács in 1526, recognized in Hungary's National Anthem, underscores the importance of memorial in the political process.[3] As such, the arrangement of tragic hero figures can create differing chains of history that can suit the needs of various political factions at a given time. The funeral of Imre Nagy on June 16, 1989, provided just the sort of occasion that encouraged a public reinterpretation of history.

The funeral successfully linked popular understandings of the 1956 Revolution and the demand for democracy with the memory of Nagy's role as a charismatic national symbol. This chapter examines how people can dramatically incorporate memory into the political process of a complex society and provide the impetus for change.[4]

THE FUNERAL OF IMRE NAGY

At 4:00 A.M. on the morning of June 16, 1989, the caskets of Imre Nagy, Pál Maléter, Miklós Gimes, József Szilágyi, Géza Losonczy, and a sixth casket representing the unknown martyr of the Revolution were placed on a bier in front of the Exhibition Hall on Heroes Square in Budapest.[5] The Nagy group was not tried and executed together. Géza Losonczy died in prison after a forced feeding on December 21, 1957, before he could stand trial with the others. József Szilágyi, who had mounted such a spirited defense that the regime decided to try him separately from the Nagy group, was convicted and hanged in April 1958.[6] Nagy's casket was prominently placed in the center of the stage surrounded by his companions, with Maléter and Szilágyi to the right and Gimes and Losonczy to the left. The empty casket of the unknown martyr was placed in a slightly raised position, so that it was above and behind the casket of Nagy and was draped with the still illegal Hungarian tricolor, the Rákosi coat of arms cut out of the center.[7] Interestingly, the stage and bier were designed by László Rajk, son of the former Interior Minister of the same name who was executed in 1949 during the reign of terror enacted by the Stalinist party head, Mátyás Rákosi. Rajk's funeral and reburial can be seen as one of the focal generators for radicalism prior to the 1956 Revolution and will be examined in detail in the next chapter. On one side of the stage and funeral bier was a large memorial torch, and on the other side, a podium for the speakers who would eulogize Nagy and his companions. The pillars of the Exhibition Hall and a large part of the building were covered with black bunting.[8] Like the funeral of the 1848 Revolutionary Lajos Kossuth, this was not an official state funeral, but like that of Lajos Kossuth, it would be a hero's funeral in every sense of the word.[9]

Nagy and his compatriots had been buried in unmarked graves in an attempt to symbolically remove them from the Hungarian community. Relatives were not permitted to visit the site to perform *kegyelet* and, worse still, the graves were desecrated. Relatives who erected grave mounds in secret would return to find them plowed into the ground. Guards posted by the regime frequently rode over the graves with their horses.[10] Statues to the new heroes of Kádár's counterrevolution were erected, and a conscious attempt was made to rewrite history in which Nagy and his revolutionaries were portrayed as traitors and an aberration of Hungarian history.[11]

The state's negative portrayal of Nagy and the revolutionaries helped further enliven the heroic status of Nagy and the legitimacy of the Revolution among many Hungarians. This, in turn, provided the opposition with a symbolic locus for dissent.[12] Hungarians by and large accepted the political reality of the time.[13] The bleak political/economic reality evidenced in other satellite states was partly ameliorated by Kádár's modified socialist economy that allowed for some small scale capitalist activity and a certain degree of independence in exchange for silence regarding the Revolution.[14] The worsening economy of the 1980s led to a split within the Communist Party, with one faction insisting that democratic reform needed to be included in any economic reform of the Hungarian economy. The end to the communist's hold on power came quickly, stimulated by the Soviet Union's Mikhail Gorbachev's reforms of perestroika and glasnost and his dramatic announcement that socialist states were free to find their own path to socialism.[15] This in turn stimulated bolder actions on the part of the reform faction within the Communist Party and provided the opportunity to challenge the regime from outside the party, leading to a burgeoning opposition by 1988–1989. Both the reform faction within the Communist Party and the opposition factions outside the government claimed the legacy of Nagy and the Revolution.

According to Minister Without Portfolio Imre Pozsgay, recognition of the symbolic power of Nagy and the Revolution led to the establishment of a subcommittee within the Central Committee whose charge was to investigate the Revolution.[16] Family members and dissidents formed the Historical Justice Committee, founded to apply pressure on the regime to reevaluate the Revolution and properly bury Nagy and his federates. Pozsgay's startling announcement in January 1989 that the Revolution was a legitimate uprising strengthened the hand of reformers within the party and opposition groups outside of the government.[17] The negotiations for Nagy's exhumation and reburial were strengthened by this announcement, and in March 1989 the bodies of Imre Nagy and his colleagues were exhumed from Plot 301 and prepared for reburial. On May 25, 1989, an agreement was signed for a public funeral to be held at the Heroes Square in Budapest. The minutes of the Political Committee of the Hungarian Socialist Worker's Party (MSZMP) on May 16 and May 29, 1989, reveal the explicit connection between the demands for Nagy's reburial and the party's legitimacy. The regime and the reform faction would have to face the past and attempt to align itself with the demands of the opposition. In the context of a discussion about an official statement about Nagy and 1956, Central Committee member György Fejti urged his colleagues to limit the political damage to the MSZMP by stating that, "mistakes should be revealed . . . the sooner we say it the smaller the damage."[18] Negotiations between the opposition parties and the regime began in June 1989. Would Pozsgay and his confederates' embrace of Nagy and the Revolution enable them to maintain their party's dominance in the context of the Republic that would be established on October 23, 1989?[19]

The construction of the Heroes Square was begun in 1896 to celebrate the millennium of the Hungarian kingdom.[20] Dominating the square is a statue group portraying Árpád and the other six leaders of the seven Hungarian tribes entering the Carpathian basin. A grave to the Unknown Soldier was placed in front of the statues in the center of the square. Directly behind the statues is a semicircular pavilion that displays the pantheon of Hungarian kings and heroes.[21] Thus a national sacred space was created appropriate for important national rituals and, in particular, for the memorialization of the heroes of the 1956 Revolution on June 16, 1989.

The tricolor so prominently displayed on the coffin was also displayed in four places along the pantheon of heroes and the pillar of Gabriel, in the center of the monument dedicated to Árpád and the conquerors of the Carpathian basin, was draped in black bunting. There was no mistaking the message that would be conveyed to the public by the funeral. The Revolution of 1956 was legitimate and Hungarians still yearned for democracy portrayed by the bier and Heroes Square.[22]

Transfer of official control of the square took place at 7:00 A.M., at which time the city police were replaced by members of the largest opposition coalition, the MDF (Hungarian Democratic Forum).[23] According to records of the secret police, telephone booths were tapped and contingency plans had been formulated in case the crowd got "out of control."[24]

Throughout that day Hungarians streamed to the ceremony. Mourners filed past the caskets from right to left with the cue starting at the right-hand corner of the pantheon of heroes. Each mourner or group of mourners was given several paces to start before the next person or group, to ensure that each would have the opportunity to pay their proper respects. In some cases individuals were overcome with grief and had to be helped away by family members and friends.[25] Mourners couldn't help but notice the Yugoslav Embassy directly across from the Heroes Square on Dózsa György Street as they exited from the cue. It was there that Nagy and his group took refuge when the Soviet army stormed Budapest on November 4, 1956. It was also from there that Nagy and his group was abducted by the Soviets on November 22 after being assured of safe conduct home. November 22 became the day that Nagy's imprisonment began.[26]

The power of the opposition had been demonstrated in its ability to have forced the regime to allow a public funeral for Imre Nagy. It was then up to the Hungarian people to decide whether to legitimize the ceremony or not. By 9:00 A.M., when the funeral began, MTV 1 estimated the crowd to be 30,000 people. By the evening they estimated approximately 320,000 had come to the funeral. As people filed past the coffins the names of those executed during the terror initiated after the Revolution were read aloud. The radio commentator for Kossuth Rádió commented at 10:00 A.M. "So many dead people [in regard to the victims of the terror] it's a wonder one can find a voice to speak. People are coming in an endless line . . . Power is awakening in the People's soul with what they want to demonstrate . . . A country is voting . . ."[27]

At 11:00 A.M. the public viewing of the caskets was temporarily interrupted so that the protocol wreathing could begin, again revealing the symbolic importance of Nagy. Hundreds of wreathes were laid by many new and recently resurrected political organizations, along with various foreign and domestic factions of the Communist Party. The general sentiment of the crowd was evident when Bettino Craxi, the Secretary General of the Italian Socialist Party, came to lay a wreath but no one applauded.[28] In solidarity with Moscow the Italian Communist Party had branded the Hungarian Revolution a counterrevolution and denounced Imre Nagy as a reactionary.[29] A wreath was also brought to the funeral by the principal members of the reform faction within the MSZMP and carried to the bier by Imre Pozsgay, Prime Minister Miklós Németh, Vice Prime Minister Péter Medgyessy, and Mátyás Szűrös, Chairman of the Parliament. The reform faction had been invited to participate in the funeral and briefly took a turn standing as the honor guard at the bier.[30] The divided sentiment within the Communist Party was revealed when Secretary General Károly Grósz decided not to attend, claiming that he did not want to give the appearance that the funeral had been officially sanctioned by the state.[31]

By the end of the ceremony the flowers and wreathes brought by the Hungarian people reached to the height of the stage. Not all who attended the funeral had a chance to file past the coffins, and as the hearses left with the coffins for the burial ceremony flowers were strewn in their path. Very few Hungarians remained unmoved by the spectacle, and though Grósz ensured that the regime did not sanction the funeral, the massive presence of the community ensured that the nation did.[32] Hungary is a small nation of less than ten million people, and any number over 100,000 represented a substantial portion of the population. Kossuth Rádió commentator László Rapcsányi commented, "Perhaps at the bottom of our souls we believe that history will make justice."[33]

At 12:27 P.M. Árpád Göncz, a leading member of the Free Democrats and former confidant of Imre Nagy who was sent to prison for his role in the Revolution spoke: "Fellow Hungarians let us pay our *kegyelet*, let us remember." At 12:30 P.M. bells tolled across the country. Traffic halted and factory sirens wailed. This was immediately followed by a minute of silence. Then an excerpt from Nagy's October 30, 1956, speech to the nation played over the sound system in which he called on "My Hungarian brothers, patriots! Faithful citizens of our country! Save the achievements of the Revolution, with all of your effort protect order and restore the tranquility! Do not shed fraternal blood in our country!" After this speech the *Himnusz* (Hungarian National Anthem) was sung (see Appendix B). Many Hungarians in Budapest stood still or faced the radio during the minute of silence and many sang along with the hymn. Stopping in the middle of a busy day, their faces betrayed a solemnity not often seen in the streets. In some cases, the expressions were of surprise, perhaps reflecting the amazement of many, that the former Prime Minister whose memorialization had been illegal only a year ago was now being given a public funeral.[34]

A series of dramatic speeches followed that explicitly called for national sovereignty and democratic rule. The first speech was given by Miklós Vásárhelyi who had been Nagy's Press Secretary and confidant. Reflecting on Nagy's speech broadcast at the funeral he began, "Thirty-three years ago Imre Nagy turned to the country in the tempest of revolution and his fellow citizens listened to him. The weapons ceased and order was restored. The reconciliation, the democratic transition started."[35] "Imre Nagy lived on in the people after our Revolution was brutally crushed . . . Hungarians do not forget, they long for quick and determined deeds. They want a free country and a constitutional state . . . dreamed about in 1956." Though making reference to the terror, Vásárhelyi called for reconciliation and the establishment of a democratic state "realized through the efforts of people with divergent views."[36]

Far more fiery was the speech of Sándor Rácz, Union leader of the Budapest Worker's Council who spent seven years in prison for his participation in the Revolution. Pointing to the presence of Soviet troops as the main obstacle to Hungarian sovereignty, he declared: "These coffins and our bitter lives are the result of Russian troops on our territory. Let us help the Soviet Union to withdraw its troops from Hungary as soon as possible. The Communist Party is still clinging fearfully to power. What it could not achieve in the past forty-four years it cannot achieve now. They are responsible for the past, they are responsible for the damaged lives of Hungarians."[37] Rácz concluded his speech with a Roman Catholic hymn, which called on the Virgin Mary to protect Hungary. The film made by Black Box showed Hungarians on the street singing the hymn as they listened to it over the radio.

Imre Mécs, who had been condemned to death during the terror for his role in the Revolution and now a leader of the Free Democrats, asserted, "We bury those who embodied the anger of the Hungarian people, the will of the people, the Revolutionaries, the martyrs, and the victims . . . This is late justice for those who mourned secretly, swallowing tears inside for several decades . . ."[38] Addressing the passive acceptance of authoritarian rule Mécs asked, "How could you [Hungarians] live without freedom for thirty-three years?" When Mécs demanded that the crowd promise to Imre Nagy that they would save the achievements of the Revolution, his audience responded—citing from the National Verse (see Appendix A) written by the volatile 1848 revolutionary Sándor Petőfi—that "they would not be held captives any more."[39]

The economist Tibor Zimányi who had been imprisoned in the Recsk Concentration Camp was even more direct in his attack against the communist regime: "Our only sin was that we took democracy seriously . . . They [the communists] destroyed the moral world . . . As they lacked a Siberia, they created Recsk."[40] Zimányi asserted that he wanted national reconciliation, but only after those who perpetrated the terror or had collaborated later with the regime left office asserting, " . . . there is a murderer where the murder is . . . though in the name of reconciliation we don't want revenge; the penalty for the murderers should be that they are named. With this funeral we do not bury you; you start to live only now."[41]

Perhaps the most passionate speech of the day was given by Viktor Orbán, representative of the Young Democrats (FIDESZ), a student opposition group. The crowd that day consisted of a large number of young people. Orbán spoke the language of the young people and connected to them in a way the older speakers could not.[42] Orbán declared that the young people in the crowd had come not only to honor Nagy but also to mourn for a future taken away by the Communist Party: "the bankrupt state that has been placed upon our shoulders is a result of the suppression of our revolution . . ."[43] He vehemently attacked the reform Communists, commenting ironically: "We cannot understand that those who were eager to slander the Revolution and its prime minister have suddenly changed into great supporters of Imre Nagy. Nor can we understand that the party leaders, who made us study from books that falsified the Revolution, now rush to touch the coffins as if they were charms of good luck."[44] His emotional speech drew seven ovations from the crowd.

The political scientist Rudolf L. Tőkés asserts that Orbán's speech helped the "survivalists" within the MSZM understand how powerful the opposition was and at the same time created a platform for FIDESZ as a political party.[45] Paradoxically, the enthusiasm for Orbán's speech was not shared uniformly by members of the various opposition groups that day, a prelude to the bitter rivalry that would soon become manifest. According to Miklós Vásárhelyi, he and many within the Historical Justice Committee felt that Orbán had gone too far, "Not only was applause inappropriate for a *kegyelet*, but the incendiary nature of the speech was inappropriate for the occasion."[46] Imre Mécs felt that the tone of Orbán's speech was wrong, "It went further than a young man's arrogance . . . This [funeral] was the victory of the opposition, but we were in mourning . . . Orbán didn't understand this . . . the funeral was not the time to launch a political party." Mécs claimed that he didn't criticize Orbán at the time because, "we did not want to put water on the wheels of the regime." It was still too dangerous for the opposition to publicly reveal differences.[47]

Orbán's speech was not the only one that irritated Vásárhelyi. He also felt that the singing of a hymn to the Virgin Mary by Sándor Rácz was inappropriate, revealing a significant rift within the opposition.[48] Identification with the Virgin Mary and Roman Catholicism is strongly connected to the medieval Hungarian kingdom and to the regime of Miklós Horthy, who was responsible for bringing Hungary into World War II on the side of the Axis powers. Horthy was titled Regent of Hungary and his politics were undergirded by an intense anti-bolshevism and the restoration of the kingdom that had been truncated at the Treaty of Trianon. Christian symbols and imagery used by Horthy are still largely anathema to Socialists and Communists alike, who blamed the destruction of Hungary on Horthy's politics.[49] Interestingly, in a telling frame of both the Black Box and Open Eye films, flags emblazoned with the Kossuth coat of arms that excluded the Crown of St. Steven and flags with the royal coat of arms that included the crown of St. Steven can both be seen waving together at the funeral.[50] Though these differences may have been keenly felt between members of the various factions making up the opposition, the unity of purpose appeared to be more important to the crowd at large.

The fear that the Communist Party had of the symbolic importance of the spectacle was revealed when they attempted to manipulate the event. According to Foreign Minister, Gyula Horn, the historian Béla Király, who had been sentenced to death in absentia for his role as leader of the National

Guard during the Revolution, had been issued a visa and allowed to speak at the funeral only on condition that he not incite against the current regime.[51] He further claimed that that there should be a meeting with Vásárhelyi to discuss the politics of the funeral.[52] More evidence of the attempt to manipulate the funeral was provided by Rezső Nyers of the Central Committee. A May meeting of that body discussed the implications of a live television broadcast. According to the minutes, Nyers claimed that Vásárhelyi had told him that the speeches to be read on June 16 would be passed to the Central Committee for scrutiny, ensuring that nothing inflammatory would be read aloud at the funeral.[53] Vásárhelyi categorically denied this in my interview with him, claiming that any meetings he had with members of the Central Committee were always in the presence of two other members of the Historical Justice Committee. According to Vásárhelyi, he was never asked for advance copies.[54] The fiery rhetoric of the speeches seems to verify his claim, but historian János M. Rainer disagrees, claiming that the Historical Justice Committee indeed requested copies of the texts in advance, but were refused both by Sándor Rácz and Viktor Orbán.

The secret police claimed that the theme of reconciliation found in the speeches given at Heroes Square was their "greatest achievement."[55] In response to this Imre Mécs said, "This type of comment is typical of the communists . . . Once they realized they were on the losing side they immediately made exaggerated claims." According to Mécs it had been the opposition that had "blackmailed" the regime, forcing them to accept the opposition's plans for the funeral by threatening to turn the proceedings over to the more radical factions within the opposition who would indeed incite the Hungarian people.[56] Both reform communists and the opposition did not want an eruption in the streets. Besides not wanting to see Budapest again "go up in flames" no one could predict what the consequences of a street uprising would be for the aspirations of the various political factions, let alone what the response would be from the Soviet Union.[57] Dissonance clearly existed within the ranks of the opposition, but the unity of purpose that was displayed publicly was reinforced by the behavior of the crowds and their determination to legitimize Nagy's funeral and the goals of the 1956 Revolution.

The burial ceremonies at the Új Köztemető cemetery were by invitation only, as the space in Plot 301 could never accommodate the crowds that had come to Heroes Square. The reinterment would include the six caskets present at Heroes Square, and forty-one other victims of the terror. Imre Nagy was interred next to the unknown freedom fighter, which is distinguished only by the inscription on the white slab that covered each of the graves. *Kopjafa* mark most of the other graves in the plot. The *kopjafa* is a richly carved post and has been used since medieval times to mark graves in the Szekély region

of Hungary, now located in Romania.[58] The Székely warriors were given special status as defenders of the eastern periphery of the Hungarian kingdom,
but it is their strong support of the 1848 Revolution against the Hapsburgs
that informs the symbolism of the markers.[59] The *kopjafa* were carved by the
dissident artist community *Inconnu* and the central *kopjafa* is inscribed,
"1956 Pro-Patria." The martyrs of the terror were to be reburied as hero warriors of the Hungarian nation.

Though not an official state funeral, an "honor guard" of soldiers lined the
roadway leading to Plot 301, again providing recognition for Nagy's status as
prime minister. The ceremony began with the reading of the names of the 231
victims that had so far been identified. As each name was read a candle for
each victim was extinguished with the bearer intoning, "You will remain with
us forever." László Rapcsányi commented, "This is the *tetemrehívás* of an
era." *Tetemrehívás*, translates as ordeal of the bier, which has its origins in the
medieval period when it was believed that if a murderer appeared beside an
open coffin, the body would provide a sign or send a message as to the be-
holder's guilt.[60]

The writer Tibor Méray delivered the eulogy for Imre Nagy. He began by
stating that Nagy had been "elected" by the will of the people. He then
launched an attack against the communist regime: "If you are without guilt,
then those that sent you to the gallows are murderers. Let their punishment be
the contempt of the nation . . . They can only guess what their judgment will
be in the unwritten history books . . . The nations of the world know that this
funeral was not a gift of the regime, but won by the people. It was only a year
ago on your 30th anniversary that Hungarian youth suffered police violence
. . . Those in power must ask your forgiveness . . ."[61]

THE MEANING OF 1956 IN 1989

Kádár has repeatedly said that Nagy Imre is free to return to Hungary . . .

—Imre Nagy to Gyula Kállai, representative from
the Central Committee, interview during Nagy's
imprisonment in Snagov, Romania, January 25, 1957[62]

When Nagy was being held in Snagov, Romania, November 23, 1956–April
14, 1957, he claimed that the Communist Party had been successful in achieving two of the goals set out during the 1848 Hungarian Revolution against the
Hapsburgs; land reform and an ending of the semi-feudal economy. What had
not been achieved were the goals of national independence, sovereignty, and

equality.[63] He said, "The meaning of the Hungarian tragedy is that socialism and national independence became antagonists. The meaning of the Hungarian uprising was to search and find an end to this antagonism and create the unity of the two. The question is, do we do this in a wisely foreseen, peaceful, and democratic way, or create it through armed struggle?"[64] The moral force of the funeral legitimized the three unfulfilled goals of the Revolution as enunciated by Nagy.[65] Though these goals were not immediately fulfilled, the presence of the Hungarian people coupled with the unique circumstances that characterized the ending of the Cold War in Hungary ensured that the path would be peaceful.

Having long been denied the ability to publicly mourn and acknowledge the consequences of the Hungarian Revolution, the Hungarian people attended the funeral *en masse*. Imre Nagy refused to acknowledge the legitimacy of the Kádár regime and was brought back to Hungary from Snagov in handcuffs in 1957. His bitter end symbolized for many the brutality of the terror enacted by the Kádár regime and the crushing of those few moments of hope that highlighted the Revolution. The communists were right to fear Nagy even in death as his public funeral explicitly demonstrated Hungarians' accord with the goals of the Revolution.[66]

Though reform communists appeared at the funeral, they had only recently attempted to repossess the symbol of Imre Nagy. As such, they were associated with the conservative members of the MSZMP, the Kádár regime, and the Soviet Union. Thus, they were fatally linked to an institution considered alien as defined by the funeral.

The dichotomy created by the funeral and burial rites that served to separate the communists from the Hungarian polity came about for several reasons. First, the Kádár and the subsequent reform communist regime had broken a deep-set Hungarian taboo by denying the families of the dead the opportunity to properly bury and remember their dead. The deliberate desecration of the graves further enraged Hungarians and only served to reinforce the former regime's image as being foreign. Second, the manipulation of national symbols by the former regimes in an attempt to woo the population away from nationalist tendencies appealed to only a small part of the Hungarian population. For example, the attempt to transform St. Steven's Day into Constitution Day (1948) or the Holiday of the New Bread under Kádár antagonized significant parts of the population. Similarly, the erection of monuments honoring the Worker's Militia, which had been formed by Kádár to assist in the demobilization of the Revolution, catered to interests of those who served the Soviet-backed regime, but openly insulted those who were in sympathy with the Revolution. State-sanctioned textbooks excoriating Nagy and the Revolution abounded through 1989, providing yet another contrast between the regime and meaning of 1956 that was brought to its full in the context of the funeral.

Nagy symbolized the Hungarian longing for national sovereignty and a democratic Republic that had been brutally crushed in 1956. Fusing the political demands for democracy with the body of Nagy was enormously successful. The Kádár regime's promises of material prosperity at the expense of deeply held cultural beliefs proved fatal in June 1989. Hungarian passivity in the wake of the Revolution's failure was first secured through an economic exchange, but also through the enactment of a terror that lasted until 1963 and a system of surveillance that could wield the power of the state against those who refused to comply. The threat of being expelled from school or ousted from one's job must have weighed very heavily on those raising children, given their absolute dependence on state social security.

Hungarians had been humiliated daily by the compromises that were necessary to continue working at the universities or within governmental institutions. Hungarians were also forced to accept a revision of history that many found unpalatable. Imre Nagy represented a Hungarian who would not compromise with Kádár and the counterrevolutionaries, and one who knew the price he would have to pay for his defiance. In this sense, Nagy's funeral in 1989 allowed for an expiation of the shame of compromise.

The official silence on Imre Nagy and the Revolution of 1956 only temporarily staved off the day when the Hungarian nation could again openly acknowledge the legitimacy of both Nagy and the Revolution. This left the communist regime fatally associated with those events that included the horror of juridical murder and the crushing of what was a legitimate revolution. Political opposition to the regime would not have been possible without the legitimacy it accrued from the Hungarian people. The funeral of Imre Nagy was critical in this regard.

The focus of the funeral was on the contents of the caskets symbolizing national sovereignty and the hopes of a democratic republic, not on the disparity of political views that abounded within the opposition, or for that matter, among the Hungarians themselves. As mentioned earlier, a number of different political symbols were displayed at the funeral, including flags bearing the royal and Kossuth coat of arms. Although members of the various factions within the opposition were well aware of political differences, this was unimportant to the vast majority of Hungarians who attended the funeral. This was borne out not only in electoral choices made by the Hungarian people in November 1989 when they stripped the Communist Party of power, but by the collapse of the MSZMP without the backing of the Soviet Union. But why then, should this story that repudiated the Communist's thirty-three–year version of Nagy and the Revolution end in yet another bitter fight over the history and memory of the same people and event that continues into the present? The story of Nagy's contested memory can be found in the bitter history surrounding Hungary's post–World War II past. It is the construction of this past and Nagy's place in it that is used to legitimate the various political platforms in the present.

NOTES

1. From Tibor Méray's eulogy at Imre Nagy's graveside. See: Hungarian Monitoring, Végtisztesség (Final honor), Kossuth Rádió Transcript, June 16, 1989.
2. Not only were the graves not marked, but false names were given to the bodies interred. János M. Rainer, *Nagy Imre 1953–1958: Politikai Életrajz II* (Imre Nagy: A Political Biography) (Budapest: 1956–os Intézet, 1999) 436.
3. The third and fourth line of the anthem states: *Balsors akit régen tép, hozz rá vig esztendőt* (Misfortune has punished them for a long time), *Megbünhődte már e nép a múltat s jövendőt* (This nation has been penalized for the past and future).
4. Ideas and parts of this chapter stem from my article "The Funeral of Imre Nagy: Contested History and the Power of Memory Culture," *History and Memory*, 12, 2 (Fall/Winter, 2000).
5. József Szilágyi was the head of the Secretariat and Géza Losonczy was Minister of State in the Nagy government. Foreign Broadcast Information Service, Daily Report for Eastern Europe (hereafter FBIS-EEU) Hungarian Information Service (hereafter MTI), "The Ceremony Begins," June 19, 1989.
6. Alajos Dornbach, *The Secret Trial of Imre Nagy* (Westport: Praeger, 1994), 16–17, 21.
7. Hungarian Monitoring, Végtisztesség (Final Tribute) Kossuth Rádió Transcript, June 16, 1989. The flag without the hated Rákosi coat of arms made its first appearance at the student rally held at Bem Square prior to their famed march on Parliament. See: György Litván ed., *The Hungarian Revolution of 1956* (London: Longman Group Ltd., 1996), 55.
8. *June 16, 1989.* Produced by Dér-Pesty. Budapest: Black Box, 1989. Videocassette.
9. John Lukacs, *Budapest 1900* (New York: Grove Weidenfeld, 1988), 120.
10. Béla Kövér, "301–es parcella Köztemető (The Public Cemetery's Plot 301), *Magyar Nemzet*, May 3, 1989, 21.
11. For example, Sándor Balogh, et al., *A Magyar népi demokrácia története, 1944–1962* (The history of the Hungarian People's Democracy) (Budapest: Kossuth Tankönyvkiadó, 1978).
12. Imre Mécs recognized the importance of Plot 301 as a form of protest early on. Mécs, himself a revolutionary originally condemned to death and subsequently pardoned as part of the general amnesty in 1963, claimed that he began visiting Plot 301 after his release from prison. Imre Mécs, interview by author, November 7, 1997.

13. George Schöpflin, *Politics in Eastern Europe* (Oxford: Blackwell Publishers, 1993), 103.

14. Charles Gati, *Hungary and the Soviet Bloc* (Durham: Duke University Press, 1986), 161.

15. Csaba Békés, "Back to Europe: The International Background of the Political Transition in Hungary, 1988–1990," *The Roundtable Talks of 1989: The Genesis of Hungarian Democracy*, András Bozoki, ed. (Budapest: Central European University Press, 2002), 242–45.

16. Imre Pozsgay, *1989: Politikus-pálya a pártállamban és a rendszerváltásban* (1989: A Politician's career in the Party-state and transition), (Budapest: Püski Kiadó Kft., 1993), 91.

17. See: Pozsgay, *1989: Politikus-pálya*, 94–95, 224, and Joshua Foa Dienstag's fine article, "The Pozsgay Affair: Historical Memory and Political Legitimacy," *History and Memory* 8, 1 (Spring/Summer, 1996).

18. Meeting of the MSZMP Political Committee, May 26, 1989. A Compendium of Declassified Documents and Chronology of Events (hereafter: A Compendium of Declassified Documents), Csaba Békés, Malcolm Byrne ed., Political Transition in Hungary 1989–1990 International Conference, Budapest, Hungary, 1999 sponsored by the National Security Archive/Cold War History Research Center/1956 Institute.

19. A conversation between Mikhail Gorbachev and Károly Grósz, General Secretary of the MSZMP reveal this desire to remain in power. Gorbachev stated, "Democracy is much needed, and the interests have to be harmonized. The limit, however, is the safekeeping of socialism and assurance of stability." Memorandum of Conversation between M. S. Gorbachev and Károly Grósz General Secretary of the Hungarian Socialist Worker's Party, Moscow, March 23–24, 1989. A Compendium of Declassified Documents.

20. András Gerö, *Modern Hungarian Society in the Making: The Unfinished Experience* (Budapest: Central European Press, 1995) 203.

21. Alice Freifeld makes the point that the "Millennium Exhibition remained in Hungarian historical consciousness as a monument to past greatness." *Nationalism and the Crowd* in Liberal Hungary, 1848–1914 (Baltimore: The Johns Hopkins University Press, 2000), 277.

22. The coalition represented by MDF and the other opposition parties and factions held a wide range of views as to what the nature of a republic should be. The empty casket perhaps provided a repository for the many conceptions embodied by this generalized yearning in the same way that the tomb of the unknown soldier provides a place to be filled by multifarious imaginings of the nation state. Benedict Anderson, *Imagined Communities: Reflections on the Origin and Spread of Nationalism* (New York: Verso, 1991) 9.

23. FBIS-EEU, MTI, "The Ceremony Begins," June 19, 1989.

24. János Kenedi, *Kis Állambiztonsági Olvasókönyv II* (Little State Security Textbook), (Budapest: Magvető Kiadó, 1996), 345.

25. *June 16, 1989*, Black Box, videocassette, and *Nagy Imre: Élete és halhatatlansága* (Imre Nagy's life and immortality), produced by Róbert Bokor (Budapest: Hungarian Television, 1996) videocassette.

26. This is shown in camera shots in the Black Box film, *June 16, 1989*, and mentioned by the historian István Rév in "Parallel Autopsies," *Representations*, 49 (Winter, 1995): 31.

27. Hungarian Monitoring, "Végtisztesség," Kossuth Rádió Transcript, June 16, 1989.

28. Ibid.

29. For example see: "Cable from Italian Communist Party Leader Palmiro Togliatti to the CPSU CC Presidium," October 30, 1956, in Saba Békés et al., ed., *The 1956 Hungarian Revolution: A History in Documents* (Budapest: Central European University Press, 2002), 294.

30. See: Hungarian Monitoring, "Végtisztesség," Kossuth Rádió Transcript, June 16, 1989, Henry Kamm, "The Funeral of Imre Nagy," *New York Times*, June 17, 1989, p. 6, and Pozsgay, *1989: Politikus-pálya*, 148.

31. Grósz and his federates were quickly losing ground to the reform faction within the Communist Party. Rudolf L. Tőkés, *Hungary's Negotiated Revolution: Economic Reform, Social Change, and Political Succession* (Cambridge: Cambridge University Press, 1996), 327–28.

32. This is clear from both the Black Box film, *June 16, 1989*, and the János M. Rainer film, *Nagy Imre: Élete és halhatatlansága*. The political scientist Rudolf L. Tőkés comments that by June of 1989 the likes of communists like Grósz were becoming an "endangered species" in *Hungary's Negotiated Revolution*, 329.

33. Hungarian Monitoring, "Végtisztesség," Kossuth Rádió Transcript, June 16, 1989.

34. *June 16, 1989*, Black Box.

35. *Népszava*, June 17, 1989, 2.

36. In addition to *Népszava* see: FBIS-EEU, MTI, June 19, 1989, and *Népszabadság*, June 17, 1989, 3.

37. *Magyar Nemzet*, June 17, 1989, 2.

38. Ibid.

39. *June 16, 1989*, Black Box.

40. *Magyar Nemzet*, June 17, 1989, 4.

41. *Népszava*, June 17, 1989, 2.

42. János M. Rainer, interview by author, April 6, 1998.

43. *Magyar Nemzet*, June 17, 1989, 3.

44. Henry Kamm, "The Funeral of Imre Nagy," *New York Times*, June 17, 1989, 6.

45. Rodolph Tőkés, *Hungary's Negotiated Revolution*, 330.

46. Vásárhelyi, interview by author, October 7, 1997.

47. Imre Mécs, interview by author, November 7, 1997.

48. Miklós Vásárhelyi, interview by author, October 7, 1997.

49. The Christian National Unity Party formed the basis of Horthy's power after the defeat of the Soviet revolution led by Béla Kun. They voted to reestablish the Hungarian kingdom in 1920. Their intense anti-Semitism was fed, in part, by the fact that Kun and others who had participated in the Soviet Revolution were Jews. Hungary passed the first anti-Semitic laws of the post-World War I era in 1920, known as the Numerus Clausus Law, which limited the number of Jews able to attend university.

32 Chapter Two

See: Thomas Sakmyster, *Admiral on Horseback: Miklós Horthy, 1918–1944* (Boulder: East European Monographs, 1994), Vera Ránki, *The Politics of Inclusion and Exclusion: Jews and Nationalism in Hungary* (New York: Holmes and Meier, 1999), 206–8, and Tibor Hajdú and Zsuzsa L. Nagy, "Revolution, Counterrevolution, Consolidation," *A History of Hungary*, 308–12.

50. *June 16, 1989*, Black Box and A temetés (the funeral) (June 16, 1989). Produced by Ferenc Székely. Budapest: Nyitott Szem (Open Eye) Különkiadás, 1989. Videcassette.

51. Király had escaped to the United States after the failure of the Revolution and later became a professor of history at Brooklyn College, City University of New York.

52. Kenedi, *Kis Állambiztonsági Olvasókönyv*, 239–40.

53. Ibid., 300.

54. Miklós Vásárhelyi, interview by author, October 7, 1997.

55. Kenedi, *Kis Állambiztonsági Olvasókönyv*, 263.

56. Imre Mécs, interview by author, November 7, 1997.

57. Tőkés, *Hungary's Negotiated Revolution*, 418.

58. Ernö Kunt, *Temetök az Aggteleki-karszt falvaiban* (Village cemeteries in the Aggtelek-karszt region) (Debrecen: Alföldi Nyomda, 1978), 9, and Nóra Kovács, "Kopjafas: The Anthropological Deconstruction of Hungarian Grave Posts as National monuments," Master's Thesis: Central European University, 1997.

59. Kovács, "Kopjafas," 57.

60. Hungarian Monitoring, Végtisztesség, Kossuth Rádió Transcript,, June 16, 1989.

61. FBIS-EEU, MTI, June 19, 1989.

62. "Lehallgatási jegyzőkönyv Nagy Imre és Kállai Gyula beszélgétéséröl (Notes of a tapped conversation between Imre Nagy and Gyula Kállai)," *Nagy Imre: Snagovi jegyzetek, Gondolatok, emlékezések, 1956–1957* (Imre Nagy: Notes, thoughts, and memories from Snagov), István Vida, ed. (Budapest: Gondolat Kiadó-Nagy Imre Alapítvány, 2006), 278.

63. *Nagy Imre: Snagovi jegyzetek, Gondolatok, emlékezések, 1956–1957*, 145.

64. Ibid., 127.

65. The sociologist János Kis asserted, "the ceremony became the moral burial of the whole post-1956 regime," in his essay, "Between Reform and Revolution," *Lawful Revolution in Hungary, 1989–1994*, Béla K. Király, ed. (New York: Columbia University Press, 1995), 45.

66. The funeral created a dichotomy pitting political goals and Hungarian traditions in opposition to the regime in power. Victor Turner's discussion of communitas is useful in this regard. See: Victor Witter Turner, *The Ritual Process: Structure and Anti-Structure* (New York: 1969), 96. The author views the theoretical perspectives offered by Turner as ways to further illuminate the political/historical processes under review, not as tools of prediction. Nagy's funeral provides "new values to space and time." See Katherine Verdery's excellent study: "Dead Bodies Animate the Study of Politics," in *The Political Lives of Dead Bodies*, 38.

Chapter Three

An Unlikely Hero

In the spirit of the revolutionary heroes of 1848–1849 . . . we should cul-
tivate the most cordial relationship with freedom loving peoples, especially with the country of socialism, the Soviet Union . . .

—Imre Nagy, Kossuth Academy, August 19, 1948[1]

The funeral of Imre Nagy explicitly demonstrated the Hungarian people's accord with the demands for a sovereign democratic state forwarded by the opposition parties and the reform faction within the Communist Party. And yet
Nagy had helped establish the Stalinist state within Hungary following World
War II. In the midst of bitter interparty struggles Nagy collaborated with those
carrying out juridical murder in a bid for both political survival and reward.
He came to power as Prime Minister in the wake of Stalin's demise and re-
pudiation by the new Soviet leader Nikita Khrushchev. His policies included
opportunities for limited political critique and an ending to the terror enacted
by his predecessor, Mátyás Ràkossi. Bitter feuding between the Stalinist faction and those backing Nagy's New Course policy led ultimately to his ouster.
Nagy continued his critique of Stalinist politics from outside the party and his
ideas continued to circulate among writers, intellectuals, and political
thinkers. Not particularly interested in democracy, Nagy believed instead that
pluralism within a one-party state provided the best chance for achieving a
socialist utopia in Hungary. How was it then that he was transformed into a
symbol associated with national solidarity and the democratic republic demanded by the student and worker councils in October and November of
1956? This chapter reviews the bitter politics that marked the ending of World
War II and the establishment of the Stalinist state, Nagy's travails within the
Communist Party, and the public renunciation of Stalinism embodied in the

33

funeral of one of it's victims that in combination lay the background for the popular interpretation accorded him in 1956.

Imre Nagy joined the Social Democratic Party in 1922 after his imprisonment in the Soviet Union as a World War I prisoner, on instructions from the Communist Party.[2] This provided him with political cover as he had become a Bolshevik in 1918.[3] He went to Vienna in 1928 for the international Union Congress, returned to Hungary for four months in 1929 and then traveled to Moscow as a representative to the Second Communist Party Congress.[4] His interest in agricultural reform and Hungarian nationalism got him into trouble with the Communist Party during his stay. While living in Moscow Nagy worked with Nikolai Ivanovich Bukharin who had been part of Lenin's elite circle and ultimately an enemy of Stalin. With Bukharin he advocated for a partitioning rather than the nationalizing of estates in an attempt to maintain the alliance between the communists and their peasant base of support, placing them both at odds with Stalinist politics.[5] Stalin insisted on a more radical policy of forced collectivization that would eradicate any traces of capitalism in the countryside; those insisting on maintaining private strips of farmland were branded as *kulaks* (wealthy peasants) interested only in the exploitation of their fellow peasants. Bukharin's refusal to recant his position ultimately cost him his life in one of the more notorious show trials of 1938, a point surely not lost on Nagy. Nagy was expelled from the Hungarian Communist Party in 1936 and according to the historian János M. Rainer, was more than likely compromised by the KGB to inform on fellow Hungarians living in Moscow during his first banishment prior to World War II.[6] Nagy became a Soviet citizen in March 1936 and appealed the Hungarian Communist Party's decision right away; he was reinstated in February of 1939.[7]

Nagy returned to Hungary at the end of World War II as part of the Debrecen government established in December 1944.[8] Nagy came away from the earlier infighting within the party unscathed and was considered fourth in rank within the party by the Central Committee of the Hungarian Communist Party, assuring him an important place within the newly formed government. He was given the position of Minister of Agriculture on December 23.[9]

The Stalinist party faced a difficult task establishing power in Hungary in the wake of national elections conducted in November 1945, which resulted in a spectacular victory for the centrist Smallholders Party. During the war years the Smallholders had aligned themselves with the Social Democrats against the pro-German factions in the Parliament. In May 1944 they helped form the Hungarian Front, a resistance movement posed against the German-dominated government and included in the Provisional Government established in Debrecen.[10] The historian Charles Gati described this ascent as indicative of "the profoundly anti Soviet attitude and overall skepticism held by the Hungarians towards the communists."[11] The election was decisive with the Smallholders taking 2,653,022 votes, the Social Democrats coming in second with 818,202, and the communists with only 792,911.[12] The sting of electoral defeat was ameliorated somewhat by the fact that the communists gained control of the Ministry of the Interior at the insistence of the Soviets.[13]

Economic problems stemming from both the war and the plight of peasants in the countryside played into the hands of the communists. Hungary's economy was in a shambles following World War II, and recovery was greatly hampered by the Soviet occupation at the end of the war. Many Hungarian civilians were abducted as prisoners of war and used for forced labor or sent to the Soviet Union.[14] Historian László Borhi asserts that food shortages were exacerbated by the Soviet's demand that the Hungarians provision the occupiers. For example, the demand for one-quarter in 1946 exceeded what the Hungarian population could consume in one year. Hyperinflation kept the country in grinding poverty, made worse by the removal of factories either as trophies or as part of reparations. The economic tensions were exploited by the communists at the local political level against the Smallholders and ultimately aided in Hungary's transformation into a Soviet dependency.[15]

Nagy was charged with devising a program of land reform, a program popular with the major political parties, and with the Soviet Union and the United States.[16] The devil was in the details, however, and the plan forwarded by the communists was designed to give them an upper hand in the countryside. Landlord and peasant categories were blurred and designed to punish anticommunists. The communists ignored the pleas for gradual reform forwarded by the Smallholders, leading to problems over who was entitled to land and how much. Land reform, though popular, had mixed results. On one hand land reform served Nagy's political interests and linked him in the minds of many as one concerned with the interests of the ordinary Hungarian peasant. On the other hand, prices set by the government kept many in poverty. Foreshadowing later turmoil in the countryside, Nagy reported that the peasants remained wary of the communists and largely stayed loyal to the Catholic Church, in spite of the fact that the church had been one of the largest landlords.[17]

The communist strategy to minimize the political significance of the Smallholders' majority in Parliament was premised on utilizing its hold on the Ministry of the Interior and the police to eliminate their opponents.[18] Set in the context of Hungary's defeat after World War II and the war crimes trials against her leading wartime prime ministers such as László Bárdossy, 1941–1942, and Döme Stójay, 1944, the communists attempted to discredit Smallholder politicians and other adversaries by rooting out fascist collaborators and criminals. The regime of Admiral Miklós Horthy, 1918–1944, had allied itself with the Axis powers in a bid to regain territory lost at the Treaty of Trianon, 1920, and as a way of forwarding the regime's policy of anti-bolshevism.[19] Hungary's declaration of war against the Soviet Union and her allies resulted in an unmitigated disaster for Hungary and resulted in Soviet occupation.[20] Both Bárdossy and Stójay were executed for war crimes in 1946.

The Communist Party began counterattacking the Smallholders immediately after the disastrous fall elections. László Rajk, who had fought fascism in the name of the communist movement both in Spain and in Hungary, addressed the Parliament in December 1945.[21] Rajk urged that the Hungarian people be vigilant of the government's actions, not their words. Pointing to Hungary's currency devaluation he asserted that, "there are some who are pleased with the inflation just because they want to make more money in the wake of Hungary's destruction." According to Rajk, the government in power had done nothing to address this problem. In a not too subtle threat as to the tactics the Hungarian communists would use he demanded, "Quick and definite measures against the reactionaries who endanger the young democracy the most are needed . . . They [the reactionaries] are fixing their lines for an attack both economically and politically [in a bid to regain power]." He claimed that the majority of the police were still "reactionaries" from the old regime. Only with the "cleansing of the ranks" can there be the possibility of a true democracy. According to Rajk, "Certain circles within the army are centers of intrigue and conspiracy against democracy . . . it is a practice to accept officers who fought with Szálasi."[22] "We must recruit young men to be officers from the workers and the peasants." In an ominous reference to the Soviet occupiers he claimed, "In the last few weeks there is a [sense of] skepticism from among our neighboring democratic foreign countries [who] are waiting for strong acts against [these] reactionary forces in order to prove that we are true democrats."[23] Indeed the Soviets backed up the communist's claims in early January 1946 in a meeting with Smallholder Prime Minister Zoltán Tildy and Ferenc Nagy, where they underlined that good relations with the Soviet Union was premised on ridding their party of reactionaries.[24] Rajk was named Minister of the Interior on March 21, 1946, a post temporarily held by Imre Nagy.[25]

On March 5, 1946, Mátyás Rákosi, leader of the Hungarian Communist Party branded the right wing faction of the Smallholders Party as "enemies of the Republic" and linked them to the politics of Miklós Horthy. On the following day he stated that the Communist Party would cooperate only with the democratic elements of the party. Demonstrating their ability to mobilize, the communists helped organize rallies and according to the newspaper *Szabad Nép* (Free Nation), 500,000 members from unions and workers' parties marched against the "reactionaries" on March 7.[26]

The Smallholder's Party was a coalition that included some politicians who were in harmony with Horthy's policies, but the majority of its membership was determined to ensure that the ruling elite associated with Horthy were barred from power. Further, land reform was a common goal of both the Smallholders and the Communists.[27] The Communist's demand for a cleansing of political opponents was stymied in part by the political success of economic programs favored by the communists and by the coalition politics being followed by the communists through 1946.[28] As the historian Joseph Rothschild asserts, the real bellicosity of communist intentions was revealed after Hungary signed the peace treaty with the allies on February 10, 1947.[29] The signing of the treaty had been viewed by the Smallholders as one of the final steps towards ending Soviet occupation and assuming full sovereignty for Hungary. Though harassed by the smear tactics and brutality of the Hungarian Communists backed by the Soviets, Hungary had been able to operate as a limited democracy.[30]

Yet, the signing of the treaty was followed by a concerted attack against the Smallholders' leadership that led to the arrest of the Party Secretary Béla Kovács. Kovács and the Prime Minister Ferenc Nagy were accused of conspiracy to overthrow the Republic, and were smeared as fascist reactionaries by their close association with Miklós Horthy. The terms of the armistice that Hungary signed with the United Nations on January 20, 1945, demanded punishment for those linked to crimes against humanity, aggressive warfare, or fascist collaboration.[31] Laws that had been designed to expand international law were now used as a tool to undermine political opposition. Details of the accusations published by the government in a White Paper included the reestablishment of the "*Nagy Magyarország*," (Greater Hungary) and the creation of Hungarian *über menchen* (supermen).[32] After Kovács was taken into custody, the charges developed by the Soviets attempted to make a link with the Horthy regime's policy of territorial revision, which played a large role bringing Hungary into World War II and the politics of eugenics that led ultimately to genocide.[33] Although the allies protested the Soviet action, the charges had their effect and resulted in both men being driven from power. Ferenc Nagy was exiled and Kovàcs was imprisoned. The odds were being stacked against the survival of parties in opposition to the communists.

From the very beginning the of the Soviet occupation the communists had been in control of the national police force that was later reorganized as the ÁVH (Hungarian Secret Police), one of the more feared weapons employed by the Communist Party. Utilizing the current problems endemic after the drastic privations of World War II that included conspirators, black marketeering, and *vetkőztetők* (robbers who literally stole the clothing off of victims), the interior minister László Rajk claimed that a new security force was necessary. The "People's Police" was portrayed as the token of true democracy. The new force would not be required to have graduated from high school.[34]

Campaigns against reactionaries and black marketeers were accompanied by mass demonstrations and what was coined as "spontaneous justice of the crowd" that included lynching. According to the newspaper *Szabad Nép* the Interior Minister was "ruthless" against his enemies because he had the "love of his people."[35] Lawless brutality was institutionalized. Not only were right wing politicians targeted and driven from office, but Jews also became targets and several brutal pogroms were deliberately instigated by the communists. Anti-Semitism was utilized to create chaotic situations and the rationale for increased security measures on the part of the state.[36]

The Roman Catholic Church in Hungary, led by the obdurate anticommunist József Cardinal Mindszenty, was a strong supporter of the Smallholders Party.[37] The communists aggressively challenged the authority of the Roman Catholic Church by using the same tactics they used against the Smallholders. For example, on December 23, 1945, when Mindszenty visited internment camps in Budapest, the press reported that he was making "common cause" with the [reactionary] criminals. In April of 1946 László Rajk ordered the police to search Catholic intermediate schools. According to Mindszenty, the police found planted weapons, which fortified accusations that the Catholic Church was linked to the reactionary politics of Hungary's World War II regimes. In July of the same year a police investigation into the murder of a Soviet soldier concluded that the perpetrator was a member the Hungarian Catholic youth organization. The Interior Ministry used this as a pretext to order the disbanding of all youth groups in Hungary.[38]

The strength of the Catholic Church in the countryside posed a real challenge to the Communist Party. The historian Peter Kenez claims that the force of this sentiment was revealed in the struggle over making religious instruction in the schools voluntary and the nationalization of Hungarian schools during the years 1947–1948. Initially popular opposition to the proposed legislation stymied calls for voluntary religious instruction. Mindszenty's call for a "Year of the Virgin" demonstrated the power of the church to mobilize hundreds of thousands of Hungarians and was perhaps decisive in determining the Communist Party's decision to nationalize the schools and silence open defiance to its authority. Mindszenty openly challenged the communists and called upon the faithful to agitate against the proposed policy. A violent demonstration in June 1948 that resulted in the death of a policeman was used to further substantiate claims that the church was infiltrated by reactionaries. How could the church be entrusted with the socialization of Hungary's youth? The destruction of the multiparty state in 1947–1948 ensured the failure of

Mindszenty's campaign and the schools were nationalized in 1948.[39] In 1949 Mindszenty himself was arrested, brutally tortured, and thrown into prison.[40]

Imre Nagy ran on the Communist Party list in August 1947. He campaigned on the Stalinist platform that included expulsion of the German Hungarians and [forced] collectivization. Interestingly, Imre Patkó of Szbad Nép called him the *"Földosztó Miniszter"* (minister of land distribution), highlighting the pivotal role he had played in the program. As we have seen, Nagy certainly had differences with Stalinist land collectivization, but his public acceptance of the communist platform certainly attested to his allegiance to the party. Overall, he was portrayed in the article as a peasant who could dance the *csárdás*, liked good wine, and affectionately called his daughter *Böske* (the informal for Erzsébet).[41]

Though again unsuccessful in gaining a majority in Parliament in the elections held on August 31, 1947, the communist position within the Parliament was fortified by a split within the Smallholders Party driven by center right Christian factions and the fact that the communists remained in firm control of security. Strong Soviet backing enabled them to continue utilizing the organs of the state to fortify their power. During the fall of 1947, the intensification of the Cold War led to Stalin's demand that the coalition governmental phase in Hungary be ended.[42] By July 30, 1948, the Smallholders had been pressured into "closer cooperation" with the communists, and Imre Nagy, Chairman of the Parliament, accepted the resignation of the President of Hungary and leader of the Smallholders Party, Zoltán Tildy. Árpád Szakasits, a Social Democrat, who endorsed unification with the communists, replaced him. Tildy had been compromised by the fact that his son-in-law had been accused of being a spy and a traitor.[43] Continued attacks against "reactionaries" were coupled with an intensive campaign to root out reactionaries within the Social Democrats, a move that would lead to the unification of the Communist and Social Democratic parties on March 7, 1949.[44] Hungary was now prepared to hold the first of many one-party elections in May of 1949.[45]

Interestingly, while the destruction of the multiparty system proceeded at full pace, the seeds of destruction were being sown for many within the Communist party. Presaged by a break in relations between Yugoslavia and the Soviet-dominated Cominform, a series of brutal show trials were planned by the regime of Mátyás Rákosi at the behest of Moscow. Yugoslavia had defied Stalin in regard to foreign policy and economic development decisions.[46] Stalin viewed Communist Party leader Josip Broz Tito's independence as a threat as he attempted to create a more uniform political system within the satellite states. Tito's refusal to accept Stalin's dominance and criticism led to Yugoslavia's ouster from the Cominform in June of 1948, and unsuccessful attempts by the Soviets to replace Tito.[47] Yugoslav intransigence led to Soviet preparations for a war with Yugoslavia and a campaign to discredit Tito and his regime.[48]

The former Interior Minister László Rajk proved to be the ideal choice for Rákosi's initial purge.[49] Stalin needed exemplars who would both incriminate Yugoslavia and dramatically demonstrate the fate that would befall those tempted to the autonomous model provided by Yugoslavia.[50] Rajk was arrested on the evening of May 30, 1949, and formally charged with war crimes, sedition, and being a leader of a treasonous organization. Mátyás Rákosi and his wife had entertained Rajk the previous day at Lake Balaton.[51]

The Rajk trial became synonymous with the brutality and coercive power of the Rákosi regime. Rajk's service against the fascists in Spain and in Hungary's underground communist movement during World War II was inverted in order to create links with the fascists and to connect him to both the Horthy and Szálasi governments.[52] In a fantastic story the accusations ranged from his being an *agent provocateur* within the underground to utilizing his position as Interior Minister to assist in a Yugoslav plot backed by the United States and Great Britain to stage a fascist counterrevolution that included the liquidation of "the present leaders of the Hungarian state and communist party."[53]

In order to substantiate the charges establishing Rajk as an agent of Tito it was necessary to create conspiratorial connections between Tibor Szőnyi, who had worked in the press department of the Interior Ministry, Yugoslav diplomat Lazar Brankov (who had defected to Hungary), and a Lieutenant General of the Hungarian Army, György Pálfy. These figures became known collectively as the Rajk gang and were subjected to brutal torture in order to extract the necessary confessions.[54] Among those entrusted to interrogate Rajk was his friend and the godfather of his son, János Kádár. In the second phase of the interrogation Kádár assured Rajk that the party knew that he was guiltless, but that he would need to accept his humiliation for the sake of the party. Though a death sentence might be meted out, Rajk and his family would be safely removed to the Soviet Union until such time that he could return to Hungary and the party. Rajk dutifully signed his confession.[55]

The trial against Rajk and his accomplices began on Friday, September 16, 1949, in the assembly hall of the Metal and Electrical Engineering Workers' Trade Union. *Szabad Nép* (Free Nation), the party organ, accused the "Enemy of the People" of "lifting a knife against the leaders of this nation and into the body of the working people, in addition to conspiring against electrified villages and white bread."[56] Foreshadowing Rajk's preordained sentence, the state prosecutor in an interview with the paper likened Rajk to a rabid dog, "the only way to defend against rabid dogs is to beat them to death."[57]

Rajk's trial consisted of his reiterative confession in a carefully staged response to questions set by the President of the Court, Péter Jankó.[58] The trial continued against all of the defendants in the same way, each one rit-ualistically linking the other to the conspiracy. For example, during World War II Tibor Szőnyi had been the leader of Hungarian communists living in Switzerland. His connection with an American Noel Field who was also a Soviet agent served to link the conspiracy to the United States through the bureau chief of the American Office for Strategic Services (OSS) Allen Dulles. Field had provided Dulles with strategic war information from his contacts with émigré groups living in Switzerland.[59] György Pálfy fortified the link between Rajk and Tito and the plot to overthrow the government, as claiming that Tito's support for the conspiracy were founded on Rajk's formation of a strong anti-party, anti-Soviet group within the police and the army "that would be at his disposal for seizing power."[60] One of the witnesses called to testify against Rajk, Sándor Cseresznyés, claimed to be a British spy who had first met Rajk in 1937 in Spain, helped establish that Rajk was an agent of the fascists asserting, " . . . Rajk hated the working class . . . he filled the Ministry of Home Affairs with former reactionary civil servants, gendarmes, and police officers . . . because he knew . . . they would gladly be ready instruments of his subversive policies."[61]

On September 24, 1949 the People's Court sentenced Rajk to death, con-fiscated his property, and ordered him to pay the costs of the prosecution.[62] János Kádár witnessed Rajk's execution on October 15. It was cast as a cele-bratory occasion that included food and drink for party members at the scene. It has been said that Rajk believed he would be saved from the gallows right until the last minute and proclaimed, "Long live Rákosi and Stalin," before the noose was tightened around his neck.[63] Kádár became a target not long af-ter, and was imprisoned in 1951.[64]

The death of Joseph Stalin on March 5, 1953, and the critique of his poli-cies by the new Moscow regime under the leadership of Nikita Khrushchev led to a change of leadership in Hungary under Imre Nagy in 1953, who un-til that point in time had been Minister of Agriculture primarily interested in issues centered on agricultural reform. Nagy had run afoul of Rákosi in the summer of 1948 when he promised that no one would take away the property of the peasants with smallholdings, a statement that was in opposition to the official policy of collectivization.[65] Nagy was accused of diverging from the party line and was forced to make a self-critique in front of the Central Com-mittee on September 3, 1949, one week before the László Rajk trial.[66] In No-vember of 1952, Nagy became a Deputy Minister for the working group re-sponsible for agriculture. The historian, István Rév, points out that it was Imre Nagy who eulogized Stalin in the Parliament after his death, providing an ad-ditional reminder of how Nagy was able to survive the Rákosi years. It concluded with these words, "The faithful and thankful Hungarian people have decided to preserve his glorious memory in law. By passing that law I have introduced . . . we are binding an imperishable wreath out of love and gratitude of our people around the deathless memory of our dear and great Comrade Stalin."[67]

The economic misery Hungarians felt at the end of the war continued under the failed policies of the Rákosi regime. Nagy's most important reforms were known as the "New Course," and involved a slowing down of collectivization and a renewed focus on light industry. The new policy was in stark contrast to the brutal collectivization and the subverting of peasant crops to fill state quotas that had exacted a cruel toll on the landed peasantry and led to food shortages. Hungary was forced to import wheat, and severe penalties were exacted on those who hoarded food. The policy of building the economy based on heavy industry was instituted without serious consideration being given to location and plants were built without ready access to railways and fuel. Hungary was still largely an agricultural economy and was not ready or able to absorb this shift in focus. A marked decline in the quality of export goods accompanied the introduction of centralized planning, characterized by breakdowns of manufactured goods such as tractors and machined tools. Hungarian agricultural products remained unsold because of low quality.[68]

Hungary's military obligation to the Soviets also played a role in Hungary's economic woes. The historian Béla Király points out that in order for Hungary to participate in a potential war against Yugoslavia the Hungarians were forced to refit their army. Ten percent of the weapons sold to Hungary by the Soviet Union were so badly damaged that they had to be repaired by the Hungarians before being used. According to Király, the Hungarians were told that this equipment was to be used for training purposes. Hungary's arms industry was restarted and began producing armaments for other socialist countries such as North Korea. Preparations for this confrontation further shifted the industrial focus from reconstruction and consumer goods.[69] As a result of these factors, by 1953 Hungary lay on the brink of economic ruin.

Nagy proclaimed an amnesty for many condemned prisoners during the hated show trials and general repression that had accompanied the Stalinists' rise to power. Well over 500,000 Hungarians suffered arrest, interrogation, forced relocation, imprisonment and execution. The terror was directed not only at political enemies among the elite such as László Rajk and Cardinal Mindszenty but enveloped the entire spectrum of Hungarian society. For example, peasants found guilty of hoarding, sometimes for only several loaves of bread, were branded as *kulaks* and sent to prison.

Sentences of internal migration for those accused of being part of past reactionary movements could mean the loss of an apartment and employment, in exchange for the life of an agricultural laborer. Rákosi reestablished concentration camps for the purpose of forced labor. According to historian László Borhi, over 40,000 Hungarians were hired as informers to assist in rooting out class enemies. Nagy's reforms were momentous when set in contrast with that of the Rákosi regime, but the "machinery of terror" had not been replaced.[70]

The Hungarian people were further distanced from the regime through the cult of personality embraced by Rákosi that trivialized or ignored national holidays in favor of important dates in the Soviet calendar. For example, St. Steven's Day was changed to constitution day, the day the Socialist constitution was enacted.[71] At the same time, however, the 1848 Revolution continued to be taught in the schools. Though viewed through a Marxist-Leninist lens, the story unintentionally fortified Hungarian nationalism with the inclusion the stirring poetry of Sándor Petőfi, the Hungarian Declaration of Independence, and the martyrdom of the Hungarian Prime Minister, Lajos Batthyány.[72] In spite of the regime's affront to Hungarian pride, many within Rákosi's inner circle, including those targeted in the show trials, and many ordinary Hungarians willingly participated in these holidays and the accompanying acts of obeisance to their leader.[73]

Nagy knew that in order to implement his "New Course" he would have to form alliances against Rákosi. In this, Nagy appeared at first to have Moscow's strong backing. Rákosi was severely critiqued by Soviet Foreign Minister Vyacheslav Molotov, at a June 13, 1953, meeting in Moscow between the Soviet Presidium and a delegation from Hungary that included Imre Nagy and Mátyás Rákosi. Molotov claimed, "There is a virtual wave of oppression against the population. They [the Rákosi regime] initiated prosecutions against 1,500,000 people in three and a half years in a population of 4.5 million adults." In regard to the economic disaster facing Hungary he pointed to outright corruption, claiming that in some cases products claiming to contain 57% wool had had the wool extracted from them. The end result however, was inconclusive, in that though Nagy became Prime Minister, Rákosi was left in place as the chairman of the Hungarian Worker's Party.[74]

Those left in power from the old regime slowed Nagy's reforms. Fifteen months after the changes had been announced, the economy remained stagnant with little material change filtering down to the people. In response, Nagy attacked those who were slowing down his changes and questioned those who claimed that the standard of living had been raised too far. There would be no turning back to the days before the New Course. Critiquing single-man rule, Nagy claimed that the collective wisdom of the party leadership had been essential in correcting the mistakes of the previous [Rákosi] regime. According to Nagy, the New Course was based on a true interpretation of Marxist-Leninist theory. In regard to the amnesty for those victimized by the terror Nagy stated, "injustices of the past must be undone . . . the Party leadership has the will to do this."[75] The illusion of party unity can be exemplified by the founding congress of the *Hazafias Népfront* (Patriotic National Front) that portrayed party rivals along with a wide array of Hungarians that included clergy all working together to strengthen Hungary and the New Course.[76]

The Soviet Union was unhappy with Hungary's economy and the constant feuding between the Rákosi and Nagy factions. Nagy's article in defense of the New Course and critique of Rákosi alarmed the Soviets to the possibility of a fractionalization within the Communist Party, a fear that Rákosi played upon and coupled to what he portrayed as Nagy's rightist tendencies. News articles appeared critiquing the New Course. For example, the danger of Nagy's policies to Hungarian socialism in the countryside were revealed in an article appearing in *Szabad Nép* by István Almási who claimed that kulaks continued to exploit the village of Jászkisér by not paying taxes and "bad mouthing the cooperatives." The village of Jászkisér had been lulled into a false consciousness that they called "class peace." Almási worried, "who would fight the kulaks?"[77] At a meeting between the Soviet Presidium and the Hungarian Worker's Party on January 8, 1955, Nikita Khrushchev severely rebuked Nagy reiterating Rákosi's claims that by trying to increase the standard of living Nagy had aided the petit bourgeoisie. Collectivization must continue, and Hungary needed to develop her heavy industry. According to Khrushchev, Nagy's policies played into the hands of the West that hoped that Hungary would provide yet another model of socialism akin to that of Yugoslavia. He demanded that Nagy either admit his mistakes or stand alone against the party. Though not demanding that Nagy step down from power, Khrushchev had helped retrench Rákosi's position within the party.[78]

The heightening of the Cold War, stimulated by West Germany's joining the North Atlantic Treaty Organization and Rákosi's claims that Nagy's reforms were undermining socialism in Hungary all played into Nagy's second ouster from the party.[79] Nagy's refusal to submit to self-criticism ensured Moscow's acquiescence. Rákosi arranged for Nagy's removal from the leadership in April of 1955 and from the party in December of the same year.

Rákosi came back into power but was unable to cope with the new political environment left in the wake of Nagy's reforms. Opposition leafleting and printed dissent had been brutally suppressed during Rákosi's terror, whereas the New Course had encouraged the formation of writer's circles such as the Petőfi Circle, named for the Hungarian revolutionary poet of 1848. These groups were made up primarily of loyal communists who had become disillusioned with the Stalinist policies of the Rákosi regime and had embraced the New Course. The Twentieth Soviet Congress in February of 1956 had provided Khrushchev with another opportunity to criticize the crimes and policies of Stalin. Fortified by this official critique, writer's circles began a concerted effort to criticize Rákosi's policies.[80]

Imre Nagy provided a focal point for these groups. The reformers planned a series of public discussions for May and June of 1956 in which issues of Hungarian economics, history, and ideology were discussed. The discussions drew capacity crowds of several thousand each evening and were viewed as Rákosi's acceptance of open dissent. For example, during the course of the first debate on economy the economist Tamás Nagy claimed that reading the government's data for the next five years was almost impossible, "the main thing is to debate the political issues that would make it possible to achieve the goals of the five year plan that include strengthening the collective leadership, expanding democracy within the party and within the country, and how to use the ideas of the Twentieth Congress."[81] Interestingly, Rákosi had been charged with de-Stalinization inside Hungary after Nagy's ouster from the leadership. The Hungarian people began to openly challenge Rákosi's legitimacy. According to Charles Gati, during performances of Shakespeare's *Richard the Third*, Rákosi was asked what he was really doing during his so-called sleepless nights searching out enemies of the state.[82] Rákosi's return to power was greeted with skepticism by a large segment of the Hungarian people encouraged to critique Stalinist policies from within Hungary, and unintentionally triggered from the de-Stalinization policies of the Soviet Union that threatened to undermine the regime.

The Hungarian Workers Party (MDP) removed Rákosi from power and sent him to the Soviet Union in July of 1956. Nikita Khrushchev based this decision on the rapidly deteriorating situation in Hungary and the Soviet Union's rapprochement with Yugoslavia. Another member of his clique, Ernő Gerő, succeeded Rákosi whom the Soviets hoped would stabilize the situation.[83] Gerő, however, had been the "architect" of many of Rákosi's policies and the earlier criticism went on unabated. For example, in an article by József Szalai entitled, "A Few Questions about Strengthening Socialist Lawfulness," Szalai asserted that, "The severe unlawfulness [of the Rákosi regime] was based on mistakes of Stalin, in which he stated that we needed to enact class struggle." In an obvious reference to Imre Nagy and the New Course he explained, "We attempted to diminish this unlawfulness after June of 1953." Rebuking the policy of terror launched against the Hungarian people he stated, "rehabilitation of these innocent workers and communists must come not only through the law, but through moral and material repatriation by our party and government." He concluded, "the most important aim in fixing this problem of unlawfulness, is to bring them back to society."[84] Criticism of Stalinist policy, fortified by the New Course, continued to transform itself into open dissent through the demand for the memorialization of Rákosi's victims, most notably László Rajk, and for the return of Imre Nagy to power.

Like Nagy and his comrades, the victims of Rákosi's terror had been buried in unmarked graves. Among those demanding a reburial was László Rajk's widow Júlia. When she confronted János Kádár, who had been rehabilitated by the party, she accused him of standing with the Stalinists in their refusal to provide her husband with a public funeral. Whether from Julia's prodding, or political expediency, Kádár pushed for Rajk's reburial.[85] The demands of the Hungarian people were clear and in an attempt to stabilize Hungary's political crisis the Gerő regime decided to rebury László Rajk and his principal co-defendants with state honors. Hungarian sentiment seemed to be captured by Ervin Gyertyán in the *Népszava*, "Oh Antigone bury your dead one. This is what is required by your morals and honor. So we will be able to grieve . . . "[86]

Rajk's funeral and reinternment explicitly transformed him from an accomplice of Rákosi to a victim of the terror. The day for the funeral was set for October 6th, the day commemorating the *Aradi vértanuk*.[87] *Szabad Nép* reported on October 7th that, "We cannot tell how many people came to the funeral, as the lines were endless; there has not been such a funeral since that of Lajos Kossuth."[88] The funeral was scheduled to begin at 3:00 P.M., but people began arriving at 11:00 A.M.[89] Over 300,000 Hungarians attended his funeral, including Imre Nagy.[90] The funeral provided a public occasion for the Hungarian people to mourn for the loss and humiliation they had suffered under Rákosi.

On the day of the funeral *Népszava* featured a picture of Rajk and his co-conspirators on the front page and announced, "On this day, officially, we will have new heroes in the pantheon of the national *kegyelet* living in our hearts . . . Communists . . . Men and Hungarians, victims of the unlawfulness . . . faithful to the ideals of our nation."[91] The *Szabad Nép* ran a headline announcing, "Never Again!"[92]

The funeral was held in the National Cemetery of Budapest, with the new "martyrs of the nation" being buried in close proximity to the tomb of Lajos Kossuth.[93] The caskets of László Rajk and his co-conspirators were laid on biers of black bunting surrounded by burning torches at each corner. In front of the caskets was a speaker's podium with a Hungarian tricolor emblazoned with a red star in the center. Other decorations at the funeral included Hungarian flags with the Rákosi coat of arms emblazoned in the center. Though wanting to distance themselves from the Rákosi regime, the Gerő regime were surrounded by symbols of the old regime. The three-minute film of the event made by the state shows mourners weeping and leaving flowers as they pass the caskets. Before Rajk's casket is covered, a wreath is tossed into the grave. The camera focuses on Imre Nagy and his wife for a brief moment.[94]

Antal Apró, speaking on behalf of the government stated, "The party is ready to jettison the mistakes of the past so there will never be a tragedy like this ever again." Ferenc Münnich, speaking for the veterans of the Spanish Civil War said, "Rajk was destroyed by those sadist criminals who were pulled into the sunshine from the cult of personality." *Népszava* branded Rákosi and his associates as "enemies of the people." Rajk and his fellow victims had become martyrs of the party.[95]

The date of the funeral coincided with the commemoration of the *Aradi vértanuk* and contributed to the burgeoning sense of national solidarity awakened by the moral bankruptcy of the terror. The 1848 Revolution had been crushed only when the Czar of Russia intervened in 1849. The historian George Schöpflin asserts that the Rajk funeral had reawakened the Hungarian sense of national unity. They saw themselves again as a nation under occupation by the same forces that had dashed their hopes more than a century earlier.[96] Béla Szász, who had been asked to speak at the funeral representing those victims who were part of the Rajk trial by his widow, Julia, claimed that it was the "passionate desire [of Hungarians] . . . to bury, lawlessness . . . tyranny . . . the moral dead of the shameful years."[97] *Szabad Nép* reported that, "the Hungarian people were filled with grief and a burning hate."[98] The unintended consequence of the funeral was the condemnation of not only Rákosi, but also the regime that followed in its place. For example, on October 19 Ernő Gerő approached Júlia Rajk in regard to a position within the Central Committee. According to Andrea Pető, Julia Rajk replied, "The people would hate and distrust me or any other compromised member of the Central Committee."[99] Béla Szasz claims that paradoxically those being buried might very well have turned against the sentiments that ultimately mobilized the Hungarian people to overthrow this hated regime.[100]

The fate of Imre Nagy was not so clear. Though the Soviets criticized the Hungarian Communist Party for creating more problems for themselves by ousting Nagy from power, they warned that an intensification of his critique could lead to imprisonment.[101] Instead, it was suggested that he be persuaded to recant his strongest critiques of the party and then be reinstated within the party in some insignificant role.[102]

During the summer and fall of 1955 Nagy wrote a series of essays entitled *On Communism* that represented not only a critique, but constituted a challenge to the regime. Defending his New Course Policy that had been defamed, Nagy warned that the MDP needed to break with the failed policies of Mátyás Rákosi while the people still trusted the party and put his reform policies into practice, the failure to do otherwise would lead to a "grave crisis."[103] Calling attention to László Rajk and the terror he asserted that, "real party unity can be established only through the exposure of crimes . . . without this

. . . there can be no talk of theoretical-political and moral unity."[104] He underscored the legitimacy of his policies stating, "Let the slanderers ask the people who is their enemy! They will hear the answer and it will not condemn me."[105]

Those within Nagy's circle had read these essays and worked for Nagy's return to power utilizing newspapers and writer's circles as mentioned earlier. His confrontation with Rákosi and his federates within the regime was in accord with the sentiment expressed at the funeral of László Rajk on October 6, 1956. As we have examined, his October reforms of 1954 included a plea for diversity within a one-party state. The partial amnesty for victims of the terror and his later demand for procedural law assured a great number of Hungarians that his reforms were to be institutionalized.[106] In this context it is not surprising that students and workers intensified their demand that Nagy be restored as the Prime Minister linked to their dream of a republican form of government after the funeral.

Acting with the Petőfi Circle, students at the József Attila University in Szeged quit the State sponsored Association of Working Youth (DISZ) and formed the University Student Association (MEFESZ) on October 16, 1956. The students moved beyond the Petőfi Circle in several important ways. Students had already begun demanding that Russian no longer be a compulsory language and that students should have choices among other European languages, indicating a desire to incorporate Hungary within the framework of an integrated Europe.[107] Students also wanted the opportunity to take part in running the country, a goal that seemed impossible under the Stalinist authoritarianism in which the government and managerial positions were subject to the ascriptive practices of the party.[108] The formation of the organization itself, as an independent political body with a democratic structure, was a major departure from authoritarian practice, but more in accord with Nagy's October 1954 platform that encouraged diversity under the blanket of a one-party state. The movement quickly spread to other universities throughout Hungary.[109] The Sixteen Points issued by students at Budapest Technical University underscores the radicalization of the movement. The students called for the withdrawal of Soviet troops, neutrality, reexamination of the planned economy, and the restoration of Imre Nagy. Interestingly, in accord with Nagy's essay, they demanded that Mátyás Rákosi be returned to Hungary to be tried by a tribunal. On the other hand, they went far beyond Nagy's reforms by reiterating the student demands of 1848 calling for new elections of the National Assembly by secret ballot, the right to strike, freedom of speech and the press. Any doubts regarding the importance of October 6th vanished when the students insisted that this date and March 15, marking the beginning of the Hungarian Revolution of 1848, be made national holidays. By meeting with workers in factories, local officials, and utilizing the network of the universities MEFESZ created the groundwork necessary for large-scale mobilization.[110]

When Soviet Ambassador Yurii Andropov and Hungarian leader Ernő Gerő discussed the accelerating pace of events, they worried that in the current climate stimulated by the Rajk funeral, many party members would look favorably on Nagy's program of reform. According to Gerő, in a conversation with Nagy on October 9, Nagy refused to admit to mistakes, insisting that he had been right all along in his assessment of Hungary's problems. According to Gerő, Nagy's program would go beyond the Yugoslav model of socialism and pull Hungary even further away from the Soviet Union.[111] Imre Nagy was reinstated as a member of the MDP on October 13. Discussions regarding Nagy's role within the party would continue until October 23, when massive student demonstrations generated a general mobilization of the people setting off a political crisis that resulted in Nagy's second tenure as Prime Minister.

The significance of the Rajk funeral was clear. According to the historian George Schöpflin, "This was the moment when thousands of atomized individuals recognized that they were not alone and lost their fear of the system."[112] Both the Nagy and the Rajk funerals were marked by strong evocations of national sentiment coupled to the tradition of memorialization that in a political sense created a moral dichotomy. In the case of Rajk the moral ending of a regime, and in Nagy's case, the moral ending of the Communist Party.

Unlike Rajk, Nagy had the opportunity to critique the regime, but only because he had survived the terror. Nagy had actively helped establish a one-party state and had remained passive in the face of juridical murder and acted only when it was safe for him to do so. In the wake of the disaster of World War II and high inflation, the communists increasingly seemed to offer a solution after the August election of 1947. According to the journalist George H. Hodos, who himself was swept up by the terror it, was difficult to foresee the tyranny that lay ahead for the Stalinist state in May of 1949. To him, Arthur Koestler's *Darkness at Noon* was simply "dirty slander."[113] Had Rajk survived the terror would he, like János Kádár, have returned to work inside the Communist Party, or like his wife turn away from the institution he held so dear? It is impossible to know as he had been brutally tortured, and so, we are unable to assess whether he went to his death a loyal servant of the party. Nagy, on the other hand, had lived in Moscow and knew the brutality of Stalinist politics first hand. Was Nagy merely an opportunist waiting to grab power, or had the trauma of the terror begun a process that slowly transformed him between the years 1953–1956? His refusal to step back from the gallows seems to indicate the later.

NOTES

1. Imre Nagy, *Imre Nagy on Communism: In Defense of the New Course* (London: Thames and Hudson, 1957), 243.
2. János M. Rainer, *Nagy Imre: Politikai életrajz* (Political Biography), *Elsö kötet, 1896–1953* (Budapest: 1956–os Intézet, 1996), 81
3. Nagy, *Imre Nagy on Communism*, 241.
4. Rainer, *Nagy Imre*, 135.
5. Ferenc Fehér and Ágnes Heller, *Hungary 1956 Revisited: The Message of a Revolution, A Quarter of a Century Later* (London: Allen and Unwin, 1983), 119, and Stephen F. Cohen, *Bukharin and the Bolshevik Revolution: A Political Biography 1888–1938* (New York: Alfred A. Knopf, 1973), 303, 384.
6. János M. Rainer, interview by author, April 6, 1998. The historian István Rév asserts that the list of names Nagy provided was a list of personal acquaintances indicating that the list was not a "willful denunciation." *Retroactive Justice: Prehistory of Post Communism* (Stanford: Stanford University Press, 2005), 15–16.
7. According to János M. Rainer Nagy was censured by the party after which his membership was restored. Rainer, *Nagy Imre*, 190, 196.
8. The Soviets had rapidly advanced after Romania joined the allies in August 1944. Debrecen and much of eastern Hungary was liberated between October and December 1944, Budapest was enveloped soon after. The Debrecen government was a coalition government whose goal in part was to lure Hungarians and those elements of the population that were not in sympathy with the German puppet government of Ferenc Szálasi to switch sides by recognizing and fighting for the Debrecen government. See: Peter Kenez, *Hungary from the Nazis to the Soviets: The Establishment of the Communist Regime in Hungary, 1944–1948* (Cambridge: Cambridge University Press, 2006), 11, 19–20, 22–23, 30.
9. Rainer, *Nagy Imre*, 255.
10. See: C. A. Macartney, *October Fifteenth* (Edinburgh: The Edinburgh University Press, 1961), 115, 271, 456–60, and Loránd Tilkovsky, "The Late Interwar Years and World War II" and Charles Gati, "From Liberation to Revolution, 1945–1956," in Peter F. Sugar et al., ed., *A History of Hungary* (Bloomington: Indiana University Press, 1990), 341, 352, 369.
11. Gati, "From Liberation to Revolution, 1945–1956," 371.
12. See: *Szabad Nép*, November 7, 1945.
13. The reality of the Soviet liberation and occupation made protestations of Hungarian Soviet friendship essential. On the other hand, the elections held in 1945 seemed to confirm the benevolence of Soviet intentions towards the Smallholders' mandate, although the author cautions us that coalition politics was a Soviet tactic utilized to gain communist ascendancy over time. Domonkos Szőke, "1945 szabad választás-szabad választás?" (1945 free elecitons-free elections?) *Tiltott történelmünk 1945–1947* (Our prohibited history), János Horváth, ed. (Budapest: Századvég Kiadó, 2006), 26, 40–42. The economist and MP (1945–1947, 1998–present), János Horváth, explained that this was part of a political deal that ensured the communists a place in the government. According to Horváth the communists were viewed as critical inter-

mediaries between the Parliament and the Soviet occupiers. János Horváth, interview by author, September 12, 2006.

14. Krisztián Ungváry, *Battle for Budapest: 100 Days in World War II*, trans. Ladislaus Löb (London: I.B. Tauris, 2005), 284–85. According to historian Peter Kenez, "People [Hungarians] expected Soviet soldiers to behave badly, and . . . they did," *Hungary from the Nazis to the Soviets*, 39–40.

15. The Soviet's profited greatly from its economic relationship with Hungary. For example, Hungarian sales of fruit pulp were financed by the Hungarians who sold it for less than half what it cost to produce. Borhi, *Hungary in the Cold War*, 145–51, 165. See also Kenez, *Hungary from the Nazis to the Soviets* and his discussion regarding Soviet long-term economic intentions, pp. 78–79.

16. László Borhi, *Hungary in the Cold War 1945–1956: Between the United States and the Soviet Union* (Budapest: Central European University Press, 2004) 66.

17. According to Kenez, by 1947 there were over 100,000 unemployed living in the countryside as a consequence of migration to the countryside due to food shortages and the loss of work resulting from the dissolution of large estates (*Hungary from the Nazis to the Soviets*, 110–117).

18. Borhi, *Hungary in the Cold War 1945–1956*, 77, 82.

19. Horthy enjoyed wide backing for these policies that were seen, in part, as redressing the unjust settlement at the Trianon Palace. István Deák, "A Fatal Compromise? The Debate over Collaboration and Resitance in Hungary," István Deák, Jan T. Gross, and Tony Judt, eds., *The Politics of Retribution in Europe: World War II and Its Aftermath* (Princeton: Princeton University Press, 2000), 48.

20. Much of Hungary lay in ruins, hundreds of thousands of soldiers and civilians had been killed in bloody battles at the Don and in Budapest and POW camps. The siege of Budapest alone cost over 100,000 lives. Over 550,000 Jews were murdered between 1941 and 1945. See: Tamás Stark, *Hungarian Jews during the Holocaust and after the Second World War, 1939–1949: A Statistical Review* (Boulder: East European Monographs, 2000), 133–38, Karl P. Benziger, "The Trial of László Bárdossy: The Second World War and Factional Politics in Contemporary Hungary," *Journal of Contemporary History*, 40, 3 (July, 2005): 467–68, 477, and Krisztián Ungváry, *Battle for Budapest: 100 Days in World War II*, Ladislaus Löb, trans. (London: I.B. Tauris and Co. Ltd., 2005), 330–31.

21. Rajk was rewarded for his work with a position in the Politburo. He and his wife had been captured for their underground activities and were interned by the Germans. Both László and his wife, Júlia Rajk, were welcomed with open arms by the party upon their return from Germany; it had been presumed that they were dead. Andrea Pető, *Rajk Júlia* (Budapest: Balassi Kiadó, 2001), 48. Some of the details of his work with the Communist Party in Hungary during World War II are outlined in Macartney, *October Fifteenth*, for example, 332–34, 364–66. See also: Jenő Györkei, "A Spanyolországi Rajk-Ügy (The Rajk case from Spain)," *Múltunk*, 41, 40 (1996): 150–51.

22. Ferenc Szálasi, leader of Hungary's fascist Arrow Cross Party replaced the regent Miklós Horthy on October 15 by the Germans after an unsuccessful attempt by Horthy to arrange an armistice with the allies. The Arrow Cross was renown for its

savage brutality towards Jews and those branded as traitors even as Budapest was in the midst of a dire struggle. Thomas Sakmyster, *Hungary's Admiral on Horseback: Miklós Horthy, 1918–1944* (Boulder: CO, 1994), 364–79, and Ungváry, *Battle for Budapest*, for example, 240–41, 248–49, 250.

23. Rajk's speech was given headline coverage see: *Szabad Nép*, December 2, 1945, 1–2.

24. Borhi, *Hungary in the Cold War*, 82–83.

25. George H. Hodos, *Show Trials: Stalinist Purges in Eastern Europe, 1948–1954* (New York: Praeger, 1987), 36–37, Joesph Rothschild, *Return to Diversity: A Political History of East Central Europe since World War II*, 2nd ed. (Oxford: Oxford University Press), 137, and *Szabad Nép*, March 21, 1946.

26. See *Szabad Nép*, March 5, 6, 7, 1946.

27. The historian László Hubai asserts that the Hungarian disaster at the Don River, in which the Hungarian expeditionary army that had accompanied the German invasion in the Soviet Union was all but destroyed, ensured the ending of the Horthy mandate to the ruling aristocracy after the war. The peasantry and the working class were encouraged to participate in civic life after 1945. "A korlátozott polgári demokrácia politikai rendszere Magyarországon: 1945–1947," (The Political system of the limited civic democracy in Hungary) *Tiltott történelmünk, 1945–1947*, 59.

28. The communists applied pressure against their political opponents gradually in a process Charles Gati has described as "salami tactics," Gati, "From Liberation to Revolution, 1945–1946," 371. See also: George Schöpflin, *Politics in Eastern Europe* (Oxford: Blackwell Publishers, 1993), 66. The historian László Borhi points out that the Soviets consistently thwarted American attempts to open up Hungarian markets to the West, effectively keeping Hungary within the Soviet economic sphere in "Soviet Expansionism or American Imperialism?" in *20th Century Hungary and the Great Powers*, Ignác Romsics, ed. (New York: Columbia University Press, 1995).

29. Rothschild, *Return to Diversity*, 100.

30. László Hubai uses the term "limited democracy" as Hungary was still under occupation and its sovereignty limited by the terms of the Armistice. There was a sense that the Soviets were honoring the terms laid out in the Declaration of a Liberated Europe as part of the Yalta agreement. For example, Law I of 1946 passed by the parliament guaranteed basic civil rights of speech, assembly, and political association. Hubai, "A korlátozott polgári demokrácia politikai rendszere Magyarországon: 1945–1947." 59. In addition, the historian István Csicsery-Rónay, reminds us that after the Smallholder victory of 1945 the *New York Times* called Hungary a "stronghold of democracy" in a region where democracy was still struggling to gain a foothold [certainly in comparison to Romania and Poland]. "Csillagos órák: a kommunisták kétszeres veresége," (starry hours: the double defeat of the communists), *Tiltott történelmünk 1945–1947*, 120.

31. See: "The Ambassador in the Soviet Union to the Secretary of State," January 4, 1945, *Foreign Relations of the United States, 1944*, III, The British Commonwealth and Europe (Washington: United States Printing Office, 1944), 965–62. Laws covering war crimes outlined in the armistice were codified in Law VII enacted by the Hungarian Parliament on September 11, 1945.

32. *Fehér Könyv: A Magyar Köztársaság és demokrácia elleni összeesküvés ok-mányai, Harmadik kiadás* (White Book: The documents . . . The documents of the conspiracy against the Hungarian Republic and Democracy) (Budapest: A Szikra Irodalmi és Lapkiadó vállalat, 1947), 1–2, 7–8. The foundation of the charges is further developed through interviews with Ferenc Kopócs that include plans to establish the Smallholders as the dominant party through means that included a black list on pages 71–72.

33. The Communists were bent on destroying the Smallholders. Witnesses against the Smallholders included members of a nationalist group called the Hungarian Community accused of plotting to overthrow the government whose ties to several of the Smallholders members aided in the development of the charges. Confessions were extracted under torture. See: Kenez, *Hungary from the Nazis to the Soviets*, 218–25.

34. Imre Patkó, "A Nép Rendőrsége," (The People's Police) *Szabad Nép*, August 15, 1947, 3.

35. "Az MKP Listavezetöi Rajk László" *Szabad Nép*, August 14, 1947, 2. Joseph Rothschild also points to Rajk's ruthless character both in his systematic destruction of opposition parties and in his encouragement of "spontaneous justice" carried out by workers against black marketeers and other targets. *Return to Diversity*, 137.

36. Borhi, *Hungary in the Cold War*, 83, and Kenez, *Hungary from the Nazis to the Soviets*, 159.

37. Horthy was a monarchist and chose to back the Smallholders as the "least undesirable," in Kenez, *Hungary from the Nazis to the Soviets*, 170–71.

38. József Cardinal Mindszenty, *Memoirs*, translated by Richard and Clara Winston (New York: Macmillan Publishing Co., 1974), 52–58. See also: Kenez, *Hungary from the Nazis to the Soviets*, 279–80.

39. Kenez, *Hungary from the Nazis to the Soviets*, 281–87.

40. Borhi, *Hungary in the Cold War*, 209.

41. Imre Patkó, "Az MKP Listavezetöi Nagy Imre," *Szabad Nép*, August 27, 1947, 3.

42. Charles Gati, "From Liberation to Revolution," 372. See also: Walter La Feber, *America, Russia, and the Cold War, 1945–2000* 9th ed. (Boston: McGraw Hill, 2002), 75–77.

43. *Politikus Pályák*, 33 and *Kis Ujság*, August 1, 1948.

44. *Szabad Nép*, March 7, 1949.

45. Among those rooted out was Anna Kéthly, a strong advocate for pluralism within the social democratic sphere. *Szabad Nép*, March 9, 1949.

46. The Yugoslavs felt that Moscow's insistence that they slow down industrial development would keep them in a "semi-colonial dependence." Rothschild, *Return to Diversity*, 129.

47. Rothschild makes the point that Stalin's actions had the unintended consequence of solidifying Tito's regime, *Return to Diversity*, 130–32.

48. According to the historian and former commander of the Hungarian People's Infantry, Béla Király, preparations for this war, which included substantial participation by Hungary and other satellite states, were complete by 1951. The author claims that the Korean War and a purge of Hungary's military leadership aborted this invasion. Béla Király, "The Hungarian Revolution and Soviet Readiness to Wage War

Against Socialist States," in *The First War between Socialist States: The Hungarian Revolution of 1956 and Its Impact* (New York: Brooklyn College Press, 1984), 8, 18–22.

49. Rajk had been moved to the Ministry of Foreign Affairs in August 1948.

50. Rajk had been accused of Trotskyism while in Spain and though cleared of the charges still had enemies who were close to his battalion commander who had leveled the charges, László Haas. Ernő Gerő was a member of the Central Committee and for ten years after World War II held key positions within the government. Prior to charges being leveled at Rajk in 1938, Gerő sent Haas a letter asking why "the Hungarian section hasn't revealed any enemies yet." Haas perished in Auschwitz after his deportation from France, whereas Rajk had survived; perhaps there was a predisposition to target Rajk. Györkai, "A Spanyolországi Rajk-Ügy," 149, 151, 159.

51. Rajk's wife was questioned by the AVH on June 6. See: *László Rajk and His Accomplices before the People's Court,* Ferenc Koltai ed. (Budapest: Budapest Printing Press, 1949), 5, Andrea Pető, *Júlia Rajk,* 79, 81 and Béla Szász, *Volunteers for the Gallows* (New York: W. W. Norton and Co., 1971), 160–62.

52. *László Rajk and His Accomplices before the People's Court,* 8.

53. Detailed accounts of the purge and show trial can be found in George H. Hodos, *Show Trials,* for example chapters entitled, "Road to the Rajk Trial," and "The Model Trial," likewise in *Volunteers for the Gallows* where Béla Szász provides riveting accounts of the events as they unfolded. *László Rajk and His Accomplices before the People's Court,* 8–16.

54. Hodos, *Show Trials,* 45.

55. Hodos, *Show Trials,* 47–49. See also: Pető, *Rajk Julia,* 51. Their relationship could be temperamental for example, Rajk and Kádár seemed to disagree as to how quickly the new security forces should expand with the later essentially dismissing Rajk's concerns, 74. Tibor Hajdú, "The Party Did Everything for You," *The Hungarian Quarterly,* 37 (Spring, 1996): 86 and William Shawcross, *Crime and Compromise: János Kádár and the Politics of Hungary since Revolution* (New York: E.P. Dutton and Co., Inc., 1974), 66–68.

56. The headline on the front page read, "Népünk Ellenségei" (The Enemy of the People). *Szabad Nép,* September 14, 1949.

57. M. Gy., "Rajk," *Szabad Nép,* September 18, 1949, 9.

58. For example, Rajk provided a blow-by-blow account of Tito's intentions to overthrow People's democracies and his specific instructions to eliminate the communist leadership that included Rákosi and Gerő. *László Rajk and His Accomplices before the People's Court,* 62–65.

59. See: Szász, *Volunteers for the Gallows,* 144–145 and an excellent article by Igor Lukes, "The Rudolf Slánský Affair," *Slavic Review,* 58, 1 (Spring, 1999): 166–72. In this article Lukes outlines Field's travails as an exposed communist in postwar America. Field decided to remain in Europe rather than face the scrutiny in the United States that would be accorded a Soviet agent. Fleeing to Czechoslovakia, he was arrested by the Hungarian AVH, chloroformed, and brought back to Budapest where he was tortured until providing the proper "evidence" needed.

60. *László Rajk and His Accomplices before the People's Court,* 89–90.

61. *László Rajk and His Accomplices before the People's Court,* 217–19.

62. *László Rajk and His Accomplices Before the People's Court*, 305–6. Rajk's wife, Júlia, was imprisoned after her husband had been taken away and their son László was placed in a state orphanage.

63. Tibor Huszár, *Kádár* (Budapest: Szabad Tér Kiadó-Kossuth Kiadó, 2001), 152. On the other hand, George Hodos points out that though Rajk agreed with the sentence he stated, "I fully agree with most of the statements of the prosecutor . . . of course I am not thinking about the secondary . . . and unimportant details, but of the substance." Hodos feels that perhaps Rajk was signaling his refutation of the charges. See: *Show Trials*, 62 and *László Rajk and His Accomplices before the People's Court*, 289. Júlia Rajk biographer, Andrea Pető, instructs us to pay attention to the fact that Rajk swore to his date of birth incorrectly, *Rajk Júlia*, 89. István Rév seems to indicate that Cardinal Mindszenty's account of an execution on October 15, 1949, was that of Rajk. In this account Rajk proclaims that he dies an "innocent man." See: *Retroactive Justice: Prehistory of Post-Communism*, 105–6 and Mindszenty, *Memoirs*, 149–51. Tibor Huszár, however, claims that it was another "conspirator," András Szalai, who exclaimed, "I die an innocent man, I have been tortured." *Kádár*, 152.

64. Interestingly, though Kádár played a major role in extracting Rajk's confession he became more suspicious and wary of his comrades after the execution. His fears were well founded as Rákosi began to complain to the Soviets in March of 1950 that he no longer trusted Kádár. Tibor Huszár, *Kádár*, 153, 154–55.

65. Rainer, *Nagy Imre*, 397.

66. Rainer, *Nagy Imre*, 418.

67. István Rév, "Covering History," Getty Conference, "Memory, History, Narrative: A Comparative Inquiry into the Representation of Crisis," Hamburg, Germany, July 3–5, 1977.

68. László Borhi, *Hungary in the Cold War*, 215–16 and Walter Laquer, *Europe in Our Time* (New York: Penguin Books, 1992), 304.

69. Béla Király, "The Hungarian Revolution and Soviet Readiness to Wage War against Socialist States," 14–6.

70. Borhi, *Hungary in the Cold War*, 208–14. See also: Schöpflin, *Politics in Eastern Europe*, 101.

71. Borhi, *Hungary in the Cold War*, 205 and Schöpflin, *Politics in Eastern Europe*, 93.

72. The story of the 1848 Revolution had been highlighted by the coalition government after World War II and was seen by the communists as an important development in the epic story of class struggle. For example see: Spira Györgyi, *A Magyar Nép Története, II Rész, 1526–1849*, Ideiglenes Tankönyv (Budapest: Tankönyvkiadó, 1951), 130–32, 158, 166, 170. Though this particular text is marked as being temporary, the treatment of the 1848 Revolution remained consistent throughout the communist period as we shall see. See also Alice Freifeld's study of March 15 and the use of the holiday by the communists in "The Cult of March 15," *Staging the Past: The Politics of Commemoration in Hapsburg Central Europe, 1848 to the Present*, ed., Maria Bucur and Nancy M. Wingfield (West Lafayette, IN: Purdue University Press, 2001), 275.

73. A point poignantly made by George Faludy as he pondered what would become of future generations socialized under the communist system in *My Happy Days in Hell*, 6th ed., translated by Kathleen Szász (Budapest: Forever Kiadó, 2002), 325–26.

74. Notes of a Meeting between the CPSU CC Presidium and a HWP Political Delegation in Moscow, June 13 and 16, 1953, in Csaba Békés et al., ed., *The 1956 Revolution: A History in Documents* (Budapest: Central European University Press, 2002), 16–17, see also the introductory essay page 5.

75. In this front page story Nagy carefully avoids naming names, although his target was clear. The article stemmed from the Central Committee. Imre Nagy, *Szabad Nép*, October 20, 1954.

76. *Szabad Nép*, October 24, 1954, 1–3.

77. *Szabad Nép*, January 11, 1955, 2.

78. "Notes of Discussion between the CPSU CC Presidium and a HWP Leadership Delegation in Moscow on January 8, 1955," *The 1956 Hungarian Revolution: A History in Documents*, 60–64.

79. Joseph Rothschild also claims that Georgii Malenkov's removal from power left Nagy bereft of one of the staunchest backers of the New Course within Moscow. *Return to Diversity*, 154–55. See also Borhi, *Hungary and the Cold War*, 236–38.

80. The MDP's journal reported on the results of the Twentieth Soviet Congress in March and specifically made connections between Khrushchev's critique of Stalin's personality cult and lack of collective decision making with that of the Rákosi regime, pointing to the travesty of the Rajk trial as an example. "Recognizing mistakes from the past provides a new way for the future." See: "A Szovjetunió Kommunista Pártjának XX Kongresszusa után," *Társadalmi Szemle*, 11, 3 (March, 1956): 16–20. (After the 20th Congress of the Soviet Union's Communist Party)

81. "A marxista politikai gazdaságtan időszerű kérdéseiről és a második ötéves terv irányelveiről," (About the current questions of the Marxist political economy and the directives of the second five year plan) May 9, 1956, *A Petőfi Kör vitái: hiteles jegyzőkönyvek alapián, Két közgazdasági vita* (Győr: Kelenföld Kiadó - ELTE, 1989), 52–53.

82. Gati, "From Liberation to Revolution," 378. See also "A Pártélet további Demokratizálásának Útjai," (further avenues to democratizing party life) *Társadalmi Szemle*, 11, 5 (May, 1956): 5–6, that warned, "real party democracy can be found only where there is no obstacle to critique . . . there are still places where they do not like critique and mute those who do so."

83. According to historian István Feitl, Rákosi's forced self-critique made his crimes manifest and paved the way for his ally Gerő's ascent. The problem being that Gerő tried to save the Stalinist faction within the MDP. See: "Szembesülés: Az MDP vezetői és a XX Kongresszus," (Facing [the facts]: The Leaders of the MDP and the 20th Congress) *Múltunk*, 2 (2006): 224.

84. József Szalai, "A Szocialista Törvényesség megszilárdításának néhány kérdése" (A Few Questions Bbout the Strengthening of Socialist Lawfulness), *Társadalmi Szemle* (June/July, 1956): 32–33.

85. Pető, *Rajk Júlia*, 142. Gerő was frightened of the revelations that would implicate himself in Rákosi's policies should the case of Mihály Farkas become public. Farkas had run the AVH and carried out their instructions regarding the unleashing of the terror and the show trials. Set against the Stalinist old guards resilience Kádár appeared to hold the moral high ground within the Party. István Feitl, "Szembesülés: Az MDP vezetői és a XX Kongresszus," 226.

86. Ervin Gyertyán "A temetés elé" (Before the Funeral), *Népszava*, October 5, 1956, 4.

87. The *Aradi vértanUK* were the thirteen generals who had fought for Hungarian independence hanged by the Austrians in the city of Arad on October 6, 1849.

88. Kossuth was a revolutionary and served as the President of the Parliamentary Republic, 1848–1849.

89. *Szabad Nép*, October 7, 1956, p. 1-2.

90. Schöpflin, *Politics in Eastern Europe*, 125.

91. "Mártirjaink," *Népszava*, October 6, 1956, p. 1.

92. "Soha Többé" (Never Again), *Szabad Nép*, October 6, 1956, p. 1.

93. A site created by the communists and named the Pantheon of the Heroes of the Labor Movement. See: István Rév, "Parallel Autopsies," *Representations*, 49 (Winter: 1995): 22.

94. *Tükörcserepek Magyarország–1956* (Cracked Mirror, Hungary 1956). Produced by Gábor Vitéz. Budapest: 1956 Institute/Hungarian Film Institute, 1996. Videocassette.

95. József Timmer, "Temetünk" (We Bury), *Népszava*, October 7, 1956, p. 1.

96. Schöpflin, *Politics in Eastern Europe*, 126.

97. Béla Szász, *Volunteers for the Gallows*, 233, 236.

98. *Szabad Nép*, October 7, 1956, p. 1.

99. Pető, *Rajk Júlia*, 157.

100. Béla Szász, *Volunteers for the Gallows*, 239.

101. See: "Report from Anastas Mikoyan on the Situation in the Hungarian Worker's Party, July 14, 1956," *The 1956 Hungarian Revolution: A History in Documents*, 145.

102. "Report from Ambassador Yuri Andropov on Deteriorating Conditions in Hungary," August 29, 1956, *The 1956 Hungarian Revolution: A History in Documents*, 166-67.

103. Nagy, *On Communism*, 62.

104. Nagy, *On Communism*, 56–57.

105. Nagy, *On Communism*, 268.

106. Especially in light of the conversations that had taken place in journals and in public forums such as the Petőfi Circle debates following the Twentieth Soviet Congress as already discussed.

107. Gati, "From Liberation to Revolution, 1945–1956," 378.

108. Schöpflin, *Politics in Eastern Europe*, 93.

109. DISZ did not entirely disappear, as not all students agreed with the more radical course outlined by the Budapest Technical University. For example, students at Eötvös Loránd University after an intense debate defeated a move to leave DISZ. See:

Nóra Némethné Dikán, Róbert Szabó, István Vida, "Egyetemisták és főiskolások Követelései: 1956 októberében," (The demands of university and college students in October 1956) *Múltunk*, 48, 4 (2003): 289.

110. "The Sixteen Points Prepared by Hungarian Students, October 22–23, 1956," *The 1956 Hungarian Revolution: A History in Documents*, 188–89 and Litván, The *Hungarian Revolution of 1956*, 52. For an excellent discussion of the Twelve Demands issued by the Revolutionaries of 1848 see István Deák's classic work, *The Lawful Revolution: Louis Kossuth and the Hungarians 1848-1849* (New York: Columbia University Press, 1979) 69–73.

111. "Record of Conversation between Yurii Andropov and Ernő Gerő, October 12, 1956," *The Hungarian Revolution of 1956: A History in Documents*, 178–79.

112. Schöpflin, *Politics in Eastern Europe*, 126.

113. Hodos, *Show Trials*, 41–42.

Chapter Four

Imre Nagy and the Revolution of 1956: A Fatal Gamble

> We have two ways to extricate ourselves from the disastrous situation brought upon the country by the Rákosi regime: we can either liquidate Stalinist policy ourselves in good time and lead the country back to the June road, by which we can avoid economic and political failure; or we can refrain from changing the course of events with the result that the increasing tension may bring the country to the verge of a grave crisis.
>
> —Imre Nagy, "Ethics and Morals in Hungarian
> Public Life," December 1955.[1]

Imre Nagy laid down a clear challenge to the Stalinists that generated sympathy within his inner circle, writer's circles, and at a more limited level within the socialist sphere. Josip Broz Tito in Yugoslavia read at least one of Nagy's essays written in 1955, and Nagy was a frequent guest of the Soviet ambassador Yuri Andropov.[2] Perhaps most importantly he remained popular with the Hungarian people. In spite of Moscow's concerns with his defiance of protocol, revealed in his refusal to submit to self-critique, his rehabilitation was assured by the political climate supercharged by Rajk's funeral. He could not have known the nature of the grave crisis that would sweep the country on October 23, leading to his brief and final ascendance as Prime Minister. A review of the Revolution and the demobilization that followed will be valuable in assessing Nagy's accord with its goals and importantly the role he plays in shaping the contemporary memories of the event.

Discontent within Hungary was fortified by events transpiring in the Soviet Union and Central Europe. Nikita Khrushchev's critique of Stalin at the Twentieth Congress in February 1956 and his insistence that Mátyás Rákosi continue a policy of de-Stalinization in 1955 served to help stay the regime's hand against the agitation of writer's circles and Nagy.[3] Within Central Europe the Soviet Union's rapprochement with Yugoslavia following the death of Stalin helped force the Gerő regime's acquiescence in the demand for Rajk's reburial.[4] The Yugoslav example of an independent path to socialism and political development outside the purview of Moscow seemed to set a precedent for other countries within the Soviet sphere.[5] The historian Johanna C. Granville points to the symmetry between the Yugoslav model and the spirit of the Bandung Conference of 1955 in which the non-aligned nations of Africa and Asia present at the conference pledged "mutual noninterference in each other's internal affairs." This hopeful theme is addressed by Imre Nagy in his essays collected together in *On Communism*.[6] Throughout his essays Nagy called for "peaceful coexistence . . . between differing social systems," explaining national difference and true patriotism from a line in a poem by the revered revolutionary poet of 1848 Sándor Petőfi, "If the earth were God's hat, then our homeland is the bouquet upon it."[7]

Secondly, the Soviet Union had agreed at Geneva to sign the Austrian peace treaty in May 1955 in which the country was neutralized in exchange for the withdrawal of Soviet troops. The Soviet excuse for leaving four divisions on Hungarian soil was that it required a secure supply route for its troops stationed in Austria. Perhaps in the context of this new reality the Soviets might agree to a withdrawal of their forces from Hungarian soil in exchange for various concessions from the Hungarians.[8]

Finally, the worker's strike in Poznan, Poland, June 1956, underscored a heated struggle for power between Stalinists and national communist reformers that resulted in the national communists gaining the upper hand. Though brutally suppressed, the strike exposed serious economic problems that lay at the heart of the strike. According to Granville, one of the consequences of the strike was a burgeoning of worker's councils and a gathering of over one million Poles at the Jasna Góra Monastary, a national shrine. In a bid to stymie the crisis, the Polish leadership rehabilitated Wladyslaw Gomulka, a national communist and former partisan during World War II who had been dismissed from the party in 1948 during the Polish equivalent of the anti-Yugoslav campaign initiated by Stalin. Gomulka as Prime Minister boldly stood up to Moscow demanding that they not interfere in Poland's sovereign affairs in mid October when armed Soviet intervention loomed.[9]

The three examples provided models of economic and political independence, or a third way of development in the bi-polar world that would be acceptable to Moscow. The Hungarian Workers' Party's journal had hailed the Bandung principles as a model for reestablishing the founding principles of the United Nations.[10] Nagy's political reforms embodied in the New Course coupled with the events taking place within Central Europe and the former colonial world encouraged many intellectuals and Hungarians in general to believe that Hungary too might hope for an independent path. Again, it should be remembered that Nagy envisioned his reforms in the context of a one-party state.

The demands of the university students in October, discussed in the previous chapter, were set in the dynamics of this international and internal context. Hungarian students organized mass meetings on their campuses in order to discuss the consequences of what was thought to be the advent of a new era of freedom in Central Europe.[11] In Budapest students at the Technical University debated the demands set out by MEFESZ and the meaning of the events taking place in Poland. It was decided to stage a mass demonstration in order to show solidarity with the changes taking place in Poland. Students would rally at the Bem monument (Bem was a Polish general who aided the Hungarians in the 1848 Revolution) located in Buda across the river from the Parliament building. The planned student demonstration coupled with their demands for the establishment of a procedural republic was clearly an affront to the Stalinist regime under Ernő Gerő who had only grudgingly allowed the demonstration to take place. The party organ *Szabad Nép*, however, supported the new student movement and their activism that responded to the critique of Stalinism at the Twentieth Congress.[12] Although, the paper warned that the movement should not be used for political ends by either left or right wing ideologues. The students' demands were not reported in full, especially those regarding freedom of the press and a plural political process, saying instead that the students' were "delighted with the Szeged [student] movement." It did, however, report the students' request that Imre Nagy should be allowed to publicize his political and economic views and that Mihály Farkas be tried publicly. Farkas had been a major figure in the ÁVH and responsible for extracting confessions during the show trials that included the Rajk gang. A public trial would further damage the credibility of the Stalinists.[13] It was in this context that Nagy and his advisors were confident that he would be appointed Prime Minister based on the Polish example.[14]

Nagy too, however, feared the proposed student demonstration. Gomulka's seeming tough stand against the Soviets was nuanced by his unequivocal loyalty to Moscow. Throughout the Polish crisis the Poles had demonstrated their ability to maintain internal security without the aid of Soviet troops. In this guise reform could be initiated, but only in a way and at a tempo that did not threaten the Soviet Union. According to historian János M. Rainer, one of Nagy's close advisors, József Szilágyi, who attended the debate at the Technical University, called for a demonstration the next day. Nagy did not agree with his advisor's actions and with the more radical demands of the students. According to Rainer, Nagy wanted someone from the Central Committee to speak with the students in order to ameliorate the situation. At his trial in 1958 Nagy claimed that he did not want to speak with the students because "he didn't have the official party answers."[15]

As the student demonstrators began their march towards the Bem statue in the afternoon, events in the streets quickly outpaced political reflections of the Nagy group or the Central Committee. Workers and the people in Budapest joined the students in the streets and the demonstration quickly grew from a nucleus of 20,000 to over 250,000 when the demonstrators moved from the Bem monument to the Parliament building.[16] The regime's refusal to meet with the students and carry the student's demands over the radio helped radicalize the crowd. Hungarian flags being flown with the Soviet star or the Rákosi coat of arms cut from the center symbolized the crowd's disillusion with Stalinism. Ernő Gerő further enflamed the passions of the crowd in an address over the radio in which he stated, "we of course want a socialist democracy not a civil democracy." Calling the demonstrators "enemies of the people," he rejected their demands that called for Hungarian sovereignty and a procedural republic.[17]

The capacity crowd at the Parliament continued their demands for an end to Soviet occupation and the return of Nagy to power. The demonstration was in part aided by the police who refused to attack peaceful demonstrators and many young people within the army who sympathized with the demands of the students. The crisis set off by the demonstrations forced the Gerő regime to act and after consultation with Moscow it was decided to invite Nagy back into the government as Prime Minister. Much to the dismay of Nagy's inner circle, Nagy cut a deal with the Gerő regime that left Gerő and other key players of the regime in the new government. On October 22, when the Nagy circle contemplated the significance of the changes taking place in Poland, it had been decided that Nagy's ascension as Prime Minister would be premised on the exit of the Stalinists. Nagy's fury against the Stalinists seems to have been tempered by what he saw as an opportunity to re-start the program of his New Course and at the same time demonstrate his loyalty to Moscow.[18] The problem with this strategy was that the crowd's demands now outpaced what he considered reasonable compromise. He was unable to capture the crowd when he addressed them at the Parliament that evening and his calls to return home went unheeded.[19]

Meanwhile, a standoff had developed in front of the radio station where students gathered to again demand that their program be broadcast to the Hungarian nation. Members of the ÁVH fired upon students who attempted to enter the radio station, whereupon students and citizens fired back and stormed the radio station. Soldiers who had been ordered to the scene to help disperse the demonstrators apparently provided the weapons to the demonstrators with some soldiers joining the assault.[20] Another crowd gathered in front of the statue of Stalin located near the Heroes Square in the city park unleashed their fury at the hated symbol and tore it apart. Equally worrying to the communist regime, the demonstrations were not confined to Budapest. In the city of Debrecen, located approximately 240 kilometers east of Budapest, three were killed and six wounded as ÁVH forces fired upon a demonstration of 20,000 in the late afternoon.[21] Police barracks and armories were stormed in search of weapons. By the time the first Soviet tanks began entering Budapest they were confronted by armed revolutionaries engaged in what was now considered a war of national liberation.[22]

Radicalization was fueled by the Gerő regime's inability to handle the crisis, a principal reason why the Soviets backed Nagy's ascension as Prime Minister. Revolutionary committees sprang up across Budapest and throughout Hungary with the demands of the students forming the nucleus of the revolutionary agenda. For example, a manifesto, publicly supporting the student demonstration of October 23rd from the city of Miskolc, an industrial city located to the northeast of Budapest, is typical and states its absolute support for the most "radical elements of the student movement."[23] The student's organization was subsumed by these overall blanket organizations in order to meet the emergency at hand, street fighting and negotiations with the government.[24]

Nagy favored an approach that would separate the demonstrators from the armed insurgents and thus supported the Soviet intervention. In a meeting with Anastas Mikoyan and Mikhail Suslov Nagy said, "We decided along with suppressing the revolt by force, to carry out a policy of reconciliation and rapprochement with the intelligentsia and the masses of people and to embrace the popular movement and national feelings, in order to surmount this popular movement and thereby defeat the counterrevolutionaries . . . "[25] Nagy drove this point home publicly in a radio address the day before when he claimed that counterrevolutionaries had taken advantage of the real grievances expressed by the workers.[26] According to the historian Miklós Horváth, it was hoped that the overwhelming force displayed by the Soviet forces would cow the resistance and force it to disperse as in the case of the Berlin crisis in 1953. But the ferocity and determination of the resistance led to casualties and an inability of the Soviets to reestablish order. Nagy's call for a return to his 1953 program no longer resonated with the street. The situation was further complicated by the seeming neutrality of much of the police force and a large part of the Hungarian army.[27] The Polish example that seemed so promising before October 23 became increasingly remote as the revolutionaries demonstrated their determination to control the political circumstances.[28]

In this light, Nagy's tempered approach was viewed as being indecisive both by his inner circle, members of the Politiburo, and the Soviet Union. On one hand, he knew that blood would be spilled in the bid to quell the insurgents, and yet, he needed to maintain the loyalty of the majority of the population. This may explain his hesitation to actually place his name on a request for Soviet aid in containing the crisis. According to András Hegedűs, who had remained in the Politburo after stepping down as Prime Minister, the Soviet Ambassador, Yuri Andropov, kept following Nagy around his office with the request for Soviet intervention in his hand. Nagy kept carefully avoiding Andropov, so he would be unable to hand Nagy the message. Hegedűs ultimately signed the request on October 26, which was then backdated to October 23.[29] On the other hand, his desire to limit the bloodshed as evidenced by his calls for amnesty in exchange for laying down arms on October 24 and 25 and ultimately his call for a truce on October 28 demonstrates his intent not to alienate the Hungarian people already sickened by the bloodshed.[30] This point was underscored by his insistence that an attack planned for the morning of October 28 against the major centers of revolutionary resistance at the Killián barracks and the Corvin Passage be called off.[31] Many Hungarians who were disturbed by the unrest or viewed the Revolution as illegitimate began to turn increasingly against the Soviets after the massacre in Parliament Square perpetrated by the ÁVH and Soviet troops on October 25 that killed 100 Hungarians. Nagy's actions in the early days of the Revolution were unable to fully satisfy the Hungarian people or the Soviets. These factors would eventually turn the Soviets and conservative members of the Communist Party against him.[32]

Nagy only gradually joined with the goals of the Revolution. His announcement of a multi-party system on October 30, 1956, marked this turning point as he urged Hungarians to "safeguard the achievements of the Revolution."[33] The seeming Soviet acquiescence to the demand for withdrawal in the context of the cease-fire and approval of Nagy's tactics led to a false sense of security that was fortified by the Soviet announcement of friendship and cooperation of October 30 published in *Pravda* on October 31. The Soviet declaration announced that its troops were being withdrawn from Budapest and were prepared to negotiate with Hungary regarding the presence of troops stationed countrywide. Throughout the document there are allusions to the "spirit of Bandung" in its assertion of the "full sovereignty of each socialist state." Less noticed and more ominous for Hungary, the declaration stated its "confidence that the peoples of the socialist countries will not permit foreign and domestic reactionary forces to shake the foundations of the people's democratic system . . . "[34] In the wake of the bitter fighting a sense of buoyancy pervaded the new government with attention focused on the negotiations that would end Soviet occupation.[35]

The procedural republic that came into being on October 30 was a far different innovation than the Polish or even the more independent Yugoslav model.[36] The October 30 government now included members of the Smallholders Party with the promise of the inclusion of the Social Democrats and other parties that had formed the coalition government of 1945. It should be noted however, that Nagy remained wary of multiparty democracy. In a meeting on October 30 with his Press Secretary, Miklós Gimes, Nagy asserted that he was not in favor of a Western type of parliamentary democracy that included an opposition, fearing that it would only strengthen the reactionary forces.[37] Soviet observers complained that revolutionaries taken prisoner by the Soviets were being released. Repellent to many supporters of the Revolution and the Soviet sphere, was the lynching of ÁVH (secret police) members taken prisoner after revolutionaries stormed the Party headquarters on October 30. The massacre served to underscore the worries of counterrevolutionary infiltration.[38] Further enflaming the fear of the more conservative members of the Soviet Politburo was the establishment of the National Guard, called the Revolutionary Committee for the Defense of the Hungarian Republic. One of their chief tasks was to incorporate the various bands of freedom fighters into the National Guard and ensure that all armed forces and police units were subordinated to the interests of the Republic. As Béla K. Király asserts, an immediate danger lay in the question of loyalty of senior Hungarian army officers and four were relieved after October 31.[39] Taken together, the new government seemed to be in danger of being toppled by a cabal of reactionaries who were now at the helm of the government and the army.[40] From this standpoint the Soviets acted. Unknown to Nagy and his coalition the Soviets had already decided to crush what it considered counterrevolutionary forces in Hungary. A Special Corps comprising 60,000 soldiers began moving towards Hungary.[41]

News of Soviet troops crossing Hungary's border began reaching Nagy in the evening of October 31. It was his inability to gain concrete information from the Soviet ambassador regarding Soviet troop movement that led to the conclusion that the Soviets had staged an invasion. Given these circumstances, Nagy's cabinet approved withdrawing from the Warsaw Pact and declared neutrality. Most vexing to the Soviets was his appeal to the United Nations and the four major powers to recognize Hungary's neutrality and address the problem of the Soviet violation of Hungary's sovereign rights.[42] Nagy understood the consequences of a direct confrontation with the Soviet Union, as did members of his party and government. János Kádár and other party notables vanished following Hungary's withdrawal from the Soviet imperium.

On November 1, 1956, János Kádár became the Secretary of the newly founded Hungarian Socialist Worker's Party (MSZMP), a position he had held in the old Stalinist party (MDP) that he helped abolish on October 28. Kádár was sympathetic to reform and had been included in the Nagy government on October 24. Like Nagy, he agreed with many of the demands of the workers and seemed to work in congress with Nagy trying to ameliorate the situation. On October 28 he addressed the MDP stating, "As a result of the fights we destroyed the mistakes of the past years . . . the new leadership will stop the Stalinist restoration." Kádár claimed that the worker's councils had placed the factories in the hands of the workers and that the new government would pave the path to real worker's power. He concluded by encouraging the membership to join the National Guard and Worker/Peasant councils.[43] In a speech on November 1 he remained firm that the Soviets should leave Hungary.[44] After the meeting, according to Kádár biographer Tibor Huszár, Ferenc Münnich, ambassador to Belgrade in the Gerő government and member of Nagy's cabinet after October 28, informed Kádár that Soviet Ambassador Yuri Andropov wished to meet them briefly at the embassy. They were picked up by a Russian car and driven to the airport and flown to Moscow. Huszár wonders if Münnich, a Stalinist *apparatchik*, had trapped Kádár.[45] On the other hand, Kádár's loyalty to the party was attested to by Béla Szász, who met him in the course of a medical examination after being released from prison. Kádár, who had replaced Rajk as Minister of the Interior, had been imprisoned by Rákosi in February 1951 and released in the wake of the partial amnesty for political prisoners initiated by Nagy's New Course. During his captivity he had been subjected to brutal torture.[46] According to Szász, Kádár told him how he had gone to see Rákosi upon his release and told that his imprisonment had been a mistake. Assured that there was a place for him in the party, Kádár seemed delighted.[47] Whether an apparatchik in the mold of Rajk or a realist with an appetite for power, by November 2 Kádár was being considered as a suitable replacement for Nagy.[48]

The Soviets entered Budapest in the early morning of November 4 surrounding important governmental buildings including the Parliament. Nagy and many of his inner circle fled to the Yugoslav embassy where he was granted asylum. The fighting was fierce and lasted through November 11.[49] Only the Minister of State, István Bibó, remained in the Parliament for two more days and issued a proclamation that encouraged the Hungarian people to passively resist the Soviet occupiers and "the puppet government" that would likely be installed by them. He appealed to the United Nations and the major powers to preserve Hungarian sovereignty.[50] The conclusion was predictable, given that the United States had indicated to the Soviet Union that they would not intervene in Hungary.[51] Large parts of Budapest were in ruins and the revolutionaries had been defeated with elements of the National Guard under Béla Király fighting a rearguard action out of Hungary. Over

200,000 Hungarians voted with their feet and emigrated.[52] Nagy addressed the nation on November 4 and informed Hungarians that, "Our troops are fighting." Interestingly, according to the commander of the National Guard, Béla Király, Nagy had issued no orders concerning the defense of Budapest or Hungary. Király claimed that Nagy was afraid of any action that would indicate that a state of war existed between Hungary and the Soviet Union, cognizant of the futility of such an action.[53] Kádár returned to Budapest on November 7 and was "officially" sworn in as Prime Minister at the Parliament.[54]

Nagy's refusal to resign as Prime Minister presented Kádár with a dilemma in that there could only be one Prime Minister. Though initially promised immunity by the Kádár regime, the fate of Nagy and his group seems to have been determined by the ferocity of the terror unleashed by Kádár in his bid to demobilize widespread disaffection unleashed by the Revolution. On November 8 the MSZMP continued to blame the Gerő/Rákosi regimes as the immediate causes of popular unrest, but indicated its new line of attack. Minister of State György Marosán explained, "Our holy mission is to completely destroy the counterrevolutionary armed bandits . . . I was imprisoned during the Gerő/Rákosi years . . . but there isn't a personal hurt that would shake my belief in Socialism. I am clearly against anyone [in reference to the Nagy group] that would use Gerő/Rákosi politics to destroy the people's state."[55] The groundwork was being laid for a public denunciation of Nagy. Kádár needed to consolidate his grip on power and at the same time demonstrate to the Soviets that he was the master of the situation, perhaps thinking of the successful Polish model previously discussed.[56] As we have already reviewed, punishment for Nagy's intransigence had been raised by the Soviets as late as July of 1956. On November 3, Nikita Khrushchev stated, "If Imre Nagy does not resign he is in the service of the enemy."[57] In this light, Nagy had to be eliminated.

Nagy and his group were lured from the Yugoslav embassy after being given assurances from the Kádár regime that they would have safe passage to Yugoslavia. Instead, they were abducted by the Soviets after boarding a bus and taken to the Mátyásföld barracks and flown the next day to Romania where they were imprisoned at Snagov, a resort outside of Bucharest.[58]

According to the Imre Nagy biographer, János M. Rainer, Nagy began composing notes that indicated he was preparing for a political struggle whose ending had not yet been predetermined, analyzing the path to the Revolution and its course from a Marxist/Leninist perspective.[59] In a conversation with Gyula Kállai of the Central Committee, Nagy was combative and seemed to relish the opportunity to defend his record claiming, "the Nagy government was not treacherous . . . the government did nothing without the party . . . ," potently noting, "Kádár was there . . . "[60] For Nagy "The meaning

of the Hungarian tragedy is that socialism and national independence became
antagonists . . . the meaning of the uprising was to create the unity of the
two."[61]

His diary indicates his unease with the radical course the Revolution had
taken. Nagy claimed that the gap between his conception of reform and the
Revolution was too wide [in spite of his bold words and actions October
30–November 4]. Indeed, democratization and national sovereignty were part
of the reforms he discussed, "Nations and countries can only accept socialism
if it guarantees and creates sovereignty, national independence, and equality
. . . " "Those democratic goals that were not solved in the 1848–1849 Revolution [and were not solved by the earlier communist regime] . . . this was
made clear by the people's revolutionary movement . . . These are historical
facts that the Hungarian communists did not understand in the past and do not
understand in the present."[62] He explained that the demands for immediate
national sovereignty and democratization that included the reemergence of
political parties were simply too radical. The people's demands were legitimate, but counterrevolutionary elements had been able to take advantage of
this situation. The demands for neutrality and withdrawal from the Warsaw
Pact were the consequences of a radicalization that had its origins in the poor
leadership prior to October 23.

Nagy, however, viewed the Soviet intervention and coup as a personal
vendetta against himself, calling Kádár a neo-Stalinist.[63] He insisted that
Gerő and his federates had planned a military coup against his government,
but when they realized this wouldn't work they called upon an outside power
to do the job, thus explaining why Münnich and Kádár switched sides. Their
actions had strengthened the reactionaries.[64] Had the New Course that he had
laid out not been waylaid by the Stalinists, the Revolution would never have
taken place. Nagy claimed, "When the party decided I would be prime minister on October 23—I had to do this in the midst of the street fights . . . I accepted the role and responsibility and I stood where they made me stand . . .
I will be the victim of anti-people, anti-nation politics and those who created
these problems escaped from the catastrophe . . . I have to bear the consequences of their sins."[65] Revealing an anger bordering on rage he damned the
Stalinists "Today's heroes, yesterday's worms . . . they ran away from the bat-
tlefield . . . they were traitors . . . their behavior is a shame to Hungarian communists . . . They personify moral death and the best they can do is shut their
mouths." Nagy asserted that the Hungarian people and communists would
never be convinced by the charges leveled against him.[66]

Nagy's anger with those who had betrayed him coupled with his great disappointment regarding the course the Revolution had taken help explain his
desire to acquit himself. But his hope for a fair hearing was certainly tempered

by his understanding of the forces arrayed against him, especially in light of his refusal to acknowledge the Kádár regime even though he no longer considered himself Prime Minister. He stated to Kállai "It is clear that they have charged me as a traitor."[67] In his diary Nagy wonders why the Polish example couldn't have worked in Hungary. "We could not stop the intervention . . . They have created a new conception [of counterrevolution] regarding the October/November events . . . that means they have to create facts as opposed to the truth . . . in order to produce evidence to strengthen their new conception." He ominously compares the "new conception" and creation of evidence with the show trials of Slánský and Rajk.[68] The reality of the situation was indeed bleak as Moscow agreed to a trial for Nagy in March 1957.[69]

Nagy and his group was flown back to Budapest and placed in solitary confinement on April 17, 1957. The planned trial included Nagy and many of the principals from his inner circle including Defense Minister Pál Maléter, József Szilágyi, head of the Secretariat, Press Secretary Miklós Gimes, and Minister of State Géza Losonczy, in addition to Zoltán Tildy and others. According to Dornbach, the physical and mental strain on the defendants was evident in film clips taken during their trial, but that only one known case of torture was made manifest in the person of Losonczy. Losonczy had apparently gone on a hunger strike and died during a session of forced feeding on December 21, 1957.[70] International events dictated the timing of the trial as the Soviet Union attempted to limit the diplomatic damage from the Hungarian invasion.[71]

On January 28, 1958, Imre Nagy was accused by the People's Republic of Hungary of "initiating and leading a conspiracy to subvert the state," and treason.[72] In preparations for the trial Kádár remained cognizant of the consequences of the Rákosi show trials. The jurist Alajos Dornbach points out that Kádár wanted to ensure that the trial be based on "facts," as opposed to the fanciful charges that were forged against Rajk and his associates.[73] Nagy's writings and actions taken during and prior to the Revolution made this relatively easy. The charges drawn up against Nagy and his federates were based on an assemblage of statements and actions that, taken out of context, could substantiate the charge. And though based on kernels of truth, the charges laid against Nagy and his federates draw conclusions that appear as fantastic as those leveled against Rajk. Further, the trial was marked by the same lack of procedure and political manipulation as those that took place under the auspices of Rákosi.

The prosecution used Nagy's essays in *On Communism* to lay the foundation of the conspiracy charges. Nagy's bid to exonerate the New Course and establish a power base to challenge the Stalinists was recast as a paper trail leading to counterrevolution. The essays composed in the summer and fall of

1955 were distributed to Nagy's group of "resentful bourgeoisie intellectuals" who then disseminated the ideas embodied in the essays to the Petőfi Circle [writer's circle] that became the "legal front organization" for the conspiracy.[74] According to the prosecutor, Nagy described the Rákosi regime as being "Bonapartist" and should be removed by force. As previously examined, Nagy had called for a thorough accounting by the regime and demanded procedural justice, warning that a failure to do so would lead to a "grave crisis."[75] Nagy's appeal to the principle of peaceful coexistence and noninterference with sovereign affairs as elaborated at Bandung can be seen as laying the basis for Hungary's withdrawal from the Warsaw Pact. The fact that the essays were published in the West is portrayed as part of a "smear campaign against the Soviet Union and Hungary."[76]

According to the prosecutor, great preparation went into staging the Petőfi Circle debates on the press in order to shape public opinion. This task was made easier by Nagy's lieutenants working in the press, such as Géza Losonczy, who was an associate editor at the *Magyar Nemzet* and reporters Miklós Vásárhelyi and Miklós Gimes (all defendants in the trial with Nagy). Through this ever-widening circle of federates, pressure was exerted to restore Nagy to the party and leadership in a bid to undermine the party and overthrow the regime.[77] The fruits of the conspiracy and its ability to put pressure on the regime and influence public opinion could be found in Nagy's rehabilitation and his group's infiltration into worker's unions and youth organizations. The student demands of October 22 could be seen as the culmination of their efforts. According to the White Paper, "The real implications of these demands became clear during the counterrevolution, through the release of fascists, war criminals . . . the sanguinary white terror, organization of reactionary parties and the publication of gutter sheets . . . "[78]

Nagy's hesitancy and his attempt to placate not only the party that had placed him in power, but revolutionaries and the Soviets as well was portrayed as a deliberate attempt to undermine the state. For example, Nagy's seeming accord with the arrival of Soviet troops and determination to subdue the armed uprising was contrasted with his attempts to negotiate with the revolutionaries that included the October 28 truce and portrayed by the People's Court as "treachery and double dealing."[79] These conclusions were further substantiated by Nagy's orders to the chief of the Budapest police to negotiate with the insurgents, who, according to a police lieutenant colonel, included handing over weapons.[80]

The prosecutor utilized the establishment of the multiparty state and the withdrawal from the Warsaw Pact as establishing without a doubt Nagy's betrayal of the state. The multiparty state was merely a front to allow the reactionary coalition parties from 1945 to reestablish their power, with the ultimate goal of realigning Hungary with the imperialist interests of the West. For example, the appointment of Béla Király to lead the National Guard provided evidence of Nagy's treacherous intent. Király had been a staff officer of Miklós Horthy who had been accused of collusion with the Arrow Cross. According to the prosecutor, Nagy had unlawfully rehabilitated him [it was Király who had been in charge of cleansing the military of Stalinists].[81] Király had organized resistance in Budapest as best he could, finally fighting a series of rearguard actions before escaping to the West and was a defendant in absentia at the trial. Demands for Soviet troop withdrawal and the Warsaw Pact clearly bespoke a coup against socialism and fears of a return to "renascent German militarism." "The decision of the Imre Nagy group to withdraw from the Warsaw Treaty was a crime not only against . . . the Hungarian people, but . . . the peace and security of Europe."[82]

The rehabilitation of Cardinal József Mindszenty was used as further evidence to substantiate the charges of conspiracy against Nagy. Mindszenty had been freed from prison on October 30, returned to Budapest that same night and received a tumultuous welcome from various revolutionary factions. He had met several times with Zoltán Tildy of the Smallholder's Party and member of Nagy's cabinet. He immediately began restoring church authority and dismissed clergy closely associated with the communists.[83] Perhaps most damning was his radio broadcast on the evening of November 3 in which he attached Hungary to a history that portrayed Hungary as the defender of the West against the [onslaught of the Tatars and Ottoman Empire]. Although calling for a policy of neutrality in which Hungary would remain non-aligned with the two superpowers, Mindszenty clearly placed Hungary's fortunes with those of the West: "a small nation has heartfelt joy that because of its love of liberty the other nations have taken up its cause."[84] Mindszenty had been convicted of conspiring to overthrow the state and had always been viewed as having fascist sympathies by the Stalinists.[85] According to the White Paper, the threat posed by Mindszenty was made plain by the fact that former Prime Minister Ferenc Nagy had been contacted by Tildy, reviving the Stalinist charges that connected the Smallholders Party to the World War II regime of Miklós Horthy.[86] As already discussed, Ferenc Nagy had been smeared as a fascist in 1947 and been forced to live in exile. Mindszenty had taken refuge in the American embassy where he remained until being allowed to leave Hungary with a diplomatic passport issued by the Vatican on September 29, 1971.[87]

Connecting Nagy to the right wing politics of the Smallholders, Béla Király, and Cardinal Mindszenty, among others, allowed the state to attach Nagy and his group to a grand design of the Western imperialists to overthrow the people's state.[88] The prosecutor charged that Radio Free Europe broadcasts and the Central Intelligence Agency's operations that floated balloons across Hungary's borders with anti-state propaganda attached had been designed to support Nagy.[89] Further, the conspiracy in its active phase had been aided by Radio Free Europe. For example, in the course of a September 19, 1956, broadcast it was stated that, "The Writer's Association has courageously embarked on the road to democratization . . . a good hope that our writers and people will achieve . . . complete freedom."[90] Perhaps most damning in the eyes of the prosecution were the Radio Free broadcasts during the fighting that encouraged the revolutionaries and included instructions for fighting a guerilla war against the Soviets.[91]

According to Alajos Dornbach, Nagy remained stoic throughout the court proceedings, whereas József Szilágyi challenged the proceedings at every opportunity, leading to a separate proceeding and execution for Szilágyi in April of 1958.[92] Imre Nagy, Miklós Gimes, and Pál Maléter were sentenced to death on June 15, 1958. Nagy refused to appeal the judgment during the right of the last word claiming, "The Hungarian people and the International Working Class will acquit me of the allegations set against me and as a result I have to sacrifice my life."[93] Under the procedure of the time, the same court that had just passed sentence decided whether its own decision was worthy of appeal. According to the historian János M. Rainer, Dr. Imre Bárd fought for his client and in his appeal argued that Nagy's actions and mind-set on October 23 were anything but conspiratorial. His lawyer delivered the court's decision to Nagy during the evening of June 15.[94]

According to György Krassó, who spent ten years in prison for his participation in the Revolution, prisoners going to the gallows often shouted their names, invoked pleas of innocence or demanded Hungarian independence. The sounds that emanated from the gallows were indescribable. The prisoner was placed on a stool with both hands tied in front with a noose around his neck, which was attached to a hook. Another rope that was placed through a pulley was tied to the prisoner's legs. After the prisoner's head was covered, the stool was kicked from under him and the rope pulled through the pulley by the executioner's assistants. The executioner then twisted and lifted the head out of the socket.[95] The three condemned men were led out to the gallows around 5:00 A.M. on June 16, 1958. In order that the executions remained secret, a leather harness was attached to each of the condemned that prevented them from opening their mouths. Imre Nagy was the first to die.[96]

Nagy had wanted to remain loyal to Moscow. For him, communism represented a path accessible to all and, in the wake of World War II, saw in the Soviet Union a strong state that could forward the political interest of Hungary. What he hadn't planned on was the reality of imperial politics that informed the Cold War. The show trials initiated by Rákosi and sanctioned by Stalin that directly affected many of his federates was disillusioning to him. Khrushchev's ascension to power represented an opportunity for Nagy in the guise of his New Course politics. Again disappointed in his political defeat at the hands of the Stalinists in 1955, he found hope in the Bandung Conference and the "peace offensive" that characterized Russia's international politics of the time. Though boisterous in its tone, his essays found in *On Communism* challenge the Hungarian Stalinists, not his loyalty to Moscow.

Rajk's funeral helped radicalize the opposition to the Hungarian Stalinists and as we have seen, outpaced Nagy's demands for change, not unusual in the politics of change. Nagy gambled as he attempted to master the events unfolding before him during the course of the Revolution. Realizing that his appeal for a return to the politics of the New Course was going unheeded, he took the unprecedented step within the Soviet Bloc of creating a plural government on October 30. Did he believe that his newly reconstituted Communist Party could dominate politics, or did he truly join with the demands for the establishment of a republic? His elation with Moscow's response in *Pravda* was short lived and his call for the withdrawal from the Warsaw Pact and appeal to the United Nations regarding the Soviet's violation of Hungary's sovereignty reveals an executive forcefully defending the state. On the other hand, his refusal to call on the army to defend Hungary against attack and his request for asylum perhaps reveals his recognition that his gamble had failed. We are left with his final actions that included his refusal to resign as Prime Minister and final words of defiance to a juridical procedure created by a regime that had predetermined his fate.

NOTES

1. Imre Nagy, *On Communism: In Defense of the New Course* (London: Thames and Hudson, 1957), 62.
2. Charles Gati, *Hungary and the Soviet Bloc* (Durham: Duke University Press, 1986), 135–37.
3. János M. Rainer, "A Progress of Ideas: The Hungarian Revolution of 1956," in Lee W. Congdon and Béla K. Király, ed., *The Ideas of the Hungarian Revolution, Suppressed and Victorious 1956–1999* (New York: Columbia University Press, 2002), 16 and Walter LaFeber, *America, Russia, and the Cold War, 1945–2000*, 9th ed. (Boston: McGraw Hill, 2002), 187–88.
4. Gerő and a contingent of the Politburo were in Yugoslavia on a state visit through the morning of October 23. Prior to the trip Gerő formally apologized for the Hungarian's past behavior towards Yugoslavia and as a conciliatory gesture readmitted Nagy back in the party. See Gati, *Hungary and the Soviet Bloc*, 137–38 and

Johanna C. Granville, *The First Domino: International Decision Making During the Hungarian Crisis of 1956* (College Station: Texas A & M Press, 2004), 56.

5. George Schöpflin, *Politics in Eastern Europe* (Oxford: Blackwell Publishers, 1993), 110.

6. Johanna C. Granville, *The First Domino*, 45. The Bandung Conference that opened on April 18, 1955, was hosted by Indonesia and included representatives from twenty-nine African and Asian countries, including the People's Republic of China, India, and Egypt and was designed to create a third faction in world politics not steered by the two superpowers. The principles of sovereignty and a strong condemnation of neocolonialism informed the spirit of the conference and can be seen as the founding meeting of the Non-Aligned Movement founded in 1962. For example see: President Sukarno's "Speech at the Opening of the Bandung Conference, April 18, 1955," found in: Modern History Sourcebook http://www.fordham.edu/halsall/mod/1955sukarno-bandung.html

7. Nagy, *On Communism*, 45–46, 237–38. The importance of Bandung on Nagy's view of international relations is underscored in a letter written to the Central Committee after the Revolution during his confinement in Snagov, Romania. Nagy stated, "Regarding international relationships between socialist states . . . I agree with the five principles of Bandung, national independence, sovereignty, equality, protection of territorial integrity, and non-intervention . . . first determined at the Bandung Conference and later in Belgrade . . . between the Soviets and the Yugoslavs . . ." "Nagy Imre levele az MSZMP Ideiglenes Központi Bizottságának, 22 Febuár 1957 (Imre Nagy letter to the MSZMP temporary Central Committee)," found in: *Nagy Imre Snagovi jegyzetek: Gondolatok, emlékezések 1956–1957* (Imre Nage notes from Snagur: Thoughts, Memoirs), István Vida, ed. (Budapest: Gondolat Kiadó-Nagy Imre Alapítvány, 2006), 298.

8. Schöpflin, *Politics in Eastern Europe*, 114 and Lafeber, *America, Russia, and the Cold War,* 178–79, 185.

9. Johanna Glanville instructs us that Gomulka's insistence on Soviet non-intervention was balanced by a pledge not to leave the Warsaw Pact. See: Granville, *The First Domino*, 48–49, 52–53; Mark Kramer agrees and adds that the Soviet's were inclined to offer a compromise after a careful examination of their military and economic options, "The Soviet Union and the 1956 Crises in Hungary and Poland: Reassessments and New Findings," *Journal of Contemporary History*, 33, 3 (April, 1998): 169, 172–74, and György Litván, *The Hungarian Revolution of 1956*: Reform, Revolt, Repression (London: Longman, 1996), 51.

10. György Göncöl, "Bandung és a békes együttlétezés elve (Bandung and the Theory of Peaceful Coexistance)," *Társadalmi Szemle*, 10, 5 (May, 1955): 95, 97.

11. The discussions taking place in the writer's circles coupled with the rapid pace of events exemplified by Poland and Nagy's readmission to the party combined to create a "liberating effect among the students." "If the masses of people could not voice their demand, then it became their responsibility." Nóra Némethné Dikán, Róbert Szabó, István Vida, "Egyetemisták és főiskolások Követelései: 1956 októberében," *Múltunk*, 48, 2 (2003): 282.

12. The political scientist, Paul E. Zinner underlines the importance of opposition representation at *Szabad Nép* in its ability to communicate with the public at large. "Revolution in Hungary: Reflections on the Vicissitudes of a Totalitarian System," *The Journal of Politics*, 21, 1 (February, 1959): 21.

13. See: "Új, Tavaszi Seregszemle," (New, Spring View) *Szabad Nép* as found in Gábor Szigethy, ed., *Jelenidőben: 1956 Október 23* (Budapest: Holnap Kiadó, 2003), 32–41, *Szabad Nép*, 23 October, 1956, 2 and Rainer, "A Progress of Ideas," 20–21, 25–27. Interestingly, the events in Poland as reported by Dénes Polgár in the same edition of *Szabad Nép* portray worker unrest as "never anti Soviet" in spite of "hopeful expectations on the part of the United States." Workers joyfully return to work exclaiming, "[now] we can finally get back to work and everyone is happy."

14. Gati, *Hungary and the Soviet Bloc*, 138–39. According to Johanna C. Granville the students chanted, "Independence based on freedom and equality! Poland shows us the way, let's follow the Hungarian way!" *The First Domino*, 55. See also: Litván, *The Hungarian Revolution of 1956*, 53–54.

15. *The 1956 Hungarian Revolution: A History in Documents* Csaba Békés et al., ed. (Budapest: Central University Press, 2002), 191 and János M. Rainer, *Nagy Imre 1953–1958: Politikai Életrajz II* (Budapest: 1956–os Intézet, 1999),, 238–40.

16. Rainer, "A Progress of Ideas," 24.

17. "Ernő Gerő Beszéde, Magyar Rádió, 23 October 1956, Este nyolc óra" as found in: Gábor Szigethy, *Jelenidőben*, 77–78.

18. Charles Gati, *Hungary and the Soviet Bloc*, 139–42.

19. The disappointed crowd left the square, but many continued demonstrating in other parts of the city. See: Békés et al., *The 1956 Hungarian Revolution*, 192–93 and Litván, *The Hungarian Revolution of 1956, 57*.

20. Béla K. Király, "An Abortive and the First Real War," in *The Ideas of the Hungarian Revolution Suppressed and Victorious, 1956–1999*, 53.

21. Békés et al., *The 1956 Hungarian Revolution: A History in Documents*, 193.

22. For example see: Zinner, "Revolution in Hungary," 29, Litván, *The Hungarian Revolution of 1956*, 57–58, and Rainer, "A Progress of Ideas," 22.

23. Bill Lomax, *Hungarian Worker's Councils in 1956* (New York: Columbia University Press, 1990), 5. A meeting had taken place in Miskolc on October 22 that included students, workers, teachers, and leaders from the county party. Dikán et al., "Egyetemisták és főiskolások Követelései," 290.

24. Rainer, "A Progress of Ideas," 26–27, Lomax, *Hungarian Worker's Councils in 1956*, 25, Litván, *The Hungarian Revolution of 1956*, 74, Granville, *The First Domino*, 90.

25. "Report from Anastas Mikoyan and Mikhail Suslov to the CPSU CC Presidium on Talks with HWP Leaders, October 26, 1956," *The 1956 Hungarian Revolution: A History in Documents*, 238.

26. "Nagy Imre Miniszterelnök Rádióbeszéde, October 25, 1956," in Zoltán Ripp, *Ötvenhat októbere és a hatalom: A pártvezetés végnapjai* (October '56 and the power: The documents of the Hungarian Workers Party Leadership) (Budapest: Napvilág Kiadó, 1997), 138–39.

27. Though Hungarian army units aided the Soviets many units remained immobile due to a lack of orders. Miklós Horváth, "Soviet Aggression against Hungary in

1956," in *The Ideas of the Hungarian Revolution, Suppressed and Victorious 1956–1999*, 70–74

28. A point fortified by Granville, *The First Domino*, 204.

29. András Hegedűs, *A Történelem és a Hatalom Igézetében* (Within the Fascination of History and Power) (Budapest: Kossuth Kiadó, 1988), 191 and Gati, *Hungary and the Soviet Bloc*, 140. Both Miklós Horváth and Béla K. Király assert that the Soviet Union was ready and did intervene in the Hungarian crisis regardless of a Hungarian request. Although Király feels that because of Gerő's request for Soviet intervention on October 23, only the second Soviet intervention can be considered an act of war. See: Horváth, "Soviet Aggression against Hungary in 1956," 67–69 and Király, "Soviet Readiness to Wage War against Socialist States," in Béla K. Király et al., ed., *The First War between the Socialist States: The Hungarian Revolution of 1956 and Its Impact* (New York: Brooklyn College Press, 1984), 3–6. Mark Kramer points out that in spite of Soviet warnings, the [Gerő] regime was unprepared for such a contingency. Over 31,500 Soviet troops responded to the crisis ("The Soviet Union and the 1956 Crises in Hungary and Poland," 182–83, 185). See also: "Working Notes from the Session of the CPSU CC Presidium, October 23, 1956," *The 1956 Revolution: A History in Documents*, 217–18.

30. Imre Nagy's first offer came with the announcement that he had become Prime Minister. The announcement of the truce of October 28 was coupled with an announcement that Soviet troops would leave and that the ÁVH would be dissolved. "Nagy Imre Miniszterelnök Rádiószózata A Magyar Néphez, October 24, 1956" and "Kormánynyilatkozat Nagy Imre Miniszterelnök Rádióbeszéde, October 28, 1956" Found in: Ripp, *Ötvenhat októbere és a hatalom*, 131–32, 153–55.

31. Horváth, "Soviet Aggression against Hungary in 1956," 75–76, 80, According to Granville the attack was initiated in spite of Nagy's order, but failed (*The First Domino*), 83

32. Johanna C. Granville asserts that whereas Gomulka was able to appease the Polish population and the Soviets, Nagy felt that appeasing the Hungarian population with a truce that included Soviet withdrawal would be enough. The Soviet's sensed that the situation was only getting worse. *The First Domino*, 84–85 and Grzegorz Ekiert, *The State against Society* (Princeton: Princeton University Press, 1996), 57.

33. "Proclamation by Imre Nagy on the Creation of a Multi-Party System, October 30, 1956," *The 1956 Revolution: A History in Documents*, 290–91.

34. "Declaration by the Government of the USSR on the Principles of Development and Further Strengthening of Friendship and Cooperation between the Soviet Union and Other Socialist States," *The 1956 Revolution: A History in Documents*, 300–302.

35. Nagy's October 31 radio address reaffirmed his commitment to non-alignment: "Hungary does not want to join any of the power blocs . . . we ask our neighbor countries near and far to respect this unchangeable decision by our nation." As reports of sizable numbers of Soviet troops were reported in *Népszabadság*, November 2, 1956, it was hoped that their direction would shift [away from Budapest] towards Kecskemét located to the south of Budapest. As discussed in the previous chapter, this sense of hopefulness had pervaded Hungary prior to the signing of the peace treaty

with the allies in February 1947 when it was assumed that Hungarian sovereignty would be restored.

36. For example, according to Granville, Tito feared that the radical developments to the north would stoke the flames of nationalism within the various ethnic groups in Yugoslavia. *The First Domino*, 101.

37. András Mink, "Keresztény Politikai Pártok és az 1956-os Forradalom," (Christian Political Parties and the 1956 Revolution) *Pártok 1956: Válogatás 1956-os pártvezetők visszaemlékezéseiből*, Zsuzsanna KŒrösi and Péter Pál Tóth, ed., (Budapest: 1956-os Intézet, 1997), 151.

38. One of Nagy's associates, Imre Mező, was among those lynched, Nagy considered him a martyr. *Nagy Imre: Snagovi Jegyzetek, Gondolatok, emlékezések 1956–1957*, István Vida, ed., 91. Would mob justice prevail over the attempts of the new government to establish order? See János M. Rainer, *Nagy Imre Politikai Életrajz: 1953–1958 II* (Budapest: 1956-os Intézet, 1999), 299. See also: György Litván, *The Hungarian Revolution of 1956*, 77.

39. Király, "Soviet Readiness to Wage War Against Socialist States," 22–23.

40. Nikita Khrushchev worried that the "imperialists" in the West would see Soviet acceptance of changes in Hungary as a sign of weakness. "Working Notes and Attached Extract for the Minutes of the CPSU CC Presidium Meeting, October 31, 1956," *The 1956 Revolution: A History in Documents*, 307–9.

41. Horváth, "Soviet Aggression against Hungary," 85.

42. According to a front page story in the *Népszabadság*, November 2, 1956, Nagy had demanded the withdrawal of Soviet troops and Hungary's withdrawal from the Warsaw Pact in a meeting with the Soviet ambassador, Yuri Andropov, on November 1st. Page 3 of the *Népszabadság*, November 4, 1956, includes a November 3rd briefing with Zoltán Tildy and Géza Losonczy in which Tildy expresses hope that the negotiations with the Soviets regarding Soviet troop withdrawals will be successful. [Tildy is referring to the negotiations being conducted between Defense Minister Pál Maléter and the Soviets. The Soviets arrested Maléter and his entourage during the course of the negotiations.]

43. "Kádár Jánosnak, Az MDP Elnökének Kiadatlan Felhívása," October 28, 1956 found in Ripp, *Ötvenhat októbere és a hatalom*, 156–58.

44. One of the front page headlines of *Népszbadság*, November 3, 1956, declares that the Communist Party (MSZMP) has "purified" itself of the sins of the MDP, asserting that anyone associated with the deeds of the past regime will not be accepted as members. Importantly, the MSZMP declares that it supports Nagy's declaration of neutrality and encouragement for workers to return to work.

45. George Lukács claimed that he resigned his post as Minister of Cultural Affairs from the Nagy government because of the presence of Stalinists. On the other hand, Lukács may have been tipped off as to the Soviet-backed coup against Nagy and acted preemptively. See: Árpád Kadarkay, *George Lukács: Life, Thought, and Politics* (Cambridge: Basil Blackwell Inc., 1991), 430.

46. William Shawcross claimed that he may have been beaten so badly about the testicles that he may have been rendered sterile. *Crime and Compromise: János*

Kádár and the Politics of Hungary since Revolution (New York: E.P. Dutton and Co., Inc., 1974), 72–73.

47. Béla Szász, *Volunteers for the Gallows* (New York: W. W. Norton and Company, Inc., 1971) 217–18.

48. Tibor Huszár, *Kádár* (Budapest: Szabad Tér Kiadó, 2001), 329–34. See also: Granville, who concludes that Kádár's time in prison and lust for power determined the course he would take (*The First Domino*), 156.

49. Resistance continued after this point with a series of worker strikes and other acts of defiance. For example see: Lomax, *Hungarian Worker's Councils in 1956* and György Litván, *The Hungarian Revolution of 1956*.

50. Interestingly, Bibó carried on his advocacy on behalf of the Nagy government until his arrest in May 1957. He was sentenced to life imprisonment and released only in 1963. "Proclamation" issued November 4, 1956, found in István Bibó, *Democracy, Revolution, Self Determination: Selected Writings*, Károly Nagy ed., András Boros-Kazai, trans. (New York: Columbia University Press, 1991), 326 and Géza Jeszenszky's, "Introduction," 8–9 in the same volume.

51. The United States was in the middle of the Suez Crisis and needed to find a way to back away from its more aggressive liberation stance that implied "rollback." Csaba Békés: "Working Paper #16: The Hungarian Revolution and World Politics," found in Cold War International History Project Virtual Archive: New Evidence on the 1956 Polish and Hungarian Crises http://wwics.si.edu/index.cfm?topic_id=1409&fuseaction=library.document&id=364 19–20, 21–22; Mark Kramer, "The Soviet Union and the 1956 Crises in Hungary and Poland," 207, and *The 1956 Hungarian Revolution: A History in Documents*, 209.

52. According to Miklós Horváth, the Soviets suffered 669 killed, 1,986 wounded, and 51 missing. Hungarian casualties amounted to over 2,500 killed, 20,000 wounded, and over 5,000 captured. "Soviet Aggression against Hungary in 1956," 85, 87, György Litván cautions that the figures may be higher given that some fighters were buried in unmarked graves or were killed in the countryside or in the bid to flee the country (*The Hungarian Revolution of 1956*, 103).

53. Király, "Soviet Readiness to Wage War against Socialist States," 28–30. "Radio Statement by Imre Nagy Announcing an Attack by Soviet forces on the Hungarian Government, November 4, 1956," found in: *The Hungarian Revolution of 1956: A History in Documents*, 383. Charles Gati states, "Nagy's cautious patriotism prevailed when he refused to order the Hungarian Army to do battle against impossible odds" (*Hungary and the Soviet Bloc*, 152).

54. See front page: *Népszabadság*, November 8, 1956.

55. Ibid., page 2.

56. Granville, *The First Domino*, 58, 150 and Ekiert, *The State Against Society*, 75.

57. "Working Notes of Imre Horváth from the Session of the CPSU, CC Presidium, 3 November 1956," found in: *The Hungarian Revolution of 1956: A History in Documents*, 360.

58. According to Johanna C. Granville, Kádár was cognizant of the KGB plan to abduct the Nagy group. "Tito and the Nagy Affair," *The East European Quarterly*, 32,

1 (Spring 1998): 41 and Alajos Dornbach, *The Secret Trial of Imre Nagy* (Westport: Praeger, 1994), 15.

59. Rainer, *Nagy Imre 1953–1958: A Politikai Életrajz II*, 354.

60. "Lehallgatási jegyzőkönyv Nagy Imre és Kállai Gyula beszélgetésér_l (Notes of a tapped conversation between Imre Nagy and Gyula Kállai)," *Nagy Imre: Snagovi Jegyzetek, Gondolatok, emlékezések, 1956–1957*, István Vida, ed., 278–79.

61. From Nagy's diary in *Nagy Imre: Snagovi Jegyzetek, Gondolatok, emlékezések, 1956–1957*, István Vida, ed., 127.

62. Ibid., 127, 145.

63. Rainer, *Nagy Imre, 1953–1958: A Politikai Életrajz II*, 359.

64. From Nagy's diary in *Nagy Imre: Snagovi Jegyzetek, Gondolatok, emlékezések, 1956–1957*, István Vida, ed., 149, 152.

65. Rainer, *Nagy Imre, 1953–1958: A Politikai Életrajz II*, 361.

66. From Nagy's diary in *Nagy Imre: Snagovi Jegyzetek, Gondolatok, emlékezések, 1956–1957*, István Vida, ed., 167.

67. "Lehallgatási jegyzőkönyv Nagy Imre és Kállai Gyula beszélgetéséről," *Nagy Imre: Snagovi Jegyzetek, Gondolatok, emlékezések, 1956–1957*, István Vida, ed., 278, 285.

68. From Nagy's diary in *Nagy Imre: Snagovi Jegyzetek, Gondolatok, emlékezések, 1956–1957*, István Vida, ed., 154–55, 158.

69. Kádár's statements against Nagy became increasingly harsh as he worked with the Soviets in regard to Nagy's fate. In March of 1957 the Soviets agreed to a trial. The time for political debate had probably ended some time earlier, although György Litván suggests that Nagy would have been punished regardless of his willingness to step down as Prime Minister. Dornbach, *The Secret Trial of Imre Nagy*, 16, 166. According to Árpád Kadarkay, George Lukács, who had been a part of the Nagy government as Minister of Cultural Affairs and held at Snagov, had advocated coming to an accommodation with Kádár during their stay in the Yugoslav embassy. Nagy refused. Lukács was allowed to leave Snagov and saved from retribution by an intervention by Bertrand Russel and his promise to stay out of politics. *George Lukács*, 431, 433, 438–40.

70. Dornbach, *The Secret Trial of Imre Nagy*, 16–17.

71. According to György Litván, the trial was postponed for the first time because the General Assembly had placed a discussion of Hungary on its agenda and a second time after the trial actually commenced in January to accommodate Italian elections and a summit conference with Yugoslavia. "The Political Background of the Imre Nagy Trial," *The Secret Trial of Imre Nagy*, 172, 175.

72. "Act of Accusation against Imre Nagy and his Associates, January 28, 1958" as found in: Dornbach, *The Secret Trial of Imre Nagy*, 52.

73. Ibid., 6.

74. *White Book: Information Bureau of the Council of Ministers of the Hungarian People's Republic, vol. 5, The Counterrevolutionary Conspiracy of Imre Nagy and His Accomplices* (Budapest) (hereafter: *White Paper, vol. 5*) 21–26 and "Judgment against Imre Nagy June 14, 1958," found in: Dornbach, *The Secret Trial of Imre Nagy*, 71.

75. Nagy, *On Communism*, 62.

76. "Judgment against Imre Nagy June 14, 1958," found in: Dornbach, *The Secret Trial of Imre Nagy*, 75–76.

77. *White Paper, vol. 5*, 30–32.

78. Ibid., 39–43, 44–45 and "Judgment against Imre Nagy June 14, 1958," found in: Dornbach, *The Secret Trial of Imre Nagy*, 80.

79. "Judgment against Imre Nagy," found in: Dornbach, *The Secret Trial of Imre Nagy*, 93–94.

80. *White Paper, vol. 5*, 54–55.

81. Ibid., 56–59.

82. Ibid., 134.

83. József Cardinal Mindszenty, *Memoirs*, translated by Richard and Clara Winston (New York: Macmillan Publishing Co., Inc., 1974), 197–200, 209–11.

84. Mindszenty's radio address as found in: *Memoirs*, 331–33.

85. According to András Mink, no one could tell what party Mindszenty would have supported. He further claims that there was an actual fear within Catholic parties of reactionary dominance [Horthy's Christian National Unity Party]. "Keresztény Politikai Pártok és az 1956-os Forradalom," 152.

86. *White Paper, vol. 5*, 16.

87. Mindszenty, *Memoirs*, 237.

88. "Act of Accusation against Imre Nagy and His Associates," found in: Dornbach, *The Secret Trial of Imre Nagy*, 53–54.

89. *White Paper, vol. 5*, 18.

90. Ibid., 35.

91. For example see: Dispatch 1086, "Balloons to Hungary," "Transcripts of Radio Free Europe Programs, Advising Military Tactics to Use against a Superior Enemy," found in: *The Hungarian Revolution of 1956: A History in Documents*, 66–68, 286–89 and Granville, *The First Domino*, 178, 180.

92. Dornbach, *The Secret Trial of Imre Nagy*, 21.

93. János M. Rainer, *Nagy Imre, 1953–1958: Politikai Életrajz II*, 430–31. See also: György Krassó, "The Memory of the Dead," *Survey*, 28, 2 (Summer, 1984): 135. The article originally appeared in the samizdat, *A Hirmondó* (The Messenger) 2 (1983).

94. Rainer, *Nagy Imre, 1953–1958: Politikai Életrajz II*, 433.

95. György Krassó, "In Memory of the Dead," 151.

96. Rainer, *Nagy Imre, 1953–1958: A Politikai Életrajz II*, 436.

Chapter Five

Reaction, Compromise, Tentative Legitimacy

Teacher: Now Józsi, if Aunt Klára's chicken dies, this is an example of a problem. On the other hand, if János Kádár's plane crashes, this would be a tragedy. Now Józsi, which word would you use if János Kádár's plane crashed?

Józsi: If János Kádár's plane crashed it would be a tragedy, but not a problem.[1]

János Kádár came to power backed by Soviet arms and was sworn in as the Prime Minister of Hungary at the Parliament on November 7, 1956. The situation he faced was bleak, given that the Revolution had obliterated the communist institutions of power in so short a time. The Stalinists had failed, and according to Nikita Khrushchev, Rákosi, Gerő, and others could not be relied upon. Khrushchev insisted that they remain in the Soviet Union and left Kádár with the awesome task of demobilizing the Revolution and rebuilding communist governance.[2] Kádár performed brilliantly, initially displaying a merciless brutality against his foes, and once his political base had been secured, benevolence towards his fellow Hungarians. His actions were encapsulated in the phrase "those who are not against us are with us."[3] The Hungarian "miracle" that sprang from his economic policies created a seeming utopia when compared to other people's democracies under Soviet sway. This chapter reviews the Revolution's demobilization and the success of *Kádárizmus*, highlighting the role textbooks and curriculum played in creating a counternarrative to the one held dear by many within the polity.

The Soviet decision to quell the Hungarian uprising by force was made October 30–31. On October 31st the massive incursion into Hungary from the

northeast enveloped Budapest's airport. The problem was who would now replace Imre Nagy. Consensus on this issue within the Soviet Politiburo was not
achieved until after Khrushchev's meeting with Tito and other socialist leaders at Brioni, Yugoslavia, on November 2. The suggestion that András
Hegedűs be returned to his position as Prime Minister, a position he had held
prior to Nagy's assumption to the post, was met with skepticism by Khrushchev
who claimed that "they [Hungarians] would have hanged him." Kádár, who
came from the "working class" and represented new leadership, was deemed to
be a better choice. Stability in the wake of the Hungarian crisis was essential to
Soviet interest and excluding the old guard such as Rákosi and Gerő was meant
to enhance the Soviet's relationship with the new leadership.[4]

It was also clear though, that strong actions were needed to demobilize the
Revolution. After the Revolution had been largely subdued by November 11,
union resistance to the Soviet incursion threatened to continue political and
economic instability. For example, energy shortages resulting from a massive
slowdown in the mining industry served to fortify the strength of the worker's
movement by demonstrating their power to bring both the railroads and industrial production to a standstill.[5] Initially unable to quell the powerful
worker's councils that formed the core of the unions' power, Kádár utilized
brute force to subdue them. One innovation recommended by Soviet advisors
was to selectively execute those who were arrested during the various demonstrations organized by the workers, advice that Kádár readily assented to.
These random executions were fortified by violence carried out against the
workers by the police and the *pufajkások*, a group of special police reorganized by the Kádár regime to aid in the consolidation of his power.[6] The *pufajkások* carried out retribution in the name of the state without the aid of the
legal system, reminiscent of the spontaneous justice advocated by László
Rajk against "enemies of the state."[7]

Judicial proceedings against those suspected or accused of revolutionary
activity became progressively severe. Special military courts and later People's Courts were established to mete out summary justice. Martial law was
established, along with general procedures that allowed for detention for
those broadly deemed threatening to the state.[8] According to political scientist Grzegorz Ekiert, the process of mobilizing the judiciary for this purpose
meant that the state had to exert direct control, as many within the judiciary
viewed many so-called counterrevolutionaries as heroes.[9] In order to survive
this period of instability, it was incumbent on János Kádár to destroy the opposition to his authority and create a distance between himself and the Stalinists. In June 1957 Kádár asserted, "Although Rákosi and Nagy are not in the
country at present, they still have followers in the country . . . they still have
followers in our party . . . they are both opposed to the present party leader-

ship . . . This is why we must safeguard the party's unity with fire and sword
. . . "[10] By establishing a reign of terror, Kádár was able to eliminate the most
dangerous threat posed by the revolutionaries and set a clear example of his
ability to wield power.

The unions and worker's councils were largely subdued by early 1957, and
an attempt to restart revolutionary activity on March 15, the anniversary of
the 1848 Revolution, was discovered by the police and quickly thwarted.[11]
Those working against the interests of the state were soon discovered by the
newly invigorated system of surveillance established by the regime.[12] Over
200,000 Hungarians left the country, 22,000 were incarcerated, and approximately 341 revolutionaries were executed.[13] By demonstrating his ability to
subdue the Revolution and assert his leadership, Kádár remained in favor in
Moscow. The Soviets, in turn, ensured that the Stalinist leadership whom
Kádár despised stayed out of power.[14] Many mid-level Stalinists remained in
the government, however, to help replenish the large numbers of bureaucrats
that either left the party during the Revolution or had been purged during the
terror. Eliminating these Stalinists would wait until 1960.[15]

Most dangerous to Kádár was Nagy and his confederates. Though Nagy accepted that he was no longer the Prime Minister, he refused to acknowledge
the Kádár government.[16] The proceedings against the Nagy group were
closed because of the potentially damaging testimony that directly implicated
Kádár in the Revolution. According to the historian Tibor Huszár, the Soviets
were inclined to encourage leniency towards Nagy in February 1958, sug-
gesting that he be sentenced to death and then later granted amnesty.[17] Even
if they subsequently changed their minds, Kádár had been provided an opportunity not to push for the death penalty. At the trial Nagy presented his defense in a deliberative manner and coolly implicated Kádár. József Szilágyi,
himself a lawyer, presented a more spirited defense that led to a separate trial
and earlier execution date. According to Szilágyi in a letter to the presiding
judge Ferenc Vida, " . . . if October was a criminal event . . . it was criminal
to lead the events [and therefore] everyone including Kádár must share responsibility." For Kádár the death penalty was unchangeable, as he felt the
need to get rid of the Nagy group in order to prevent them from forming a
new center of opposition.[18]

The announcement of the execution of Nagy and his federates was placed
on page three of the June 17, 1958, edition of all major Hungarian dailies including the *Népszabadság*, *Magyar Nemzet*, and the *Népszava*. The full-page
story was designed to shock and certainly constituted an explicit advertise-
ment for the power of the Kádár regime.[19] Subsequent articles appeared in the
newspapers explaining the need and importance of ridding the state of such
criminals.

In a speech given on July 1, 1958, Kádár claimed, "I think we were patient enough, we nicely asked the leaders and participants of the counterrevolution to lay down their arms . . . If they had done so forgiveness would have been theirs . . . They did not, and if the enemy doesn't put down their weapons they should be destroyed." Explaining why Nagy had been put to death he explained, "Some people claim we did not keep our word to Imre Nagy, but this is a lie." This is in reference to a letter of safe conduct signed by Kádár and Ferenc Münnich on November 21, 1956. Kádár and the Soviets had already decided to arrest Nagy and his group when they left the Yugoslav embassy where they had taken refuge.[20] Kádár continued reiterating several of the allegations against Nagy, "Who really knew what Imre Nagy wanted. On October 23 he promised to help suppress the counterrevolution. He did not say at the time that he had written a paper in December 1955 which said that we have to withdraw from the Warsaw Pact and that the coalition parties had to be restored . . . Imre Nagy and his group were not called to account for their point of view, but because they broke their oath to uphold the constitution: and nobody can do that." Referring to the people's justice he exclaimed, ". . . what kind of justice would it be if the person [Nagy] who had thought out, decided, organized the whole thing would not be charged . . . He could have avoided the trial if he had not lied."[21]

The Revolution had been transformed into a traitorous conspiracy. Memorials were erected throughout Budapest and the country in honor of those who had stood fast during the time of crisis, including the *pufajkások*.[22] A monument in front of the Party (MSZMP) headquarters at Köztársaság Square that featured a figure of a hero being shot memorialized those communists who had been "martyred" in their attempt to save the state. As late as November 4, 1988, commemorations for the suppression of the counterrevolution were held on Köztársaság Square.[23]

Ridding the state of criminals like Imre Nagy continued until the last execution in 1961. Perhaps the most odious of these was that of Péter Mansfeld, who was arrested in 1958 for his participation in the Revolution and held in custody until his eighteenth birthday in 1959, when he could be legally hanged.[24] In 1963 a general amnesty was declared for those who had participated in the Revolution; however this amnesty was not offered to all prisoners. Further, former revolutionaries and their families were reminded of their special status when their pensions were cut in 1977.[25]

In an interview with Andre Fontaine of *Le Monde*, Kádár explained his interpretation of the October events and the suppression that followed: "The Hungarians who were faithful to the People's Democratic Republic won. Development [in the People's Republic] can be explained by the suppression of the counterrevolution. We convinced the undecided in an open ideological fight . . . and have provided a realistic future for the faithful people." After discussing the role of the Communist Party in supporting the suppression of the counterrevolution, Fontaine asked about the role of the Soviet tanks. Kádár claimed "the request for Soviet troops came from the legitimate government to an ally of our country."[26]

Fontaine then turned his attention to Imre Nagy and his companions, asking whether the notes of the trial would be made public and whether there would be any kind of rehabilitation. To this Kádár replied, "Soon after the judge's verdict, the fifth white book was issued dedicated to Imre Nagy and his counterrevolutionary conspirators. They were guilty of inexcusable sins . . . there was so much blood and material damage . . . that we cannot speak of rehabilitation." Going into more detail Kádár said, "The 56 events, including the trial, were debated in public and went into the deepest details. For us, this is completely a closed question . . . It's better to leave it where it is . . . you have to know that the situation at the time was not normal because of the international community's hysteria. It wouldn't have been right to have an open trial. However, I can assure you that the trial was lawful and composed only of Hungarians." Kádár pointed out of his office window to show the reporter the building in which the trial took place. He finished the interview by saying, "Not a single person in Hungary would not know that those who were condemned, were condemned because they broke Hungarian laws. We never wanted revenge . . . Whenever we stepped into the events; we did so to declare amnesty."[27] The severity of the terror ensured that no one would forget the terror inflicted on Hungary, setting a clear example of Kádár's ability to wield power. But what was this realistic future that would be provided to the Hungarian people?

The fearful toll exacted by the demobilization and the reality of Soviet occupation ensured that a majority of the population would not view the Kádár regime as legitimate on these terms.[28] Kádár recognized that his continuation in power would have to rely on something other than the repressive techniques that undergirded his first five years of power. Instead, his legitimacy would be founded on providing the Hungarian population access to material goods, relative freedom of movement, and a certain *laissez faire* in regard to matters of the home. Intellectuals were co-opted by the state through publishing, travel, and other professional opportunities offered in exchange for their support. All of this was encapsulated by a policy that not only supported or banned various artistic and intellectual endeavors, but provided a category of activities that were tolerated.[29] Józsi's interpretation of a tragedy and a problem (quoted at the beginning of the chapter) encapsulates this idea of tolerated dissonance. Stories told on a street car or other informal situations would not bring the weight of the state against the individual. Kádár stated,

"We fought the major criminals [of 1956] . . . We didn't care who and what was said on the trolleys . . . We had to work with that."[30] Kádár remained in full control of political power, yet appeared to be lenient in regard to local autonomy.[31] In exchange for these concessions, the Hungarian people would "publicly forget" the events of 1956.[32]

Restarting collective farms, a process that had been reversed during the Revolution, was accompanied by an allotment of land for each peasant. Initially, the individual plots used for cultivation and limited animal husbandry provided a critical supplement to the peasants' diets. Ultimately, these plots provided the basis for additional income. After a series of failures threatened to undermine the regime's stability, Hungary's need for hard currency to purchase Western technology led to limited decentralization of the economy.[33] The Kádár regime's New Economic Mechanism emphasized modernization of industry and agriculture that encouraged innovation and independence motivated by profit.[34] The ability to provide consumer goods to the Hungarian people was viewed as a measure of success. The Hungarian system provided healthcare and schooling, so income could be reserved for consumables, and even the possibility of owning an automobile or getting into better housing. Interestingly, it was the Soviet demand for Hungary's agricultural and industrial products that helped stoke the economy and provided Hungary with a favorable balance of trade until the mid 1970s.[35]

Kádár could be seen as an advocate of the Hungarian people against the more conservative economic policies of the Soviet Premier, Leonid Brezhnev, who followed Khrushchev into power in 1964. The Brezhnev Doctrine of 1965 declared that the Soviet Union had the right to defend the Soviet satellite states and maintain the integrity of socialism within them. Kádár very carefully balanced Hungarian concerns with those of the Soviets. He not only towed the line regarding foreign policy, but encouraged Soviet military presence in Hungary. Hungary was able to appease Soviet concerns regarding Hungary's loyalty and at the same time ignore the Soviet demands for greater participation in the country's defense. The end result was that Hungary could channel more resources to its domestic programs.[36] Stability within their sphere of influence proved to be precious, given the Soviet's deteriorating relationship with the People's Republic of China and the expense of maintaining dominance within the satellites as exemplified by the Hungarian example.

Social mobility accelerated during the Kádár era. A professional class developed, along with an economy that encouraged entrepreneurship. Access to schooling increased the number of children from working-class backgrounds attending institutions of higher learning, and became part of what political scientist Rudolf L. Tőkés calls Hungary's "new post totalitarian middle class." Party membership helped ensure access to power and status.[37] The focus on economic well-being led to the encouragement of a second economy that allowed Hungarians from all strata to earn extra cash. Stability had followed Kádár's terror, and a feeling of well-being was provided by setting the Hungarian standard of living in contrast to the other client states within the Warsaw Pact.[38]

The unintended consequence of these policies, however, was a stratification of society in which those at the upper levels of the professional classes and skilled professions benefited most.[39] As the sociologist Zsuzsa Ferge noted, the desire for social mobility created a contrast between the socialist values of the state and that of many Hungarians marked by individualism in which consumerism played a major role. Ferge challenged the notion that Hungarians viewed the Soviet economic system as legitimate stating "traditional capitalist values are hard to transform [into the Kadarist formula]."[40] According to the educator Péter Szebenyi, in a study conducted in 1984 of 500 school children between the ages of ten and fifteen, 67% named a socialist country when asked to respond to the question: "Name a happy country where people live very well, where there are no needy people, and everyone lives a free and happy life." However, when asked where you would like to live for a year, 78% of the children named one of the developed [capitalist] countries.[41] The seeds of dissatisfaction were embedded in Kádár's economic programs.

How successful was Kádár's pact with the Hungarian people? On one hand, his modernization program had a positive impact on a substantial number of Hungarians. And yet, the regime's interpretation of the Revolution was in stark contradiction to what many, who had either actively or passively supported it, knew to be true. Control over interpretation of the event was considered essential for the longevity of the regime.[42]

Textbooks, which were controlled by the state and mandated for use in all public schools, reveal a fairly accurate picture of the way in which the regime arranged the narrative of the Revolution to legitimize its authority. The first reference to the Revolution appeared in gimnázium textbooks in 1961.[43] Over time the sections dedicated to the discussion of the counterrevolution grew from several paragraphs to two full sections of at least ten pages. Though revised and ultimately enlarged, the storyline remained essentially unchanged.[44] The stories told mirror the charges laid out in the *White Book*, Kádár's speeches, and histories by party members such as János Berecz.[45] For example, the rise of Nagy into a position of power is explained by Hungarian's "feeling of disappointment with the internal crisis" of 1953 that stemmed from the political and economic mistakes made by the Rákosi regime. The ensuing erosion of worker solidarity was evidenced by the ". . . certain sympathy [between] the less conscious workers and the remaining bourgeoisie which threatened a revival of anti-socialism."[46] Nagy's ascension as Prime Minister was marked by tension between the revisionists and the dogmatists. The textbooks indicate that Nagy was "misled" by the economic development of the capitalist countries, which led him to advocate for a national socialist democracy over the Soviet model. Ultimately, these problems led to his removal in 1955.[47] By using the national socialist descriptor, the text lays the foundations for charges that Nagy was in sympathy with the restoration of a "Horthy type" regime and that his sympathy with capitalism fostered an anti-Soviet feeling among the people.

The university text tells the same story, but provides more detail. For example, textbook writer Sándor Balogh detailed the political infighting between the Rákosi and Nagy factions. He then further damned Nagy by claiming that he and the editor of the *Magyar Nemzet*, Géza Losonczy, illegally formed a political faction sympathetic with the establishment of a national socialist economy. The text chided the Central Committee for not openly criticizing Nagy's ideas after his ouster from the party in December 1955.[48] Reflecting Kádár's two-front strategy whereby he eliminated the revolutionaries and the Stalinists, the Rákosi and Nagy factions are portrayed as being extremist, thus paving the way for Leninists such as Kádár to provide a reasonable alternative to extremism and the path to socialism.

In these textbooks the Revolution is portrayed for high school students as the "The Counterrevolutionary Riot" and backs up the conspiracy charges against Nagy stating that "a revisionist group instigated massive student demonstrations on October 23, 1956."[49] The university text claims that though most students felt they were participating in an anti-Stalinist demonstration, "right wing civic groups hidden in the crowd," began chanting anti-Soviet slogans exhorting the crowd to follow them.[50] The crowds are led to places where "armed counterrevolutionaries" had prepared attacks against the radio station, telephone exchange, armories, and police stations. Nagy and his supporters promised to quell the rioters and though the Central Committee "was still mistrustful of his [Nagy's] revisionist ideas," they made him Prime Minister. The Committee's fears were "well founded" as Nagy was unable to stem the rebellion from spreading into the countryside, "setting the stage" for the reemergence of "extreme right wing parties" and the bloody "white terror" that swept the streets of Budapest. The charge that Nagy betrayed his country is made explicit by his forming a government with the extreme right wing parties and his demands that those responsible for the creation of "People's Democracy" be held to account.[51]

The notion that the 1956 Revolution was a popular uprising is discounted as the text explains how the Hungarian people were outraged by the program of the counterrevolution. "The Central Committee broke with Imre Nagy because of his decision to turn away from the Hungarian people."[52] Kádár's decision to request Soviet intervention was based on the government's resolve to "stay the course with a program based on national independence, socialism, and the worker's alliance with the Soviet army," and is set in contrast with Nagy's further betrayal of Hungary with his request for United Nations assistance.[53] Kádár's new government successfully defeats both the "dogmatists [Stalinists] and the revisionists [Nagy group]." Workers Councils that had been most influenced by the revisionists were the hardest to bring back into the Hungarian Socialist community. Patient reasoning was used to instill "healthy reasoning" in the workers. In a frightening reminder of how "healthy thinking" could be enforced the high school text states, "Those who continued to resist were met with summary courts and the force of arms." Ninety-five percent of those arrested for counterrevolutionary activities were released, but those that were politically responsible and committed crimes were put to death. The policies of the MSZMP and the majority of the Hungarian people had led to the quick consolidation of power that is responsible for the "Hungarian Miracle" of today.[54]

Discussion of 1956 on terms beyond those sanctioned by the state was not tolerated. On national holidays guards were placed around national monuments associated with the 1848 and 1956 Revolutions.[55] This was especially true for those buried in Plot 301 with Imre Nagy in the Új Köztemető. Imre Mécs stated, "On All Souls Day (day of the dead), June 16, March 15, and October 23, the guards wouldn't let you anywhere near the plot."[56] Yet, the state's negative interpretation of the Revolution and its official acts of prohibition helped sustain the Revolution's memory in both acts of passive acceptance and passive resistance to the state's interpretation.[57]

According to Gábor Gyapay, a renowned Hungarian gimnázium history teacher and writer, many history teachers in the secondary schools simply ended teaching about the contemporary period with the end of World War II and the establishment of the People's Republic by "running out of time at the end of the school year."[58] Péter Szebenyi, who worked in the field of curriculum and development at the Hungarian National Institute for Education from mid-1964 onward, claimed that in the 1960s "the party lost control of the sciences, mathematics, and history . . . ," explaining, "As long as we followed the taboos of discussing the 1956 Revolution and Imre Nagy, we could do as we wished with Roman and Medieval history . . . there was really no difference between our texts and those used in England in regard to these topics." At one point in the 1960s Gyula Kállai from the party complained that the textbooks contained too much Roman history and nothing about agriculture and the liberation of Hungary. Szebenyi said that he and his colleagues responded in a letter addressing this issue to the party, promising that something would be done to rectify the problem. But as there was no reply: "we continued to create what we wished." Further emphasizing the benefits of avoidance he claimed that, "many historians turned to writing encyclopedias and bibliographies rather than address the history of contemporary Hungary." Szebenyi himself preferred to work on texts suitable for children in grade school, requesting that someone else handle curriculum and texts for students in the gimnázium or technical schools.[59]

Though nationalism was considered one of the great taboos of the regime, the 1848 Hungarian Revolution and the struggle against the Hapsburgs figured prominently in the public school curriculum during the communist period 1948–1989.[60] The narratives are consistent in their analysis of the event as being pivotal in the construction of national solidarity. The twelve points of the students and the Declaration of Independence figure prominently in the narratives. Imperial Russia's role in suppressing the Revolution is replete with Russian military leaders announcing to the Czar that "Hungary is at your feet."[61] Poetry of the 1848 Revolution is filled with imagery that was similar to the events of 1956.[62] For example, Mihály Tompa's poem about a stork, that was written in the wake of the Hapsburg victory, admires the fact that the stork has two homes, whereas the writer bemoans that the one he had is now lost.[63] On one hand these narratives and poems fortified Hungarian nationalism, but as gimnázium teacher Leo Zacharia emphasized the reading of these poems or discussion of 1848 was "not accompanied by a wink," a point emphasized by many educators that I have spoken with.[64] Perhaps the most acceptable sympathetic expression one could use in the classroom was to describe the counterrevolution of 1956 as the "sorrowful October events."[65] Students reading between the lines either kept their understanding to themselves, or confirmed their dissonant interpretations through questions asked in the home or from someone close. The danger posed to teachers or students who dared to defy the regime was not to be underestimated.

Éva Rostáné Földényi and her colleague Józsefné Kelemen, both secondary history teachers, reported that they had heard of teachers being interviewed and investigated by the police. In several instances, teachers had actually been imprisoned for expressing opinions contrary to the regime.[66] Leo Zaccaria also knew of stories about teachers being dismissed over such allegations. The vice director of the Móra Ferenc Gimnázium in Kiskunfélegyháza introduced himself to me as one of the "counterrevolutionaries." According to István Geray, he had access to stamps that would allow vehicles to travel to Budapest. The vehicles were transporting food and medicines to the inhabitants during the fighting. After the Revolution had been crushed he was dismissed from his teaching position for these actions and forced to leave the village where he was working. He obtained another job at a nearby school, but when the authorities learned of his participation in the Revolution, he was given twenty-four hours to leave. According to him, the success of the Russian language program in Kiskunfélegyháza led to his forgiveness. He was quick to add that under the consolidation [under Kádár] he had had a good living.[67] Dismissal from a teaching position could mean being consigned to menial work and not being able to work in the profession that one was trained in, or worse. Though the state no longer exacted punishments that characterized the first five years of the Kádár regime, loss of status and the accompanying economic sanction were often enough to enforce compliance.[68] Student resistance could lead to dismissal from school. For example, on March 15, 1985, a student at Ságvári Gimnázium in Szeged emblazoned the walls with demands similar to those made by students in 1848, and by extension 1956. According to Péter Zoltán the student was expelled from school, almost ensuring that he would not be admitted to the university.[69]

In this light many parents chose not to speak with their children about 1956. Instead, under such circumstances focus was placed on improving life. Éva Molnár, formerly of the Hungarian News Service, told me that she wanted her children to have a chance for the future and at that time the future was a Hungary under Soviet hegemony.[70] Many Hungarians benefited or were active members of the government and accepted the official view that 1956 was a counterrevolution. For example, the school director at the Néri Szent Fülöp Általános Iskola, Attila Dudás, whose father was a lieutenant colonel in the Hungarian army, learned the official state interpretation of 1956 and claimed that he had to relearn history after 1989.[71]

The silence regarding 1956 was utilized to create the perception that many within Hungary viewed the event as a counterrevolution and is a testament to the effectiveness of Kádár's ability to co-opt the Hungarian people. A poll taken in 1988 indicated that over 50% of Hungarians in Budapest viewed the 1956 Revolution as a counterrevolution.[72] Certainly, acceptance of the Kádár pact by many Hungarian people, both for those who remembered their lives under the Stalinists, and for a younger generation interested more in consumables than ideology, seemed to hold real promise in a world subordinated to the Soviet Union. On the other hand, fear of retribution coupled with a long-practiced passive acceptance must also factor into these poll results. Dissonance with the state's interpretation of 1956 certainly existed, but was subdued. For many, escape was not an option and led to a tentative compromise with this contemporary reality. A film by Miklós Jancsó, *The Round Up* made in 1965 seems to capture this predicament. His film portrays the struggle of the *honvéd* (1848 revolutionaries) who are trapped by their Austrian captors on the seemingly endless Hungarian *puszta* (plains) in a not too subtle allusion to the plight of those who would oppose the regime.[73]

What is interesting is that, the state unintentionally fortified Hungarian national sentiment by its inclusion of the 1848 Revolution as an integral part of its national curriculum. Connections between the 1848 and 1956 Revolutions could be made by the curious, and in private conversations in the home, but only at one's peril in public. Silence however, could only temporarily forestall a public reckoning as we shall see. What accounted for the ending of the "pact of silence?"

NOTES

1. A joke current among high school students in the 1970s and emblematic of the kind of humor that was tolerated by the regime as told to me by my brother-in-law Ágoston Gendur while visiting the grave of Imre Nagy on June 5, 1996.

2. *Molotov, Malenkov, Kaganovich. 1957. Stenogramma iiun'skogo plenuma TsK KPSS I drugie dokumenty Molotov, Malenkov, Kaganovich. 1957.* (Stenographic Report of the June Plenum of the Central Committee of the Communist Party of the Soviet Union and Other Documents) A. N. Iakovlev, ed. (Moscow: Mezhdunarodnyi fond "Demokratiia," Guverovskii institute voiny, revoliutsii i mira, Stenfordskii universitet, 1998) (Moscow: International Fund "Democracy," and the Hoover Institute of War, Revolution and Peace, 1998), 477. I am grateful to the historian Peter B. Brown for his translation of these documents.

3. See: Charles Gati, *Hungary and the Soviet Bloc* (Durham: Duke University Press, 1986), 158–61.

4. Ferenc Münich, whom Khrushchev personally knew and liked, became Kádár's deputy after Khrushchev was persuaded of Kádár's leadership qualities at Brioni. *Molotov, Malenkov, Kaganovich*, 477, 535 and Gati, *Hungary and the Soviet Bloc*, 156.

5. Johanna C. Granville, *The First Domino: International Decision Making during the Hungarian Crisis of 1956* (College Station: Texas A & M University, 2004), 146.

6. The *pufajkások* were known as the quilt-jacketed men and were the forerunner of the worker's militia. Massacres of demonstrating workers occurred at places such as Salgótarján, where forty-six workers were killed when the police opened fire into a demonstration. See: Attila Szakolczai, "Repression and Restoration, 1956–1963," in Lee W. Congdon and Béla K. Király, ed., *The Ideas of the Hungarian Revolution, Suppressed and Victorious 1956–1999* (New York: Columbia University Press, 2002), 170–71 and Granville, *The First Domino*, 152.

7. Given sanction by the Chief Prosecutor, the *pufajkások* activities often included a penchant for sadistic behavior and the number of Hungarians tortured and murdered in their actions against "enemies of the people" is not known. Szakolczai, "Repression and Restoration, 1956–1963," 172.

8. For example see: Szakolczai, "Repression and Restoration, 1956–1963," 172–74 and Grzegorz Ekiert, *The State against Society: Political Crises and Their Aftermath in East Central Europe* (Princeton: Princeton University Press, 1996). 77–78.

9. The judiciary was exhorted to be swift and merciless in the repression. Ekiert, *The State against Society*, 90.

10. As noted in the preceding chapter, Imre Nagy had already been arrested, removed from Romania, and was being held in the Fő Street Prison in Budapest. János Kádár, "Reply to the Discussion at the National Conference of the Hungarian Socialist Workers' Party," found in *János Kádár: Selected Speeches and Interviews*, Robert Maxwell, M.C., ed. (Oxford: Pergamon Press, 1985), 195–96.

11. Szakolczai, "Repression and Restoration, 1956–1963" 177.

12. The Soviets reorganized the Hungarian internal security forces providing for more agents working incognito. Granville, *The First Domino*, 154–55.

13. *The 1956 Hungarian Revolution: A History in Documents*, Csaba Békés et. al., ed. (Budapest: Central University Press, 2002), 375. The historian Attila Szakolczai claims that 230 persons were executed on the basis of the death sentence, 13,000 interned, and over 20,000 imprisoned ("Repression and Restoration, 1956–1963," 186). These figures do not include summary proceedings enacted during the fighting or by the *pufajkások*.

14. The political scientist Rudolf L. Tőkés asserts that acceptance of Soviet dominance and the success of the terror was the price Kádár had to pay to remain in power. *Hungary's Negotiated Revolution: Economic Reform, Social Change, and Political Succession* (Cambridge: Cambridge University Press, 1996), 22.

15. Bill Lomax, "Hungary: The Quest for Legitimacy," in Paul G. Lewis, ed., *Eastern Europe: Crisis and Legitimation* (New York: St. Martin's Press, 1984), 86.

16. "Lehallgatási jegyzőkönyv Nagy Imre és Kállai Gyula beszélgetéséről," January 25, 1957 in *Snagovi jegyzetek: Gondolatok, emlékezések 1956–1957*, István Vida, ed. (Budapest: Gondolat Kiadó – Nagy Imre Alapítvány, 2006), 282.

17. Tibor Huszár, *Kádár: A hatalom évei 1956–1989* (The years in power, 1956–1989) (Budapest: Corvina Kiadó Kft., 2006), 76. Johanna C. Granville argues that Khrushchev was predisposed to sanction Nagy's execution given his unwillingness to cooperate with the Kádár regime and to demonstrate both his resoluteness in foreign policy and to assuage Kádár's anxiety. *The First Domino*, 140, 143.

18. Huszár, *Kádár: A hatalom évei 1956–1989*, 79.

19. One is reminded of Michel Foucault's interpretation of absolute power: "The atrocity of the expiation organized the ritual destruction of infamy by omnipotence." *Discipline and Punish* (New York: Vintage Books, 1977), 57.

20. See the essay: "Hungary in the Aftermath," and "Situation Report from Georgii Malenkov, Mikhail Suslov, and Averki Aristov, November 22, 1956," in *The 1956 Hungarian Revolution: A History in Documents*, pages 366 and 449, respectively.

21. "Hazaérkezett a Magyar Párt-és Kormány küldöttség" (The Hungarian Party and Government Delegation Has Arrived Home), *Népszava*, July 1, 1958, p. 2.

22. For example the statue erected to the *pufajkások* on Thököly út. The statue was taken down and can now be viewed in the Statue Park in Budapest.

23. "Koszorúzási ünnepségek Budapesten" (Wreathing Celebrations in Budapest), *Népszava*, November 5,1988.

24. In 1957 juveniles who had been sixteen when they had committed a crime against the state were eligible for the death penalty. Szakolczai, "Repression and Restoration, 1956–1963," 179 and György, ed., Litván, *The Hungarian Revolution of*

1956: Reform, Revolt, and Repression, 1953–1963 (London, longman Group Ltd., 1966, 204.

25. See: Szakolczai, "Repression and Restoration, 1956–1963," 185–86 and the 1956 Institute's excellent website: *A Private History: 1956 and the Kádár Period*, György Bindorffer, Pál Gyenes, ed., http://server2001.rev.hu/oha/index_eng.html, Mária Wittner. The current FIDESZ parliamentarian and former revolutionary, Mária Wittner, was originally sentenced to death for her role in the Revolution and not released from prison until 1970. According to Wittner, her pension was cut in 1977 in order to pay for her incarceration. Mária Wittner, interview by István Lugossy, 1991–1992.

26. Andre Fontaine, "Törvénysség, létbiztonság, reális távlat mindenkinek (Lawfulness, Security, A Realistic Future for Everybody): Kádár János interjúja a Parizsi LeMonde-nak," *Magyarország*, February 23, 1964, 4.

27. Ibid., 5.

28. See: Iván Völgyes, "Never Again '56: Cooptation, Privatization, and Terror in Hungarian Society since the Revolution," Béla K. Király, et al., eds., *The First War between Socialist States: The Hungarian Revolution of 1956 and Its Impact* (New York: Brooklyn College Press, 1984), 522 and Ferenc Fehér and Ágnes Heller, *Hungary 1956 Revisited: The Message of a Revolution a Quarter of a Century After* (London: George Allen and Unwin, 1983), 136.

29. Known as the three t's *Támogatott, tűrt, tiltott* (supported, tolerated, prohibited) in Völgyes, "Never Again '56: Cooptation, Privatization, and Terror in Hungarian Society since the Revolution," 522–24. Charles Gati calls the toleration of less than hostile activities a system of "supervised steam letting," providing religion as an example. Gati, *Hungary and the Soviet Bloc*, 162–63.

30. Tibor Huszár, *Kádár: A hatalom évei 1956–1989*, 275.

31. Iván Völgyes calls this exchange the "Greyhound Effect" (leave the driving to us). "Never Again '56: Cooptation, Privatization, and Terror in Hungarian Society since the Revolution," 521. See also: Ekiert, *The State against Society*, 109.

32. The sociologist János Kis discusses this tradeoff known as the "pact of forgetting" in his book, *Politics in Hungary: For a Democratic Alternative* (New York: Columbia University Press, 1989), 75. The historian George Schőphlin claims that ultimately Hungarians accepted the inevitability of Soviet dominance. *Politics in Eastern Europe* (Oxford: Blackwell Publishers, 1993) 103.

33. Sándor Szakács, "From 'Goulash Communism' to Breakdown," in Congdon and Király, ed., *The Ideas of the Hungarian Revolution, Suppressed and Victorious, 1956–1999*, 195–97, 200–202. See also: Andrew Felkay, "Hungary and the Soviet Union in the Kádár Era," *20th Century Hungary and the Great Powers*, Ignác Romsics, ed. (New York: Columbia University Press, 1995) 274, 276.

34. Gati, *Hungary and the Soviet Bloc*, 165–66.

35. Szakács, "From 'Goulash Communism' to Breakdown," 205–6.

36. Tőkés, *Hungary's Negotiated Revolution*, 40–42.

37. The changes were dramatic as Tőkés points out "between 1970–1980 the number of white-collar employees increased by 27 percent . . . and that by 1980 8.1 percent of all wage earners were university or college graduates" in: *Hungary's Negoti-*

ated Revolution, 134–35. András Bozóki and Gergely Karácsony underscore the fact that the "second generation" of Hungarian Communists saw membership in the party as a "prerequisite of advancement in the party hierarchy, and upward mobility" in their essay, "The Making of a Political Elite: Participants in the Hungarian Roundtable Talks of 1989," *The Roundtable Talks of 1989: The Genesis of Hungarian Democracy* ed. András Bozóki (Budapest: Central European University Press, 2002), 192–93.

38. Ekiert, *State against Society*, 113–15.

39. For example see: Völgyes, "Never Again '56: Cooptation, Privatization, and Terror in Hungarian Society since the Revolution," 525 and Tőkés, *Hungary's Negotiated Revolution*, 136.

40. Zsuzsa Ferge, *A Society in the Making* (New York: M.E. Sharpe Inc., 1979), 317–19. The book is striking because it was published at a time when an open discussion of the contradictions that existed in Hungarian society was forbidden. According to Benő Csapó, chair of the Education Department at the University of Szeged, Ferge simply reported her findings without comment, and in this way, was able to have her work published in the academic community. Benő Csapó, interview by author, October 25, 1997.

41. The historian and educationalist Péter Szebenyi cites this study in his article, "Crossfire of Debates, History Teaching—The Volcano of Hungarian Schooling," *Studies in Education Evaluation*, 18 (1992): 106.

42. Policy statements related to propaganda, ideology, and education issued by the regime ranked second only to party management in order of importance between 1956 and 1989, Tőkés, *Hungary's Negotiated Revolution*, 62–63.

43. Tibor Szamuely et al., *Történelem Általános Gimnázium IV* (Budapest: Tankönyvkiadó, 1961), 276.

44. For example see: Ágota Jóvérné Szirtés, *Történelem IV* (History 4) *Dolgozók Középiskola részére* (Budapest: Tankönyvkiadó, 1987), Endre Balogh and Miklós Mann, *Történelem IV* (Budapest: Tankönyvkiadó, 1982) written for technical high school students, Endre Balogh, *Történelem Általános Gimnáziumok, IV* (Budapest: Tankönyvkiadó, 1974), János Almási, *Történelem Az Általanos Gimnáziumok IV* (Budapest: Tankönyvkiadó, 1965) written for gimnázium students, and Sándor Balogh et al., *A Magyar népi demokrácia története, 1944–1962* (The History of the Hungarian People's Democracy) (Budapest: Kossuth Könyvkiadó, 1978) written for university students preparing for positions as secondary school history teachers. The books were recommended to me by Péter Zoltán, a history teacher at the Jószef Attila Bilingual Gimnázium in Szeged, interview by author, July 11, 1996 and the Senior Archivist of the Pedagogical Archive in Budapest, László Horváth, interview by author, November 30, 2006.

45. Berecz wrote a book entitled *Counter Revolution in Hungary: Words and Weapons* (Budapest: Akadémia Kiadó, 1986) originally published in 1969 *Ellenforradalom tollal és fegyverrel, 1956* (Budapest: Kossuth Kiadó, 1969). Berecz became the Central Committee's Secretary for Ideological Affairs in the 1980s.

46. Balogh and Mann, *Történelem IV*, 159.

47. Ibid., 160.

48. Balogh et al., *A magyar népi demokrácia története*, 161.

49. Balogh and Mann, *Történelem IV*, 161.

50. Balogh et al., *A magyar népi democrácia története*, 276–77.

51. Balogh and Mann, *Történelem IV*, 162–64.

52. Balogh et al., *A magyar népi democrácia története*, 285.

53. Balogh and Mann, *Történelem IV*, 164.

54. Ibid., 165, 167–68.

55. Ágoston Gendur, interview by author, June 15, 1996, and more recently by Lászlóné Motajcsek, an administrator Néri Szent Fülöp Általános Iskola, Budapest, interview by author, October 27, 2006.

56. Imre Mécs, interview by author, November 7, 1997.

57. "Heresy is as much of a child of orthodoxy in politics as it is in religion," Clifford Geertz, "Centers, Kings, and Charisma: Reflections on the Symbolics of Power," *Local Knowledge: Further Essays in Interpretive Anthropology* (New York: Basic Books, 1983), 144.

58. Gábor Gyapay, interview by author, August 5, 1996, and Péter Zoltán, interview by author, July 11, 1996. This has been mentioned to me in many conversations that I have had with Hungarians, most recently in an interview with Leo Zaccaria of Tóth Árpád Gimnázium located in Debrecen, interview by author, October 31, 2006.

59. Péter Szebenyi, interview by author, February 9, 1998.

60. For example see: György Spira, *A Magyar Nép Története , II, 1526–1849* (The History of the Hungarian People) (Budapest: Tankönyvkiadó, 1951), Mátyás Unger, *Történelem—Az Általános Gimnáziumok III* (Budapest, Tankönyvkiadó, 1964) through the 12th edition published in 1978, and Géza Závodszky, *Történelem III, Gimnázium* (Budapest: Tankönyvkiadó, 1980). This strong sense of nationalism is evidenced not only in textbooks, but in movies shown in Hungary such as Miklós Jancsó's *The Roundup*, Budapest: MOKÉP Zrt., 1965. Another epic movie that celebrates Hungarian resistance to overwhelming odds is *Egri Csillagok* (Stars over Eger) made in 1968, in this case depicting the siege of Eger castle in 1552 against the Ottomans. As mentioned earlier the Ottomans had occupied Hungary for close to 150 years following the disastrous Battle of Mohács in 1526. The film is rich in Hungarian folk imagery and is based on a much-loved novel of the same name by Géza Gárdonyi. See: *Egri Csillagok*, directed by Zoltán Várkonyi, Budapest, MOKEP, Rt., 1968.

61. Mátyás Unger, *Történelem a gimnáziumok III* (Budapest: Tankönyvkiadó, 1971), 197.

62. The narrative found in the texts features poetry by the revolutionary poet Sándor Petőfi, a point made explicit by the students on October 23, 1956 as already discussed.

63. Pálné Vidor, ed., *Irodalmi Szöveggyűjtemény III* (Collection of Literature) (Budapest: Tankönyvkiadó, 1970), 25. The Petőfi Verse and the Hymnus already cited were known and often recited by Hungarian school children.

64. Leo Zaccaria, interview by author, October 31, 2006. Béla Jazimicky, who taught at the Radnóti Gimnázium in Szeged during the 1980s, said that making direct references between the 1848 and 1956 Revolutions would have been too dangerous

for him to use in the classroom in light of a very conservative director of his school. Béla Jazimicky, interview by author, February 2, 1988.

65. From an interview with Éva Rostáné Földényi and Józsefné Kelemen from the Móra Ferenc Gimnázium located in Kiskunfélegyháza, interview by author, January 28, 1998.

66. Ibid.

67. István Geray, interview by author, January 28, 1998.

68. For example, administrative sanctions could include the loss of an apartment or driver's license. See: Huszár, *Kádár: A hatalalom évei, 1956–1989*, 274.

69. Péter Zoltán, interview by author, July 6, 1996. The Kádár regime often tolerated dissent, but viewed nationalism, especially in this light, as a threat. For example see: Tőkés, *Hungary's Negotiated Revolution*, 172–74. The plight of students publicly expressing their nationalist sentiments is also mentioned by Alice Freifeld in "The Cult of March 15," ed., Maria Burcur and Nancy M. Wingfield, *Staging the Past: The Politics of Commemoration in Hapsburg Central Europe, 1848 to the Present* (West Lafayette, IN: Purdue University Press, 2001), 277.

70. Éva Molnár, interview by author, August 9, 1996. Leo Zaccaria's family also never discussed the issue in the home.

71. Attila Dudás, interview by author, October 25, 2006.

72. László Deme, "Liberal Nationalism in Hungary, 1988–1990," *East European Quarterly*, 32, 1 (Spring, 1998): 63–64.

73. *The Round Up*. Directed by Miklós Jancsó. Budapest: MOKÉP Zrt., 1965.

Chapter Six

The Demand for Memorial

The vast majority is dumbfounded, and not because they have heard the results of an academic research from the Historical Subcommittee, but because they feel that a pillar of the institutionalized political system is about
to be uprooted. Party members feel that our political system is somehow
based on 1956. And now they have the impression that this foundation is
being removed from underneath.

—Mihály Jassó, Meeting of the MSZMP
(Hungarian Socialist Worker's Party) January 31, 1989[1]

Dissident constructs of the state's interpretation of Imre Nagy and the 1956
Revolution had largely been subdued throughout the 1970s and early 1980s.
János Kádár feared the symbolic power of Nagy, and demonstrated this by the
stories he fostered in which it was the Soviets, not himself, who had insisted
on his execution and by his insistence that the legitimacy of the action not be
discussed.[2] In many ways this silence had been obtained through a certain
economic prosperity and openness not found in other countries under the
sway of Soviet rule. Though it was the Historical Justice Committee com-
prised of dissidents and the families of the victims who demanded proper burial for Nagy and his confederates, it was the announcement from Central
Committee member Imre Pozsgay, working to reform the party from within,
that instigated a very public reexamination of the period with his statement
that 1956 had been a popular uprising. In this light, Mihály Jassó was right to
worry that the foundation of the party was being removed from underneath,
for by the end of 1989 the one-party state had been destroyed. What had
opened this Pandora's Box? There was no one causal factor but instead the
confluence of several that included Hungary's uneasy economy, the demands
for reform from within the party, and the far-reaching consequences of Soviet

reforms that collectively ended the "pact of silence" and paved the way for democratic change in Hungary.

The rise in oil prices triggered by the Yom Kippur War in 1973 and the Iranian Revolution in 1979 was devastating to the Hungarian economy. Hungary had continued modernization projects that included an emphasis on the expansion of heavy industry. Though profit was used as a motivating factor in Kádár's policies, centralized planning that seemed to ignore global market conditions remained.[3] For example, in a joint venture between Hungary and the Soviet Union in the Zala oil fields very little profit was generated, and yet funds were allocated to build a car wash for company employees.[4] Further complicating Hungary's increasing need for energy was the decision by the Soviets to increase oil prices in 1975. In order to pay for these investments Hungary borrowed capital from the West. As the historian Andrew Felkay asserts, Hungary's modernization was premised on antiquated technology, and the investment merely exposed an economy that was seriously in trouble. For example, part of the money was used to "cover" Hungary's burgeoning deficits.[5] The legitimacy of the regime was intimately connected to increasing the Hungarian's living standard and Kádár could not accept anything that smacked of downsizing living standards or social security.[6]

Hungary's favorable trade balance with the Soviet Union and within COMECON disappeared in the second half of the 1970s. Throughout the same period Western technology continued to outpace goods manufactured within Hungary and led to a decreased value for Hungarian exports.[7] By 1979 Hungary had a 5.9 billion dollar trade deficit.[8] Hungarians' wages stagnated as prices increased leading to 40–50% of the population engaged in some type of enterprise to supplement their income.[9]

The urgency of the souring economy paved the way for a challenge to Kádár and his old guard. Hungary's innovative use of capital had tied it closer to the Western banking system and capitalism.[10] In order to emerge from the economic nightmare of the 1970s Hungary joined the International Monetary Fund and the World Bank in May 1982, obligating the country to Western regulation in order to obtain credit.[11] Reformers within the Central Committee such as Imre Pozsgay, Secretary of the Patriotic People's Front, believed that an introduction of democratic reforms paired with economic liberalization was essential to save the economy. In fact, Kádár's policies had exacerbated stratification within Hungarian society in contrast to the egalitarian principles espoused by the party that contributed to a growing sense of unease among the Hungarian population.[12] The continued economic downturn played to Pozsgay's hand.[13] Pozsgay utilized the Patriotic People's Front to gain a wide base of support both within and outside the party.[14] Initially,

Kádár attempted to quash dissonance within the party. In 1983 he announced that there would be "no more reform of the reform," but the ascension of Mikhail Gorbachev in 1985 and his introduction of glasnost and perestroika helped disarm efforts of conservatives within the Central Committee to somehow maintain a status quo.[15] Kádár who vigorously opposed fiscal strategies that he felt threatening to state social security and political legitimacy was outpaced by economic and political changes, which made his policies obsolete.[16] Ultimately, the Central Committee admitted to itself that its economic policies had been disastrous and policy planning was placed in the hands of experts that included Péter Medgyessy as Minister of Finance, and by 1986 the reform faction was gaining the upper hand.[17]

The disastrous economy and the recognition of a new generation of experts helped set the stage for Kádár's ouster as the party's Secretary General. At the Third Conference of the MSZMP, May 1988, he was replaced by Károly Grósz who became the new Prime Minister and Secretary General of the party. Though wanting to reform the party and the economy, Grósz also wanted to maintain the preeminence of the communists. Kádár had wanted to limit the political power of Pozsgay and the reformers within the party, and went so far as to compare Pozsgay with Imre Nagy. Grósz also portrayed the opposition as the enemy, whereas reformers such as Imre Pozsgay believed in a more democratic process and were willing to work with the opposition.[18] The conservative platform championed by Grósz was marked by a hard line towards 1956 as revealed by the texts we have examined, setting a marked contrast between the regime and the opposition both within and outside the party.

Dissent had been tolerated in Hungary as long as it did not constitute a direct challenge to the regime. The events in Poland that resulted in that regime's forceful suppression of the Solidarity movement in 1982 were closely watched in Hungary. According to Tibor Huszár, Kádár understood from the Polish experience that though the Soviets remained deeply involved in the internal politics of their satellites, they could not count on Soviet military intervention to back up the regime. Instead, other tactics would be needed to thwart the opposition that "threatened party unity." In a meeting of the Politburo on March 30, 1982, Kádár exclaimed, "We have to step on them [the opposition]!" He went on to compare how the Revolution had been suppressed and the Hungarian people won over. In his mind the taboos established in the context of his dictatorship needed to continue.[19]

The demand for democratization within the regime coupled with Moscow's new stance towards open dialogue emboldened intellectuals to challenge the regime from outside the government and further undermined Kádár's "pact of silence." Many younger intellectuals were inspired by the writings of István

Bibó, who had been silenced by the state after his release from prison in 1963. In a taped lecture published outside of Hungary in 1986 he asserted, "The student movements in the Socialist countries exhibit such extraordinary demands for liberty, [with] such humanity and depth . . . and their programs are so concrete, because in these countries the institutions of freedom have been operating under numerous constraints."[20] The demand for the reburial of Imre Nagy and his comrades was utilized as a lever by the democratic opposition to unhinge the regime, a strategy made easier by the ascendancy of conservatives like Grósz and Berecz within the communist party.[21]

Imre Mécs claims that he began using Plot 301 as a site of protest and memorial in the 1970s. Though he began visiting the site after his release from prison in the general amnesty of 1963, "it was in the 1970s when we began formally requesting a human burial for the legitimate Prime Minister and Pál Maléter, Defense Minister . . . " Some of these letters went unanswered, or were answered with statements claiming that the records of these affairs did not exist.[22] When Júlia Szilágyi, daughter of József Szilágyi, wrote a letter to the Central Committee asking for the remains of her father, a letter was sent back claiming that they did not know what she was talking about. In a second letter she requested information as to when, how, and why her father was executed. To this she and mother received a letter stating that they were looking for documents, but that the people who had been present at the execution and burial were now dead.[23]

Samizdat and the Western press were critical in publicizing the call for the proper burial of Nagy and his fellow revolutionaries.[24] For example, in "The Messenger," which appeared in December 1983, György Krassó described four graves in Plot 301 that were "different from all of the rest." The graves were adorned with flowers and the author thought that these must be the graves of Nagy and his principals.[25] The graves, in fact, belonged to four less well-known revolutionaries.

Radio Free Europe amplified the demand for Nagy's proper burial in 1985. According to the report, mothers of two of the revolutionaries, Béla Békési and Géza Pech, watched where their sons were buried after they had been hanged at the Gyüjtőfogház Prison. Though the authorities regularly plowed and bulldozed the mounds of the graves, the mothers repeatedly repaired the mounds using a high tension utility post as a guide to remember where the graves were located. Eventually, Aliz Halda, the companion of Miklós Gimes, and Judit Gyenes, the wife of Pál Maléter, began leaving flowers at the site for lack of a better spot. The sight of the four mounds led others to conclude that this was where Imre Nagy and his comrades lay. In spite of the regime's refusal to tell the families of the victims where their loved ones were buried, the author of the news story "Searching for the Grave of Imre Nagy," Béla

Lipták was able to examine an official register of executions performed around the time of Nagy's execution, and speculated where the graves could be found in Plot 301. The story ends with a demand that the remains of Nagy and the others be turned over to their families for proper burial.[26] Hungarians would not learn the full story of Nagy's execution or where he lay until 1989.[7]

By 1986 the opposition began utilizing legal procedures to challenge the regime. For example, Mécs challenged the regime's right to deny him his obligation to perform *kegyelet* on All Souls Day, 1986. According to Mécs he had wanted to light a candle and leave flowers at Plot 301, but a guard prevented him from doing so, telling him that "the right of *kegyelet* does not apply to Plot 301." Mécs challenged this in court and in December 1986 he was called into the Ministry of Internal Affairs where he was told that the reason he had been prevented from lighting a candle was the danger of fire. Mécs exclaimed, "the guy's face went red . . . you could tell that the officer knew this was nonsense." Though there were no repercussions from his legal challenge, he had already paid a price for speaking openly about the Revolution earlier that year.[28] Mécs was fired from his job for speaking at the funeral of fellow revolutionary, Miklós Péterfi. According to the story published in the *Herald Tribune*, two hundred people and fifty police attended the funeral where Mécs praised the patriotism and valor of his comrade.[29] The same story reported problems the BBC had encountered while making the film "Cry Hungary" on June 16, 1986. While the crew was filming at Plot 301 the crew and journalists from the *New York Times*, *Wall Street Journal*, and the *Christian Science Monitor* had their film and notebooks confiscated by the police. The resulting publicity drawn from the international papers and Radio Free Europe embarrassed the government and stepped up pressure for the reburial of Nagy and his comrades.

Concurrent with the demand for the reburial and reevaluation of Nagy and the Revolution was an increasingly vibrant sense of populist nationalism among Hungarians, especially regarding the treatment of Hungarian minorities living in Czechoslovakia, Romania, and Yugoslavia.[30] The Helsinki Accords of 1975 that sanctioned border arrangements after World War II also provided specific instruction regarding the treatment of minority populations. As the historian Andrew Ludanyi asserts, closer attention was given to Ceauşescu's treatment of Hungarians living in Transylvania. Harassment of Hungarian minorities and their institutions ultimately ended in a threat to eradicate Hungarian settlements in Romania, which stimulated outrage both inside and outside of the government.[31] Similarly, the decision to build the Nagymaros dam on the Danube River in 1983 by Czechoslovakia and Hungary served to stoke the outrage of both environmentalists and nationalists. The Danube Circle formed to oppose the project served to further challenge the regime.[32]

Though real differences existed between the various interest groups that composed the opposition to the regime, one of the principal mouthpieces of the democratic opposition helped create a sense of unity by paying close attention to populist issues. The samizdat publication *Beszélő* was persistent in its call for a reevaluation of 1956 and its demand for democratization.[33] A conference held at Monor in June 1985 exposed significant differences between populists and the democratic opposition, but at the same time attempted to articulate consensus.[34] The political parties that developed from these movements within the opposition reflected the wide variety of views regarding economy and politics that existed at the time (see Appendix C). The largest of these groups, the Hungarian Democratic Forum (MDF) established in September 1987, represented this diversity with factions strongly dedicated to populist causes and the establishment of democratic governance. They embraced a platform that called for gradual change and compromise in contrast to the Free Democrats (SZDSZ) established in November 1988, which sprang from the democratic opposition that insisted on the establishment of procedural republic unhindered by communist hegemony. The threat posed by the democratic opposition can be seen in the brutal suppression of the alternative March 15, 1987, celebration. Again, it is important to note that the legitimacy of 1848 was accepted by both the communists and those opposition factions forwarding democratic and populist issues. Over time this consensus helped undermine the communist regime's selective interpretation of 1848 and its linkage with 1956. In this light, control over the public interpretation of 1848 and 1956 was essential.

As mentioned earlier the reform movement within the Communist Party believed that democratization was essential in order to initiate economic reforms. This led to the decision to revise the constitution in order that a general election could take place in 1990. A key part of their strategy was to unseat the conservative faction within the party and create a broad base of support by co-opting populist intellectuals outside the party. In response to the outside pressure being brought to bear regarding Nagy and 1956, and also as a way of further undermining the conservative faction, the Central Committee created a subcommittee to investigate the historical interpretation of 1956 under the leadership of the historian Iván Berend.[35] This was crucial, given that dissidents to the regime had created the Committee for Historical Justice founded on June 5, 1988 and backed by a coalition of opposition groups. This organization joined with the families of the deceased to advocate for a reexamination of 1956 and the reburial of Nagy and the martyrs.[36]

Both the opposition and the reform faction within the government would lay claim to Nagy and the legacy of 1956. A conscious attempt was made by the post-Kádár regime to play on the divisions within the opposition to prevent a united front that could threaten the survival of the envisioned communist-dominated democracy. The establishment of the New March Front was an attempt to link Kádár's economic reforms with populist issues such as the Nagymaros dam and the plight of Hungarians outside the borders. The official party line regarding Nagy and the Revolution, however, would cost them dearly. The samizdat *Beszélő* taunted the new regime's refusal to publicly confront the demands set out by the Historical Justice Committee: "A few years ago it would have demonstrated the power and willingness of the regime to effect reconciliation, but now, the longer this is put off . . . it demonstrates weakness. Do not wait for the reburial of Imre Nagy, as it may become another Rajk funeral."[37]

June 16, 1988, was the thirtieth anniversary of Nagy's execution, and the Committee for Historical Justice marked this occasion with a poignant protest at Plot 301 where the graves and their contents were acknowledged. The event was filmed by the underground film group Black Box, and reveals an overgrown cemetery plot with depressions marking the locations of the graves.[38] Protests took place later that day at the Batthyány Eternal Light Memorial and the Hungarian television station where the names of the martyrs were read aloud. The police forcefully broke up those rallies, by using tear gas and beating demonstrators that got in their way. Approximately sixteen demonstrators were arrested.[39] The demonstration nevertheless continued in the nearby Vörösmarty Square, a place frequented by tourists, and served to "showcase the brutality of the police." The day ended in a Franciscan church where despite pressure the priest there refused to read a requiem mass for Nagy and the martyrs. According to organizer, Imre Mécs, "the priest was afraid of the political repercussions."[40]

Increased international attention was drawn to the memory of Nagy and the 1956 Revolution with events in Paris and Washington, D.C. In Paris on the same day as the demonstrations in Budapest a symbolic funeral for Nagy was held in Pére Lachaise cemetery that included not only those close to Nagy, but Nobel prize winners such as Saul Bellow, Ellie Weisel, and Joseph Brodsky. The ceremony included the unveiling of a monument to Nagy.[41] Later in July during a state visit to the United States, Grósz was pressed by President Ronald Reagan to attend to the demands for a proper reburial of Nagy and his companions.[42] The year 1956 was being linked to Hungary's desire to establish closer economic ties to the West.

On June 28, 1988, over 60,000 people gathered at Heroes Square to protest human rights abuses being perpetrated against the Hungarian minority living in Romania for a rally sanctioned by the government and MDF.[43] The rally tacitly demonstrated the government's responsiveness to a populist issue and demonstrated explicitly what kind of public activity would be tolerated. But it also stimulated mass participation, as was evidenced by the size of the crowd.[44] Many who participated in the crowd were also sympathetic to the demands of the Committee for Historical Justice. The cooperation with the MDF did not necessarily mean that the organization could be used as a means to divide an increasingly aggressive opposition.

Despite the police action on June 16th, increased openness in Hungarian society was difficult to suppress and the rapidly deteriorating economy that had contributed to Kádár's downfall was forcing the regime into a defensive posture. Further undermining Grósz and the communists was Mikhail Gorbachev's abandonment of the Brezhnev Doctrine. The urgency with which Gorbachev wished to hasten reform led to his momentous statement in June 1988 that, "any nation had the right to choose its own social economic system," a point he reiterated in December of that year.[45] The demand for a proper burial for Nagy and his companions became a demand for a public reburial.

The pace of change seemed to overwhelm Grósz, and his resistance to a reevaluation of 1956 continued in his explanation to ban all demonstrations on October 23 stating, " . . . counterrevolution cannot be commemorated as a memorable anniversary."[46] On November 29 he warned that the reform process was the herald of a "white terror." Later in December he reaffirmed his commitment to Marxist-Leninist ideology and declared that there were no problems in Hungary.[47] Conservative intransigence over 1956 provided the opportunity for Pozsgay and his federates within the party and the opposition without to strike a crippling blow. Unable to stabilize the economy and recover Kádár's illusory social contract with Hungarians meant that moral and political legitimacy would rest on interpretation of the Revolution of 1956 and the legacy of Imre Nagy.

Conservatives had reason to feel overwhelmed by the pace of change. On October 8 the economist Tamás Nagy, an architect of Kádár's New Economic Mechanism, announced on the popular radio program "168 Hours" that in 1956, "the Stalinist regime had collapsed" and that rather than being a counterrevolution, "The aim of the uprising was a democratic society and the independence of Hungary."[48] The announcement served as a harbinger of what was to come. On November 24 Imre Pozsgay proposed a package of democratic reforms that included a multiparty system to the Parliament on behalf of the government, providing the legal basis for the transition to the "new democracy."[49] The rug was about to be pulled from underneath Grósz and his allies. On January 27, 1989, the historical subcommittee of the Central Committee met and the overwhelming majority agreed that the 1956 Revolution was a popular uprising. Unsure of how to disseminate the information, the committee decided to go through the traditional channels of the Communist

Party.[50] Pozsgay knew that this would have meant a rejection of these findings by the conservatives, or at best a compromise with the research. He claimed, "I decided that after the debate I would look for a newspaper, the radio or, television and I would say out loud what was impossible to say, what the people always knew . . . " A leader of the party needed to forcefully back Tamás Nagy's assessment of 1956. Pozsgay stated, "the real importance here will be that one of the leaders of the party will say that the legitimacy to rule was based on the lie that it, the party, saved the nation from a fatal counterrevolution."[51]

Pozsgay's startling announcement on "168 Hours" on January 28, 1989, affected not only those within the Central Committee, but the Hungarian public as well. If the 1956 Revolution was a popular uprising, on what ground had Nagy and the Revolutionaries been executed?[52] As Mihály Jassó remarked during a meeting of the Political Committee, ". . . I got phone calls today asking how we are going to call the monument on Köztársaság Square," in reference to a monument erected to the communist martyrs killed during the revolutionaries attack on the Party headquarters on October 30, 1956.[53] The announcement strengthened both the reformers within the government and the opposition groups outside the government.

Grósz rushed home from an economic conference in Switzerland to try and put out the fire, but it was too late. The Central Committee issued a statement claiming that the events of 1956 had begun as a popular uprising but ultimately had devolved into a counterrevolution.[54] This is a line that Grósz and his allies seemed unable to deviate from and was supported by Mikhail Gorbachev who agreed that no historical revision was needed regarding the official Hungarian interpretation of 1956.[55] The rift between members of the Central Committee became more marked both in meetings and in public. Rezső Nyers claimed that though he disagreed with Pozsgay's decision to broadcast the committee's findings he stated, "If 1956 is our foundation . . . it is a weak foundation indeed . . . Imre Nagy was not a counterrevolutionary."[56] On February 15 during the course of a television interview Pozsgay contradicted Grósz's claims that his interpretation enjoyed popular support.[57] The opposition pounced. SZDSZ issued a statement on February 5 followed by the other major opposition groups warning that any government statements that were contrary to Pozsgay's January 28 statement would only escalate the crisis.[58]

The communists' goal of negotiating separately with the various opposition groups in a bid to remain in power through the formation of a multiparty democratic system was stymied in large part by the crisis of legitimacy uncapped by Pozsgay's announcement and pressure exerted by the opposition. The issue was intensified by a host of articles and books that reexamined the Kádár

years and the fate of Nagy and his compatriots, making the demand for reburial a moral imperative for those previously intimidated by the regime. The
potential power of the Hungarian people was demonstrated on March 15, the
national day commemorating the 1848 Revolution, when hundreds of thousands of Hungarians joined the opposition parties in the streets for rallies in
Budapest. The Hungarian people were energized by the event and affirmed
the legitimacy of the opposition's demands, a point not lost on those in
power.[59]

An Opposition Roundtable was established at the invitation of the Independent Lawyers Forum for the purpose of negotiating the transition to multiparty democracy with the regime. The roundtable was established on March
22 and included the major opposition groups such as MDF, SZDSZ, and
FIDESZ (Young Democrats) along with parties resurrected from the
1945–1947 Republic such as the FKgP (Smallholders). An attempt by the
communists to sideline the new organization through separate negotiations
was thwarted at the end of March with the acceptance of an SZDSZ proposal
that the roundtable negotiate collectively with the regime, and that the new
constitution be created after general multiparty elections. Importantly, the
rules of the transition would be through consensus achieved through roundtable negotiations with all parties.

The demand for a public funeral for Imre Nagy and his federates became a
reality on May 25, 1989.[60] Up until the last moment the hardliners within the
party had tried to lay the main reasons for reburial aside to avoid the political
consequences. For example, at a Central Committee meeting on December
15, 1988, György Fejti proposed that the Committee inform the party and
public that the reburial of Imre Nagy and his comrades would be an act of reconciliation, honoring the requests for a proper burial, not a political rehabilitation.[61] At another Central Committee meeting on April 28, 1989, Jenő Fock,
who had been Prime Minister during the Kádár era and well understood the
political danger posed by a public funeral stated, "First we said that there
would be no rehabilitation of the Nagy case, that the funeral would be a
purely humanitarian act. The family agreed with this, but then requested that
a monument be put up. The families continue to pressure us . . . if we agree
[that a memorial ceremony] would be held on Kossuth or Heroes Square, then
there will be no stop [to the demands of the opposition]."[62] In spite of continued resistance by Grósz and other hardliners, however, the reform faction
understood that the importance of spiritual attachment with Nagy and the
Revolution was critical to their survival. The past that Kádár had feared had
now caught up with him and those who had inherited his regime.[63]

The government's fear as for what might transpire at the June 16 funeral
played into the Opposition Roundtable's hands, deciding that it would give

them an upper hand in negotiations.[64] Conciliation would be expressed from a point of strength fortified by association with the past. At the Plenary Session of the National Roundtable Negotiations three days before the funeral on June 13, 1989, Imre Kónya, MDF stated, "After thirty years of numbness, our society has finally risen. The formation of independent organizations, and of large-scale demonstrations indicate that it [our society] wants to control its own fate . . . Burying the martyrs of the Revolution and commencing these talks can mark the beginning of national reconciliation. Real reconciliation, however, can be achieved by burying the existing dictatorial power system."[65]

Kádár's popular economic reforms that had assuaged an oppressed population after the suppression of the Revolution were outpaced by the reality of global politics and the fact that Hungarian prosperity had become linked to global capitalism. Ignoring the economic downturn only temporarily staved off the day of reckoning for the Hungarian economy and the Hungarian people's satisfaction with their lot. Ultimately, many Hungarians became dissatisfied with the struggling economy and linked it to the failed policies of the communists. Tibor Huszár is probably right in his assertion that Kádár did not fully understand the global forces that helped undermine his regime. The call for democracy from inside and outside the party helped thwart his attempt to maintain the taboos that were the firmament of his "pact of silence." Whether in 1982 or with Gorbachev's declaration ending the Brezhnev Doctrine in 1988, and in spite of the continued Soviet occupation, the communists were no longer propped up by the Soviet army. This forced them to utilize different strategies that ultimately resulted in negotiations with the opposition. glasnost and perestroika fortified the opposition's boldness and opened the door for discussions regarding the plight of Hungarian nationals outside Hungary's borders, which served to fortify a Hungarian nationalism that had been controlled, but not subdued during the Kádár period. As we have seen, the 1848 Revolution played a prominent place in the national curriculum.

The question of Nagy and the revolutionaries was raised by dissenters outside the party and directly challenged Kádár's political legitimacy. The moral imperative for proper burial was fused to the question as to whether the Revolution constituted a popular uprising or a counterrevolution. Political socialization had been successful to a point, and many Hungarians accepted the regime's explanation regarding the "sorrowful October events." But the continued challenge to the regime's paradigm, ultimately conceded by those within the regime itself, served to validate the opposition's claim that 1956 was a War of Independence in every sense that 1848 was. This concession by the regime and the ability of Hungarians to gather and speak freely demonstrated on March 15, 1989, and later at the funeral of Imre Nagy, confirmed the opposition's claim. Despite the sense of horror to hardliners within the Communist Party who recognized that their political power was now seriously jeopardized, it served as a confirmation to many who had remained silent out of expediency or fear. The announcement by Pozsgay provided permission and a moral justification for those formerly intimidated by the regime to openly back the opposition. In this way, the "pact of silence" ultimately backfired.

The ending of the communist regime raised a host of questions regarding national identity and economy in Hungary. Not all Hungarians accepted the new paradigm posed by the opposition, or were ready to jettison Kádár's ideology, especially as it related to the economy. On July 13–14, 1989, over sixty thousand Hungarians filed past Kádár's coffin, and even more came to his burial at the Kerepesi cemetery, indicating the still strong allegiance that many held for him and his ideas.[66] Among the opposition, that included a wide range of beliefs regarding economy and politics. Sovereignty and the establishment of a democratic state were issues of consensus; all else was up for debate. It is this debate over the nature of the Hungarian state that occupies the remainder of this story

NOTES

1. A Compendium of Declassified Documents and Chronology of Events (hereafter: A Compendium of Declassified Documents) Csaba Békés, Malcolm Byrne ed., Political Transition in Hungary 1989–1990 International Conference Budapest, Hungary, 1999 sponsored by the National Security Archive/Cold War History Research Center/1956 Institute.

2. Roger Gough, *A Good Comrade: János Kádár, Communism and Hungary* (London: I.B. Tauris, 2006), 116–18.

3. Sándor Szakács, "From 'Goulash Communism' to Breakdown," in the Ideas of the Hungarian Revolution, suppressed and Victorious, 1956–1999. Lee W. Congdan and Béla K. Király ed. (New York: Columbia University Press, 2002) 206–7.

4. L. Cooper, and A. Kinesei, *Hungarians in Transition* (New York: McFarland and Co., Inc., 1993) 148.

5. Andrew Felkay, "Hungary and the Soviet Union in the Kádár Era, in *20th Century Hungary and the Great Powers*, Ignác Romsics, ed. (New York: Columbia University Press, 1995)," 279.

6. Tibor Huszár, *Kádár: A hatalom évei, 1956–1989* (Budapest: Corvina Kiadó Kft., 2000), 268.

7. For example see: Paul Jonás, "The Hungarian Economy in Transition," in *The First War between Socialist States: The Hungarian Revolution and Its Impact*, Béla K. Király, et al., ed. (New York: Brooklyn College Press, 1984), 478–79. Jonás makes the point that the need for energy in the command economies was twice that of the West. See also: Szakács, "From 'Goulash Communism' to Breakdown,"209.

8. Charles Gati, *Hungary and the Soviet Bloc* (Durham: Duke University Press, 1986), 201.

9. George Barany, "Epilogue, 1985–1990," *A History of Hungary*, Péter F. Sugar et al., ed. (Bloomington: Indiana University Press, 1994), 401.

10. This was something that Kádár understood and he repeatedly tried to persuade the Soviet Union to allow Hungary to join the World Bank and the International Monetary Fund, the Soviets finally relented in fall of 1981. By this point the Soviets were unable to provide the Hungarians with more loans and had to cut back on oil shipments to Hungary. See Huszár, *Kádár: a hatalom évei, 1956–1989*, 269–71.

11. According to Sándor Szakács Hungarian liabilities amounted to 85 million dollars against export income of 15 million dollars ("From 'Goulash Communism' to Breakdown," 211).

12. Hungarians supplemented their decreasing buying power with jobs in the second economy that resulted in Hungarians working the longest hours in Europe. Economic stress translated into social stress that had a significant impact on health. Gough, *A Good Comrade*, 222 and Gati, *Hungary and the Soviet Bloc*, 167. See also the Zsuzsa Ferge study cited in chapter 5.

13. See Rudolf L.Tőkés, *Hungary's Negotiated Revolution: Economic Reform, Social Charge, and Political Succession* (Cambridge: Cambridge University Press, 1996), 224–25, 236.

14. Ibid., 237.

15. George Schöpfin, *Politics in Eastern Europe* (Oxford: Blackwell Publishers, 1993), 211. According to Tibor Huszár, Kádár underestimated the changes taking place in world affairs. *Kádár: a hatalom évei, 1956–1989*, 276.

16. Gough, *A Good Comrade*, 226.

17. Tőkés, *Hungary's Negotiated Revolution:* Economic Reform, Social change, and Political Succesion (Cambridge: Cambridge University Press, 1996), 275. Medgyessy would later become the Hungarian Republic's fifth Prime Minister in 2002.

18. According to Roger Gough he seemed to favor Károly Grósz, appointed to the Politburo in 1983 and János Berecz, appointed Secretary for Ideological Affairs in 1985 as possible successors. *A Good Comrade*, 225–26, 235.

19. Kádár worried more about internal party unity than outside opposition, which he claimed could be crushed within twenty-four hours. On the other hand, Kádár worried about dissent and according to Huszár became increasingly obsessed in silencing dissent utilizing administrative measures all the while resurrecting memories of 1956. He most certainly worried that questions raised by the opposition regarding 1956 posed a threat to his political legitimacy. Huszár, *Kádár: A hatalom évei, 1956–1989*, 272–76.

20. István Bibó, "Reflections on the Social Development in Europe (1971–1972)" and Sándor Szilágyi, "Postscript," in István Bibó, *Democracy, Revolution, Self-Determination: Selected Writings*, Károly Nagy, ed., András Boros-Kazai, trans. (New York: Columbia University Press, 1991), 495, 542 respectively. See also: Tőkés, *Hungary's Negotiated Revolution*, 186.

21. Rudolph Tőkés asserts that widespread outrage followed a television documentary in 1956 produced for the thirtieth anniversary of the event. Triumphed by

Berecz, it was met with "public outrage," especially among young people whose parents had "tried not to remember" the event (*Hungary's Negotiated Revolution*, 241). Tőkés uses democratic opposition to denote the intellectual dissident movement in Hungary. See his explication in the same book on pages 188–89. The sociologist Maurice Halbwachs reminds us that constructions of historical events must be informed by traces of the past that are held in common in order for the interpretation to gain widespread legitimacy. Maurice Halbwachs, *On Collective Memory*, trans. and ed., Lewis A. Coser (Chicago: The University of Chicago Press, 1992) see "The Legendary Topography of the Gospels in the Holy Land," especially 194, 231–35. In this light the negative interpretation of the Revolution openly exposed one of the major frailties of the regime through a strategy approved by Kádár to prevent this from happening.

22. Imre Mécs, interview by author, November 7, 1997.

23. Judit Ember, *Menedékjog* (Right of Asylum) (Budapest: Szabadtér Kiadó, 1989), 33. This is a book of published interviews that became a script of a documentary by the author.

24. The clear challenge to the regime's legitimacy was in 1956. The opposition recognized that they needed to dramatically expand their base from the relatively small number of dissidents in Hungary. Kádár initially felt that they could be contained relatively easily, although he became enraged at their brazenness as already examined. See Gough, *A Good Comrade*, 212–13, Tőkés, *Hungary's Negotiated Revolution*, 189, and Huszár, *Kádár: a hatalom évei, 1956–1989*, 273.

25. György Krassó, "The Memory of the Dead," *Survey*, 28, 2 (Summer, 1984): 135. The article originally appeared in the samizdat *A Hirmondó* (The Messenger) 2 (1983). Krassó spent ten years in prison for his role in the Revolution.

26. Béla Lipták, "Searching for the Grave of Imre Nagy," *Wall Street Journal*, 15 October 1985. F-520, Radio Free Europe.

27. Nagy and his companion's burial in the prison yard was only revealed on June 15, 1989, one day before his funeral by Gyula Borics, State Secretary of the Justice Ministry on Kossuth Radió, Esti Magazin, 6:30 P.M., June 15, 1989.

28. Imre Mécs, interview by author, November 7, 1997. This story also appeared in the *Magyar Nemzet*, February 25, 1989.

29. Michael T. Kaufman, "Forgotten in Weedy Cemetery," *The Herald Tribune*, June 28–29, 1986.

30. Serving to stimulate the long-forbidden dialogue regarding Hungary's misfortune at the Treaty of Trianon as discussed earlier.

31. Andrew Ludanyi, "Programmed Amnesia and Rude Awakening," *20th Century Hungary and the Great Powers*, Ignác Romsics ed. (New York: Columbia University Press, 1995), 318, 321–24.

32. Gough, *A Good Comrade*, 229.

33. János Kis, the principal editor of *Beszélő* worried about a fragmented opposition from the very beginning. See: Tőkés, *Hungary's Negotiated Revolution*, 187.

34. Ibid., 190–91.

35. Imre Pozsgay, *1989: Politikus pálya a pártállamban és a rendszerváltásban* (Budapest: Püski, 1993), 91.

36. Family members such as Erzsébet Nagy, Judit Gyenes (widow of Pál Maléter), and Aliz Halda were members of the committee.

37. The article is centered on Aliz Halda's frustrated search for the remains of her companion, Miklós Gimes in 1985 and is titled, "Halda Aliz levelezése Gimes Miklós sirhelyének helyszinéröl" (Aliz Halda's correspondence about the location of Miklós Gimes' gravesite), *Bészelő*, 24 (1988).

38. The dissident artist community Inconnu had carved a *kopjafa* that was to be erected on the site and was confiscated by the police. According to the samizdat *Demokrata*, photos of the *kopjafa* were distributed to the protesters. The police returned the *kopjafa* only after Tibor Philipp, who had been arrested, refused to leave the police station until his artwork had been given back to him. See: Virág kedvelö (flower lover), "A Nap Története" (The days news), *Demokrata* (1988). The protest in all of its phases was preserved in the film *June 16, 1988* (Budapest: Black Box, 1988). Videocassette.

39. See: "Police Report" in János Kenedi's, *Kis Állambiztonsági Olvasókönyv* (Budapest: Magvetö Kiadó, 1996), 213 and *June 16, 1988*.

40. Imre Mécs, interview by author, November 7, 1997.

41. Kenedi, *Kis Állambiztonsági Olvasókönyv*, 215.

42. Tőkés, *Hungary's Negotiated Revolution*, 287.

43. Tőkés, *Hungary's Negotiated Revolution*, 287.

44. Benő Csapó told me that "when we heard that Hungarians were gathering freely in the square, we immediately decided to drive up to the demonstration from Szeged." Interview by author, October 25, 1997.

45. Csaba Békés, "Back to Europe: The International Background of the Political Transition in Hungary, 1988–1990," *The Roundtable Talks of 1989: The Genesis of Hungarian Democracy* (Budapest: Central European University Press, 2002), 242–45.

46. Dezső Pintér, "Miniszterelnöki mérleg 16 hónap után" (Review of the Prime Minister after 16 months), *Magyar Hirlap*, October 28, 1988, 5.

47. See: S. Agocs, "The Collapse of Communist Ideology in Hungary," *East European Quarterly*, 27 (1992): 190 and Tőkés, *Hungary's Negotiated Revolution*, 196–97.

48. Hungarian Monitoring. Kossuth Rádió. "168 Hours," 4:00 P.M. October 8, 1988.

49. Pozsgay, *1989: Politikus-pálya*, 86.

50. Ibid., 94.

51. Ibid., 95.

52. Ibid., 224.

53. Meeting of the MSZMP Political Committee, January 31, 1989. Compendium of Declassified Documents.

54. See Joshua Foa Dienstag's fine article, "The Pozsgay Affair: Historical Memory and Political Legitimacy," *History and Memory* 8, 1 (Spring/Summer, 1996): 61.

55. According to Gorbachev, "Democracy is much needed, and the interests have to be harmonized. The limit, however, is the safekeeping of socialism and the assurance of stability." Memorandum of Conversation between M. S. Gorbachev and

Károly Grósz General Secretary of the Hungarian Socialist Worker's Party, Moscow, March 23–24, 1989. A Compendium of Declassified Documents.

56. Meeting of the MSZMP Political Committee, January 31, 1989.

57. "Pozsgay Defends his Assessment of "56," Hungarian television B, 19:30, February 15, 1989.

58. Joshua Foa Dienstag, "The Pozsgay Affair," 57.

59. The historian Zoltán Ripp explains that prior to this point in time SZDSZ made gains because of the weakness of the regime as opposed to mass-based support. See: "Unity and Division," in *The Roundtable Talks of 1989*, 9.

60. The agreement was signed by the Historical Justice Committee, the Ministry of Internal Affairs, The Ministry of Justice, and the City Council of Budapest.

61. Kennedi, *Kis Allambiztonsági Olvasókönyv*, 228.

62. Ibid., 245.

63. On April 12, 1989, an ailing János Kádár addressed the Central Committee for one last time. Throughout his rambling speech he referred to Nagy as "that man who has since deceased." He claimed that, "he could have let those two people [Nagy and ?] go home freely, but he couldn't allow that . . . they opened the gate to counterrevolution." He concluded by saying that it was disturbing to hear questions being raised as to whether the events of 1956 were a counterrevolution or a popular uprising. See: Mihály Kornis, "Kádár" (Magyar Dràma), *Beszélő*, 3 (May, 1996): 86, 89, 91. Kádár was officially removed from the Central Committee on May 8, 1989. Until the end he believed that he had acted for the good of Hungary and was innocent of any wrongdoing. Gough, *A Good Comrade*, 247–48.

64. Meeting of the Opposition Roundtable, May 31, 1989. A Compendium of Declassified Documents.

65. Opening Full Session of the National Roundtable Negotiations, June 13, 1989. A Compendium of Declassified Documents.

66. Gough, *A Good Comrade*, 256–57.

Chapter Seven

The Imre Nagy Bill and the Politics of Memory

Nagy probably knew his forthcoming destiny, as he knew his communist comrades would never forgive his desire to remain Hungarian.

—Ottó Sándorffy, Smallholders Party[1]

Imre Nagy is a symbol of 1989–90 . . . at his coffin and at his companion's coffins . . . Hungarian society made a judgment about the past and future generations.

Imre Szekeres, Socialist Party[2]

The two statements above appear to be in accord with the place of Imre Nagy in Hungarian history. Yet they create differing narratives in which political association is central. Soon after the Republic of Hungary was declared on October 23, 1989, a fierce dispute emerged between the various political factions about Nagy's place among Hungarian heroes. History up to this point had been written to serve the needs of the one-party state. With sovereignty established and ultimately vouchsafed by the final withdrawal of Soviet troops in June 1991, the concrete reality of communist power vanished. Not surprisingly, association with the 1956 Revolution and Nagy became entwined with political debates regarding the nature of the state. The twentieth century had been rife with disaster for the Hungarian nation, and 1956 provides a redemptive moment with its uncompromising demands for sovereignty and democracy against overwhelming odds. And yet, the very nature of the coalition politics that had characterized the opposition served to provide points of contest in the new democracy. Those factions that espoused the success of the Western liberal model at the expense of the failed Soviet model tended to view social welfare models warily, and from this point of view Nagy as a national communist is problematic. On the other hand, how could those formerly associated with the communist regime embrace Nagy? In this light, control of Nagy's image remained paramount, because even after the establishment of the Republic the story of the Revolution could not be told without him. The parliamentary debate over the Imre Nagy memory bill of 1996 that made him a martyr of the nation encapsulates the contest over the political interpretation and memory of Nagy and the Revolution. Each faction battled fiercely to create chains of history favorable to themselves; a battle that has continued unabated into the present, underscoring the perceived stakes that might accrue to the winner in a contest over the history of Hungary in the twentieth century.

The roundtable discussions began three days prior to Imre Nagy's funeral. The MSZMP had tried negotiating separately with the various opposition groups in a bid to maintain power. Realizing that time was not on their side, the Political Committee determined to conclude the negotiations quickly. In an attempt to stem their political retreat, the communists dug in their heels and rejected opposition demands that the party abandon their institutions found in the workplace, disband the Worker's Militia, and provide a detailed accounting of the party's assets.[3] In order to capitalize on the popularity of Imre Pozsgay as the icon of democratic reform within the party, the communists wanted the current Parliament to elect a President for the new state.[4] Hoping to safeguard the work of the negotiations that would ensure the establishment of a democracy, MDF leader József Antall urged the Opposition Roundtable to accept a compromise that included the MSZMP position. Antall's plea for compromise on these issues was rejected by both FIDESZ and SZDSZ who instead called for a referendum, foreshadowing the partisanship that would mark the politics of the Republic.[5] In an address to the Plenary Session of the National Roundtable Negotiations on September 18, 1989, Péter Tölgyessy of the SZDSZ attacked the MSZMP asserting, "Under these circumstances we do not see guarantees for the freedom of the elections or for the equality of chances of the parties . . . The negotiations have been necessary because this Parliament is not suitable for expressing the will of the people. Our proposition is to hold a referendum on the matters that fundamentally determine the democratic transition."[6]

The decision not to sign the Roundtable Agreements highlighted the radical nature of the democratic change foreseen by FIDESZ and SZDSZ.[7] Imre Pozsgay had attempted to engineer a modification of this position by the MSZMP in which all party organizations would operate outside the workplace, but was voted down in a meeting of the Central Committee.[8] Pozsgay rightfully worried that the referendum campaign would be marked by a deliberate campaign that painted the Socialist Party as a monolithic structure inextricably linked to its past.[9] Politburo member Rezső Nyers, on the other hand, insisted that FIDESZ and SZDSZ were grandstanding, knowing full well that the Worker's Militia would ultimately be dissolved through legislation proposed in Parliament.[10] There were also revelations that the MSZMP was attempting to hide its assets through investment schemes that called into question the party's sincerity to establish democracy. This helped to fortify the demand for a referendum.[11] Fearing the growing power of the SZDSZ and FIDESZ, József Antall and the MDF found themselves working in tandem with the Socialists and Pozsgay to defeat the referendum.[12] Pozsgay's assurances to those signing the Roundtable Agreements seemed to be confirmed by the actions of the government. On the day the Republic was declared October 23, 1989, the Worker's Militia was disarmed and disbanded.[13] Why then should the referendum be considered a pivotal moment in the establishment of the Republic?

In a bid to explicitly break with its past the MSZMP dissolved itself on October 7, 1989, and created the Socialist Party (MSZP). As the referendum approached, the MSZP and Imre Pozsgay's popularity was second only to the MDF. In this light, the referendum was important for both SZDSZ and FIDESZ as they competed for the political limelight with the two large parties.[14] But the Hungarian people were adamant in their demand for an end to the one-party state or any variation that would allow the Socialist Party to maintain preeminence in the political sphere. The moral imperative of Nagy's funeral had been fulfilled by the Hungarian people through an electoral process and had helped seal the fate of the MSZP's chances in the coming parliamentary elections; it also legitimized the position taken by SZDSZ and FIDESZ. The referendum had allowed the Hungarian people to address the political process directly, rather than through a Parliament associated with the old state, and in this sense represented movement from below. The matter of when to elect the President was decided by just over 6,000 votes and certainly indicated the sympathy that the Hungarian people had for Imre Pozsgay. The President would be elected only after the new Parliament was seated. According to political scientist Rudolf L. Tőkés, the referendum began the decline of Pozsgay's fortunes and fortified those of the MDF and József Antall. Disengaging from its relationship with Pozsgay allowed the MDF to reclaim its position as the largest coalition against the one-party state and fortified its position as the most popular party in the newly founded Republic.[15] Pozsgay remarked that he "felt as if he had been punched in the stomach."[16]

The national elections in March and April of 1990 brought the center-right MDF in coalition with the Independent Smallholders (FKgP) and Christian Democrats (KDNP) to power. József Antall became Prime Minister.[17] The other big winners, the SZDSZ and FIDESZ, sat in opposition with the Socialists. The campaign was infused with progressive rhetoric and the "fatal traditions of Hungarian political culture" marked by anticommunism, virulent nationalism, and Christian tradition.[18] The infighting that had marked the opposition prior to the Republic began in earnest with the writing of the First Act of Parliament, which officially recognized the Revolution of 1956 as a War of Independence.

The original drafting of the bill had recognized Nagy as the symbolic leader and embodiment of the Revolution. The bill also named the perpetrators of the terror that followed in the wake of the failed Revolution. In a last minute maneuver the committee responsible for writing the bill under the leadership of the nationalist playwright István Csurka removed Nagy's name and the names of the perpetrators from the bill, most likely with the assent of Antall. Their conception of the new Republic was one based on the free market systems of the West. Nagy as a national communist did not fit into their construction of history in which communism is considered an aberration. It was reasoned that removal of the names of those who had participated in the terror would prevent the initiation of political trials reminiscent of the old regime.[19] Though he continues to deny the charges, Csurka was accused of collaborating with the old regime.

The deletions outraged parliamentarians from the center left wing factions of the MDF and the center left parties, most notably the Free Democrats and the Socialists. Explaining why the bill passed in this form Miklós Vásárhelyi of the Free Democrats claimed that at a meeting he had with Antall he thought that Csurka would be allowed to raise his objections and then allow the proposal to come to a vote. Given the symbolic power of Nagy, "very few would have voted for the Csurka proposal." Instead, at the end of the meeting Nagy's name had been removed from the bill. Though angered at the result he decided to vote for the bill, not wanting to set off a divisive debate, stating "At the time we were concerned with the prestige of the Hungarian government in front of the diplomatic corps."[20] The majority agreed and the measure was passed 366 to 2, all but ensuring that the symbolic image of Nagy would be used as a pivot on which to base factional legitimacy and to those various interpretations of what the nation-state should be.

The seeds of division planted by this political maneuver were further deepened by what was perceived by the center left parties as the government's obsession to construct a past that reconnected the Hungarian state to the anticommunist regimes of the twentieth century with the memory of the Hungarian kingdom. The new Prime Minister, speaking on St. Steven's Day August 20, 1992, encouraged Hungarians to view the thousand-year-old history without remorse, as the sacrifice of Hungary's martyrs had been for freedom. The reburial of Miklós Horthy in his hometown in the fall of 1993 can be seen as emblematic of this revision.[21] Antall proclaimed that rehabilitation for Horthy was unnecessary as he had not been condemned either by the Nuremberg International Tribunal or by the Hungarian courts after World War II, " . . . rehabilitation is not a matter of law, but historic research."[22]

In this light, Horthy should be viewed as the preserver of the nation who wisely guided the Hungarian state through the treacherous waters of the interwar years. Blame for the Holocaust rests with the Germans who occupied Hungary in March 1944. The Hungarian alliance with the Axis is excused as a way of regaining territory lost at Trianon. Hungary's participation in the invasion of the Soviet Union is considered part of the fight against international communism, an action made prescient by the Cold War.[23]

The historical revisions proposed by Antall enraged members of the SZSDZ and the Socialist Party. According to Miklós Vásárhelyi it was the debate over the Hungarian coat of arms in 1990 that was the beginning of the alliance between "two enemies . . . The Hungarian people were not interested in an updated version of the Horthy regime."[24] The majority of the new Parliament disagreed and on July 3, 1990, the crown of St. Steven was incorporated into the coat of arms of the new Republic. For many within the Free Democrats and the Socialists, the ancient symbolism had been tainted by its association with Horthy. The Kossuth coat of arms, created for the short-lived Republic during the 1848 Revolution, had eliminated the crown. As the historian Ignác Romsics points out the Kossuth coat of arms was used by the revolutionaries in 1956 to explicitly connect their Revolution with 1848.[25] In a forty-five-minute speech given on October 23, 1991, Antall spoke about the 1956 Revolution without mentioning Nagy's name once.[26] The attempt to distance Hungary from its communist past included creating distance between itself and Nagy. According to the historian István Rév, Antall would have preferred to memorialize Zoltán Tildy instead.[27]

The new government was plagued by economic difficulties, many of which stemmed from Kádár's economic policies and its "budgetary disequilibrium."[28] What was perhaps most damning for the MDF was the distance it placed between itself and the welfare of the Hungarian people. As the large-scale enterprises that were begun by the communists failed and closed, Antall said, "let the rotten apples fall." The fact that nearly one million workers were out of a job in a population numbering less than ten million seemed appallingly brutal to many Hungarians.[29] Hungarians watched helplessly as their social reality premised on a welfare state was seriously eroded.

Not surprisingly, a certain nostalgia for the good old days under Kádár took hold among many of those disaffected.[30] For example, the political scientist Gábor Tóka asserts that when asked the question "To what extent do you agree that the government should subsidize branches of industry in crisis in order to save jobs?" 69% of those surveyed agreed, compared to 48% in 1990.[31] The Socialists promised a government of specialists, in contrast to a regime seemingly more interested in the past than the current problems faced by the polity; the Socialists captured 54% of the parliament.[32] The Socialists made formal their uneasy truce with the Free Democrats by inviting them into a coalition government.

The Socialists' return to power was in part predicated on the Hungarian people's expectations that they would be better guardians of social security than the MDF coalition they had replaced. For them their ties with Nagy would be used to create a chain of history linking them to the goals of the Revolution. It also made them a symbol of national and social renewal, made easier by the jettisoning of his name from the First Act of Parliament in 1990. On the centennial year of Nagy's birth and the mille centennial of the Hungarian nation the Socialists proposed the Imre Nagy memory bill in Parliament, which would make Imre Nagy a martyr of the nation. The measure passed on June 26, 1996, with a vote of 167 yes, 77 no, and 64 abstentions. Passage of the bill had been viewed as a "moral imperative" by the Socialists.[33] The bill infuriated members of the opposition and many within the Socialists' coalition partner the Free Democrats. The partisanship that informed the debate was confirmed by political scientist György Fábián, one of the architects of the bill, who explained, "This bill was meant to be a current reflection of the Socialist Party . . . The opposition regarded this bill as an historical evaluation of 1956 and used the debate to attack the Socialist Party."[34]

Before its formal introduction in Parliament the MDF Party newspaper *Új Magyarország* launched a frontal assault on the bill. Jenő Fónay, a leading member of POFOSZ (Political Prisoners Society) wrote, "he continually hears about what never happened during the 1956 Revolution from those who fought against the Revolution." Fónay asserted that the current debate was fought not with "God and reality," but with ideas created to cater to political interest. "The further we get from the miracle [the Revolution] the more differently we remember. . . . Only the true ones are silent [the martyrs of the Revolution]." The Socialist bill named only Imre Nagy and not his fellow confederates. He concluded, "A bill can be born that hurts Imre Nagy . . . We will still celebrate, but not with them [the Socialists] . . . who not only shocked the whole world by killing the Prime Minister, but by killing the sons of the Prime Minister [victims of the terror] as common enemies . . . our symbol forever is Plot 301 . . . "[35] For Fónay, reconciliation after 1989 had been shortchanged by leaving perpetrators of Kádár's terror untouched. Aiming his invective at the Socialist Prime Minister Gyula Horn he asserted, " . . . they are still in power." Horn had been a member of the notorious *pufajkások* (people's militia) that was used by Kádár in the demobilization of the Revolution. According to Fónay, compromises with the Socialists such as the Imre Nagy Bill represented further surrender of the goals of the Revolution.[36]

The stage was set for a battle royal.[37] Imre Szekeres who introduced the bill for the Socialist Party explained that it was the responsibility of the Parliament to promote "the values that represent loyalty to the fatherland in the highest sense . . . " though "national consensus about 1956 is in process . . . the Parliament should . . . place Nagy out of reach of those who would use his image for political gain."[38] He continued by recounting the life of Nagy beginning with the introduction of his New Course politics, his ouster from the party in 1955, and his heroic stand against Mátyás Rákosi and the Stalinists. Throughout all of this Nagy remained loyal to communism. Szekeres then likened the transformation of Nagy, and by inference the Socialist Party, to that of St. Paul. Using the allegory of Saul's conversion to St. Paul he asserted, "From the time Nagy accepted the crowd's demands outside the Parliament that he resume his role as Prime Minister he began to change . . . accepting and implementing the national and democratic goals of the Revolution . . . which ultimately concluded with his martyrdom."[39] Szekeres' peroration concluded by linking Nagy's martyrdom to that of Hungarian Prime Minister Count Lajos Batthyány, who was executed on October 6, 1849, and to the Smallholder parliamentarian Endre Bajcsy-Zsilinszky who had actively opposed the Hungarian fascists and was hanged on December 24, 1944. "Imre Nagy is a symbol of 1989–90 . . . at his coffin and at his companion's coffins . . . Hungarian society made a judgment about the past and following generations."

The Free Democrats (with the exception of Imre Mécs and Péter Zwack) broke ranks with their coalition partners and led the attack against the bill. Aliz Halda, the companion of Miklós Gimes who was executed with Nagy, began her explication by reading from the Joseph Stalin memory bill passed by the Hungarian Parliament in 1953 in which he was honored for liberating the Hungarian people and aiding them in their bid for independence. She highlighted the absurdity of memory bills by claiming that "a prominent lawyer" had claimed that the Hungarian people would be breaking the law if it was publicly stated that they despise Stalinism. Halda exclaimed, "we state here the consensus is perfect."[40] To legislate the memorialization of a political figure smacked of coercion. The Socialist proposal was merely an "official gesture."[41] Nagy himself would never have wanted his name associated with this type of legislation. Halda then zeroed in on the Socialists. At the "shameful" trial of Imre Nagy "he was judged by those not worthy to untie his sandals. . . . The Hungarian people deserve to know who Imre Nagy really was. . . . Nagy's memory would be much better served if the country

could see the movie that was made at his trial . . . ," raising the not too subtle question of who the perpetrators were.[42] For the majority of Free Democrats who had been at the forefront of dissent prior to 1989, a memorialization of Nagy by many of those who were responsible for the destruction of
the Revolution that they had taken part in was unpalatable. Halda finished by
stating that Imre Mécs who had been condemned to death for his role as a
Revolutionary "was generous . . . to support this bill . . . It is more difficult
however, to say that others who bear grievances should forget . . . especially
those who have been put to death, as in the case of Imre Nagy and others."[43]

The Smallholders, MDF, and FIDESZ opposed the bill on different
grounds. In an interesting parliamentary maneuver, Ottó Sándorffy of the
Smallholders Party connected Imre Nagy to the martyrs of the Revolution executed during the terror. In a stirring speech, Sándorffy compared the Hungarian people's demand for Nagy's restoration as Prime Minister to the ac-
clamation of King Matthias Corvinus by the Hungarian people and their lords
and bishops in January 1458. This linked Nagy to a chain of history extend-
ing to the Middle Ages.[44] Sándorffy then drove the point home by separating
the communists from the Hungarian nation. "Nagy probably knew his forthcoming destiny, as he knew his communist comrades would never forgive his
desire to remain Hungarian . . . Nagy who fought against the cult of personality would never have wanted to be separated from his companions who
fought by his side." Sándorffy then proceeded to read, the names of those who
had been executed for their role in the Revolution into the minutes of Parliament. *Kegyeleti* tradition in Hungary demands respect for the dead, and so,
the entire Parliament stood as the names were read which took the rest of the
afternoon and early morning next day. Sándorffy then stated that the Smallholders would support the bill as long as Nagy and all 278 names were included in the bill. In an interview with Sándorffy, he stated that he had pur-
posely read the names in order to ensure that the martyrs were properly
memorialized even though he realized at the time that his amendment to the
bill was sure to be defeated.[45]

Sándorffy's tactic served to incense the Socialists. They responded by
charging that Francia Kis, whose name had been included was, in fact, a fascist and anti-Semite. The Socialists' objections were strikingly similar to the
apologies found in the Kádár era textbooks that smeared the revolutionaries
as fascists. Interestingly, Francia Kis had participated in the white terror that
accompanied the defeat of the short-lived Hungarian Soviet State in 1919 and
had been brought up on murder charges. His crime was pardoned by a general amnesty issued by Miklós Horthy after his assumption to power in 1920.
Francia Kis was eventually hanged for this crime in 1957 although the purpose was to demonstrate that the 1956 Revolution was largely the work of

fascists that had their origins in the rise of Horthy regime.[46] Iván Vitányi in speaking for the Socialists claimed that the Socialists owed Nagy the honor of maintaining his name and the memory of 1956, " . . . what happened in 1958 was no small thing. The legitimate Prime Minister of Hungary was executed . . . this is a sin screaming to the sky!"[47] He then punched back at the MDF stating " . . . let's not search out who removed his name [from the First Act of Parliament] . . . let's fix it . . . "[48]

László Varga of the Christian Democrats rose next and explained why his party would not support the Socialist bill, stating that Nagy "wasn't the leader from the Revolution's point of view. This is the only Revolution in world history which didn't have leaders, only ideas . . . Imre Nagy cannot be separated from the known and unknown martyrs of the Revolution . . . Our proposal was not to separate and state in law the memory of Imre Nagy and all the executed martyrs. It is the Socialists responsibility . . . that they are not in a big common memorialization."[49]

FIDESZ and the MDF joined the Smallholders in their demands that the martyrs be included in the bill. Miklós Csapody from the MDF launched into a blistering attack against the Socialists, demanding that they apologize for the brutality of Kádár's terror and the Soviet-backed repression of the Revolution, "There can be no reconciliation without confession . . . It is impossible to remember the victim and the murderer with the same soul."[50] On the issue of Francia Kis, Csapody turned the tables on the Socialists by directly attacking the Prime Minister and comparing the *Pufajkások* to Hitler's storm troopers: "Honored Parliament! I think along with others that it is unavoidable for Gyula Horn to not speak about this question."[51] FIDESZ reiterated its claims made at Nagy's funeral that the Socialists were responsible for the death of civic society. Both parties explicitly linked the Communists and the Socialists with foreign Soviet influence.[52] László Kövér claimed that the purpose of the debate was to "make history begin in 1953 [with Nagy's New Course politics] . . . this has become a trial to found the Socialist Party's political legitimacy . . . they refuse to face 1956, this is because their history extends from 1945–1989 . . . It is a lie that communism is part of mainstream Hungarian history."[53]

The debate grew more rancorous as the charges of collaboration with the communists and fascists once again rose to the surface. The general debate finished with Iván Szabó speaking for the Hungarian National Democratic Party (MDNP) who claimed, "It is not a coincidence that there was no consensus [in regard to the bill], as this was a political action by the Socialist Party . . . they are the ones who made it possible for those who had participated in the revenge and ordered the shooting to begin in various towns of Hungary . . . to walk freely with the widows . . . in Mosonmagyaróvár and

Salgótarján."[54] Szabó concluded by asking that the bill be withdrawn and that
the debate be postponed indefinitely, and reminded his colleagues that Joan
of Arc became a saint only after five hundred years had passed![55]

A detailed debate began on June 11 and focused on the proposed amendment to the bill that would have listed those executed during the terror along
with Imre Nagy. Ottó Sándorffy reminded the Parliament that his party would
only support the bill with the acceptance of this amendment. He then proposed that the bill address the issue of the *vérbíró* (blood judges) who had
handed down summary judgments during the terror, such as Ferenc Vida who
had condemned Nagy to death. Gábor Gellért Kis responded for the Socialist
Party asserting that two more victims that Sándorffy had read into the minutes were not victims of the revenge.[56] Sándorffy retorted, "Perhaps these
names irritate you, but don't allow this to happen as they are lying there [in
Plot 301] for some reason." Imre Mécs attempted to clarify the problem for
the Socialists by explaining that reconstructing the lives of those executed
was difficult. According to Mécs, though the lists were largely accurate they
also contained criminals such as László Zsendovics who had a National
Guard I.D., but had been executed for "chopping up his wife."[57] And there
was Francia Kis, who again was executed not for his participation in the Revolution, but for a crime committed thirty-five years previous. In spite of these
mistakes Mécs now strongly supported Sándorffy's proposal explaining that
like the *Aradi Vértanú* the revolutionaries of 1956 were not homogenous, but
died for the common cause of Hungarian independence.[58]

The spirit of compromise was not in the air and the most the Socialists were
willing to concede was to add the phrase "fellow martyrs" to the bill. Gellért
Kis asserted, " . . . Sándorffy's proposal would change the goal of this bill
. . . This Parliament needs this bill." In response, members of the Christian
Democrats shouted, "the biggest faction [needs this bill]. . . . Speak only in
your name."[59] The SZDSZ now proposed an amendment that addressed Sándorffy's concern regarding the *vérbíró* and demanded that the perpetrators of
the terror be named. Ferenc Kőszeg dramatically stated, "It was not a stroke
of fate . . . which suppressed the Revolution . . . it was human guilt and villainy . . . there are no martyrs without executioners . . . even Pilatus name is
mentioned in the credo."[60] The opposition, including the MDF, was now demanding that what had been deleted from the First Act of Parliament be restored in the Memorial Bill.

The bill's introduction had served to resurrect ideological differences
within the opposition. For example, in an article that appeared during the debate the historian Mária Schmidt, director of the House of Terror Museum in
Budapest, helps explain how Nagy was perceived by the right wing at the
time of the debates. Schmidt argued that both the Socialists and the Free

Democrats who were then in power, were grateful to Imre Nagy for "saving the idea of socialism by his martyrdom . . . The victorious soldiers of the failed idea are still in power." She attacked the Free Democrats as being "Janus faced," explaining that though members of the party called the Socialists traitors for their responsibility in the suppression of the Revolution, they are still, "members of the same team." She concluded that in order for the liberal left to stay in power they needed Nagy, the martyred Prime Minister for political legitimacy.[61] Then in an interesting twist, much of the fractious coalition that had brought the communist government down in 1989 had momentarily been restored over what they considered a dangerous revision of history by many who had been their bitter enemies only a few years before.

As the debate concluded, László Surján from the Christian Democrats broke the tension by commenting, "This will make for an odd law in which we talk about Imre Nagy and his fellow martyrs and János Kádár and fellow executioners."[62] The end result of the debate, however, was a foregone conclusion and the Socialist version of the bill was passed on June 26, 1996, with a Socialist majority of 165.

From the opposition's point of view, Imre Nagy was now being honored by the party most closely associated with the authoritarian regime of János Kádár. The casting off of Nagy in 1990 had provided the Socialists with the opportunity of appropriating Nagy's symbolic status and his attachment to the Revolution with its explicit demand for a procedural republic like the one in 1848. The Imre Nagy memory bill served the Socialists as a way of rationalizing their association with communism, an association that ultimately led to Hungarian national sovereignty through the sacrifice of patriots such as Nagy and the reform communists. In this version of events, the period of reform communism begun by Nagy was a necessary step in the progression to Hungarian independence after World War II. Democratic socialism coupled with an implicit promise to finding an economic third way becomes the fulfillment of Nagy's legacy. The illegality of his execution is portrayed as "a sin screaming to heaven." Emphasizing Nagy's transformation was critical in explaining how it was that the Prime Minister and others within the Socialist Party actively collaborated with the terror. This was skipped over in their telling of the story. In the Socialist narrative Horn became a member of the *pufajkások* to restore order in the wake of chaos. At the same time his role in opening Hungary's borders in 1989 to East Germans wishing to leave for the West was widely celebrated in the press and recognized as yet another indication of democratic change in Hungary.[63]

Charges of collaboration with the communists were further deflected by linking Nagy to Bajcsy-Zsilinszky and his fight against fascism. Raising the specter of the Horthy regime reawakens memories of white terror, alliance

with the Axis powers, and genocide. In this light the Socialist agenda is portrayed as progressive rather than being locked in the past. Nagy's transformation and patriotism is linked with the renewal of the nation in 1989 seemingly confirmed by the Socialist victory at the polls in 1994.

The Socialist bill made plain the importance of Nagy's symbolic status as evidenced by the furious battle for his possession staged by those in opposition
that included the majority's coalition partner. They saw the bill as an oppor-
tunistic attempt by the Socialists to shape public opinion and further legitimize
their standing with the Hungarian people. Even more disturbing for the opposition was the common memorial that sidestepped issues of guilt and collaboration. In order to counter the Socialist position, they needed to use the well-worn
tactic of linking the Socialists to the communists and to reemphasize how the
Revolution had been shaped by the Hungarian people. In this construction,
Nagy was a follower of events who ultimately joins with the revolutionaries
and then confirms his patriotism through his final act of self-sacrifice. For them,
his fate and memory is inextricably joined to his confederates.

Despite some of its inconsistencies, the reading of the martyrs' names into
the Minutes of Parliament recalled the poignant protests of the 1980s in
which the names were read out loud at the risk of arrest. More important, it
also placed the Socialists on the defensive. Charges of linkages with the Horthy regime were countered by comparing the *pufajkások* with Nazi storm
troopers. Those who collaborated with the Kádár regime were fatally linked
to a foreign power and the cruelty of the terror. "They were not even worthy
to untie your sandals." The momentary unity displayed during the debate was
just that. The Free Democrats remained, albeit uneasily, in coalition with the
Socialists and certainly did not accept the historical revisions regarding the
authentic conception of the Hungarian nation put forth by the Smallholders
and the other parties displayed during the debate. Likewise, the Smallholders,
FIDESZ, and MDF found the Free Democratic conception of the state too
close to that of the Socialists, ensuring that battles over Hungary's history
were far from finished.

Reflective of the uneasy alliance between the Socialists and the Free
Democrats, the annual ceremony at Imre Nagy's graveside on June 16,
1996, was fraught with tension. As the President of the Republic and member of the SZDSZ, Árpád Göncz, who had been imprisoned during the terror, and Prime Minister Gyula Horn walked through a gate at Plot 301 to lay
a wreathe at Nagy's graveside emblazoned with the adage "Only a Hungarian soul may pass through these gates," a close-up of the two men revealed
expressions of real discomfort.[64] In 1997 Miklós Vásáhelyi commented on
the televised ceremonies and explained how glad he was that he no longer
had to make compromises with those he still considers his enemies. He as-

serted that he never attends memorial ceremonies such as these with former communists.[65]

Uneasiness with who would tell Nagy's story remained. A 1996 television documentary based on János M. Rainer's two-volume biography of Nagy resulted in a lawsuit brought by his daughter Erzsébet Nagy to stop the program from being broadcast. She felt parts of the film might damage the memory of Nagy. The lawsuit was ultimately dropped in early July 1996, as the court declared that Rainer had not damaged the memory or memorial of Nagy and had lawfully exercised his freedom of speech. The decision resulted in the documentary being shown on television.[66]

The film begins with Nagy's exhumation at Plot 301 and continues with his funeral in 1989. At this point the film reviews Nagy's life, ending with death row and his place of execution.[67] Perhaps what might have concerned Erzsébet Nagy was that in the course of the documentary, the film portrays her father as a loyal member of the Communist Party. In the film Nagy not only survives, but also helps establish a Stalinist state in Hungary, and his eventual transformation comes slowly. His patriotism is not in question but the story seems to live with the Socialist Party's claim that Nagy belongs to them.

Political commentator Zsófia Szilágyi claimed that the Hungarian Revolution was losing significance because it has been "abused by political parties for their own purposes." For Szilágyi the Revolution remains a divisive issue among Hungarians and more importantly, "[Hungarians] didn't consider historical justice to be among the most crucial elements the country is now facing."[68]

Certainly issues of economy loomed large for many Hungarians in 1996. The debate might well have seemed unimportant in the context of the transition after all; the procedural Republic was well established. But the specters of the Revolution had not been put to rest. The nature of the transition all but ensured that those responsible for the suppression of the Revolution would not be punished.[69] How could punishment be conferred when so many had actively or passively cooperated with the regime that replaced the short-lived Republic of the sad October days? The unsettled scores revealed by the bitter political contest all but guaranteed a continued debate over the Revolution and Imre Nagy.

At the same time a consensus began to emerge from the bookshelves of textbook publishers writing for gimnázium and university students. Though differences certainly exist between texts and the curriculum actuated in the classroom that reveal shadings of the debates revealed here, there seems to be a real concern to portray the national drama in a way that highlights the War of Independence and the heroism of the actors who fought for national sovereignty, including Nagy. How is this story to be passed on from one generation to the next?

NOTES

1. Az Országgyűlés tavaszi ülésszakának 41. Ülésnapja 1996, Június 3-án, hétfön (hereafter: Minutes of Parliament), 21203.
2. Ibid., 21201.
3. The retreat appeared more like a rout after the events of June 16th.
4. Zoltán Ripp, "Unity and Division: The Opposition Roundtable and Its Relationship to the Communist Party," *The Roundtable Talks of 1989: The Genesis of Hungarian Democracy* András Bozóki ed. (Budapest: Central European University Press, 2002), 13–14, 25–26.
5. Zoltán Ripp, "Unity and Division," 30–32. MSZMP began giving way on the issue of the Worker's Militia stating by August that the organization would be abolished and integrated into the Hungarian defense forces. SZDSZ and FIDESZ remained unmoved by this overture that in essence was based on word rather than a written settlement. See András Bozóki, Hungary's Road to Systemic Change: The Opposition Roundtable," *Lawful Revolution in Hungary, 1989–94*, Béla K. Király and András Bozóki, ed., (New York: Columbia University Press, 1995), 85–87.
6. "Plenary Session of the National Roundtable Negotiations, September 18, 2007," A Compendium of Declassified Documents and Chronology of Events (hereafter: A Compendium of Declassified Documents) Csaba Békés, Malcolm Byrne ed., Political Transition in Hungary 1989–1990 International Conference Budapest, Hungary, 1999 sponsored by the National Security Archive/Cold War History research Center/1956 Institute.
7. According to Rudolf L. Tőkés, by not vetoing the agreement both FIDESZ and SZDSZ "benefited from the achievements of the negotiations . . . " and " . . . reserved the option to modify objectionable points of the agreement," in *Hungary's Negotiated Revolution: Economic Reform, Social Change, and Political Succession* (Cambridge: Cambridge University Press, 1996), 347.
8. Ádám Masát, "Beyond the One-Party System: The Debate on 'The Party Law," *The Roundtable Talks of 1989*, 151.
9. See: "Meeting of the MSZMP Political Executive Committee, September 19, 1989" in A Compendium of Declassified Documents, page 4, Imre Pozsgay, *1989: Politikus-pálya a pártállamban és a rendszerváltásban* (Budapest: Püski Kiadó Kft., 1993), 160–61 and Zoltán Ripp, "Unity and Division," 33.
10. "Meeting of the MSZMP Political Executive Committee, September 19, 1989," A Compendium of Declassified Documents, page 13.
11. András Bozóki, "Hungary's Road to Systemic Change: The Opposition Roundtable," *Lawful Revolution in Hungary, 1989–94*, Béla K. Király and András Bozóki, ed. (New York: Columbia University Press, 1995), 80.
12. The Socialists urged a no vote while the MDF recommended a boycott of the referendum. Ádám Masát, "Beyond the One-Party System," 153.
13. Tőkés, *Hungary's Negotiated Revolution*, 362.
14. A point fortified by Imre Pozsgay in *1989: Politikus-pálya a pártállamban és a rendszerváltásban*, 185.

15. Tőkés, *Hungary's Negotiated Revolution*, 363–65. The conservative Antall outmaneuvered SZDSZ whose membership included intellectuals with a pronounced Marxist tradition. Szonja, Szelényi, Iván Szelényi, and Winifred R. Poster, "Interests and Symbols in Post-Communist Political Culture: The Case of Hungary," *American Sociological Review*, 61, 3 (June, 1996): 475.

16. Imre Pozsgay, *1989: Politikus-pálya a pártállamban ésa rendszerváltásban* (Budapest: Püski Kiadó Kft., 1993) 186.

17. The six major parties gaining over 5% of the seats were: MDF 42%, SZDSZ 23.8%, Independent Smallholders Party (FKgP) 11%, MSZP 8.5%, FIDESZ 5.7%, and the Christian Democrats (KDNP) 5.4% For a detailed analysis of the election see: Tőkés, *Hungary's Negotiated Revolution*, 388.

18. István Stumpf, "Evolution of Political Parties and the 1990 Parliamentary Elections," *Lawful Revolution in Hungary, 1990–94*, Béla K. Király and András Bozóki, ed. (New York: Columbia University Press, 1995), 110.

19. Gábor Murányi, "Második helyben futás/Törvények Nagy Imréről" (Running in place for a second time/Bills about Imre Nagy), *Heti Világgazdaság*, 12 (March 24, 1996): 94.

20. Miklós Vásárhelyi, interview by the author, Budapest, Hungary, October 7, 1997.

21. Tamás Ungvári, "Culture and Crisis: The Pains of Transition," in *Lawful Revolution in Hungary*, 285. Political scientist Katherine Verdery asserts that post-socialist legitimacy is based on rejection of the immediate past, making reburials an essential part of this process in *The Political Lives of Dead Bodies* (New York: Columbia University Press, 1999), 52.

22. The quote is from an interesting web site titled "Országgyűlési felszólalások" (Collection of József Antall's speeches in Parliament) November 12, 1991 kedd, az őszi ülésszak 23 napja, válasz Dr. Jánosi György (MSZP) (Reply to György Jánosi, MSZP) http://www.antalljozsef.hu/1991/1991_november_12_vi.html. Horthy's family had requested that he be rehabilitated so he could be buried in Hungary. Miklós Horthy had died and was buried in Portugal in 1957.

23. István Rév, Paralel Autopsies, *Representations*, 49 (Winter, 1995): 33–34 and Randolph L. Braham, "An Assault on Hungarian Memory: Hungarian Nationalists and the Holocaust," *East European Quarterly*, 33, 4 (Winter, 1999): 411, 416.

24. Miklós Vásárhelyi, interview by author, October 7, 1997.

25. Ignác Romsics, "The First Four Years of Democratic Transformation," *The Ideas of the Hungarian Revolution, Suppressed and Victorious 1956–1999*, Lee W. Congdon and Béla K. Király, ed. (New York: Columbia University Press, 2002), 315.

26. Murányi, "Running in place for a second time," 96.

27. István Rév, interview by author, August 27, 1997. Tildy was the leader of the Smallholders Party and President of Hungary during the short-lived Republic 1945–1948. He had been placed under house arrest during Rákosi's terror, but came back into government with the establishment of a multiparty state during the Revolution on October 30, 1956.

28. János Kornai, "The Dilemmas of Hungarian Economic Policy," *Lawful Revolution in Hungary*, 338.

29. László Szamuely, "The Costs of Transformation in Central and Eastern Europe," *The Hungarian Quarterly*, 37 (Winter, 1996): 67. See also: Barnabás Rácz, "Regional Voting Trends in Hungarian National Elections 1985–2002, *East European Quarterly*, 37, 4 (Winter, 2003): 446.

30. Ignác Romsics asserts that the voter's punished government parties in the national elections of 1994 in "The First Four Years of Democratic Transformation," *The Ideas of the Hungarian Revolution*, 344.

31. Gábor Tóka, "Parties and Their Voters in 1990 and 1994," in *Lawful Revolution in Hungary*, 142–43. This point is strongly fortified by sociologists Szonja Szelényi, Iván Szelényi, and Winifred R. Poster who claim that Hungarians were "reluctant to abandon social benefits." For example, a May 1990 survey indicated that "91% of Hungarians wanted a continuation of price controls" in "Interests and Symbols in Post-Communist Political Culture: The Case of Hungary," 469–72.

32. Ferenc Glatz, "Multiparty System in Hungary, 1989–94," *Lawful Revolution in Hungary*, 22 and Romsics, "The First Four Years of Democratic Transition," 345.

33. According to Socialist MP, László Donáth, see: "Nagy Imre Törvény Hatályba Került (Imre Nagy Law is Passed)," *Magyar Nemzet*, June 26, 1996.

34. György Fábián, interview by author, Szeged, July 31, 1996.

35. Jenő Fónay, "Nagy Imre emberi nagyságat sértő törvény születhet" (A bill may be born that would hurt Imre Nagy's greatness), *Új Magyarország*, May 18, 1996, 4. Fónay had been condemned to death for his role in the Revolution and only learned that his sentence had been commuted to life in the shadow of the gallows.

36. Jenő Fónay, interview by author, September 16, 1997.

37. Ideas and parts of this section are informed from an earlier study I wrote entitled, "Imre Nagy, Martyr of the Nation: Contested Memory and Social Cohesion," *East European Quarterly*, 36, 2 (June, 2002). The historian István Rév also includes an account of the debate in his chapter titled "The 'Necronym'" in *Retroactive Justice: Prehistory of Post Communism* (Stanford: Stanford University Press, 2005), 84–90.

38. Minutes of Parliament, June 3, 1996, 21199.

39. Minutes of Parliament, 21200.

40. Minutes of Parliament, 21201.

41. Minutes of Parliament, 21202.

42. Biblical references seemed to abound in this debate. Halda's attack begins with a reference to the New Testament story in which John the Baptist says to Jesus, "Christ I am not worthy to tie up thy sandals." John 1:27.

43. Minutes of Parliament, 21203.

44. The fields of Rákos were a traditional meeting place of the Hungarian nobility during the Middle Ages and were located in what is now Pest. It was here that the king was acclaimed. Kálmán Benda, *Magyarország Történeti Kronológiája I* (Budapest: Akadémiai Kiadó, 1983), 273.

45. Ottó Sándorffy, interview by author, September 16, 1997.

46. See: "A Rule of Law," in Rév, *Retroactive Justice: Prehistory of Post Communism*, especially pages 202–3, 210–14.

47. Minutes of Parliament, June 4, 1996, 21313.

48. Minutes of Parliament, 21314.

49. Minutes of Parliament, 21315–21316.

50. Minutes of Parliament, 21317.

51. Minutes of Parliament, 21319.

52. Minutes of Parliament, 21321.

53. Minutes of Parliament, 21324, 21327.

54. This is a reference to the massacres perpetrated by the communists against workers demonstrating in support of the Revolution. Gábor Jobbágyi claimed that 132 workers were killed at Salgótarján on December 8, 1956. Gábor Jobbágyi, "56' Vérontó sortüzei (Bloody Massacres of 56'), *Heti Magyarország* 43 (October 23, 1993): 6. Attila Szakolcai places the figure at forty-six in "Repression and Restoration, 1956–1963," *The Ideas of the Hungarian Revolution,* 171–72. The journalist József Bozsik named István Dudás as the commander of the garrison that opened fire on the workers of Mosonmagyaróvár, in "Hagyjanak Békén mondja Dudás" ("Leave me in peace," says Dudás) *Heti Magyarország*, 44 (October 29, 1993): 7.

55. Minutes of Parliament, 21333–21334.

56. Minutes of Parliament, June 11, 1996, 22066.

57. The National Guard had been created to provide security in the newly established Republic and unify the various revolutionary militias. See chapter 4.

58. Minutes of Parliament, 22067.

59. Minutes of Parliament, 22070.

60. Minutes of Parliament, 22073.

61. Mária Schmidt, "Miért kell a kormánypártoknak Nagy Imre?/Miért nem támogatjak a szabad Demokraták az MSZP initványát?" (Why do the governing parties need Imre Nagy?/ Why the Free Democrats do not support the MSZP proposal?) *Népszabadság*, June 4, 1996, 10.

62. Minutes of Parliament, 22077.

63. Konrad H. Jarausch, *The Rush to German Unity* (Oxford: Oxford University Press, 1994), 15–16, 27.

64. "The Imre Nagy Memorial Service," 1 hour, 7 min., MTV/DUNA Television, Budapest, 1996.

65. Miklós Vásárhelyi, interview by author, October 7, 1997.

66 "Megszüntették az eljárást a Nagy Imre film történésze ellen" (The lawsuit has been dropped against the historian of the movie), *Népszabadság*, July 9, 1996, 5.

67. Róbert Baló and János M. Rainer, *Nagy Imre élete és halhatatlansága* (Imre Nagy's Life and Immortality), Magyar Televízió, 1996.

68 Zsófia Szilágyi, "For Hungarians, Memories of 1956 Lose Significance," *Transition*, 23, 2 (November 15, 1996): 38–39.

69. The historian János M. Rainer feels that this "moral deficit" weighed heavily on Hungary. See his essay, "Regime Change and the Tradition of 1956" in The *Roundtable Talks of 1989*, 219.

Chapter Eight

Imre Nagy, Textbooks, and the Next Generation

Talpra Magyar, hi a haza!
Itt az idö, most vagy soha!
Rabok legyünk, vagy szabadok?

Rise Hungarians, the homeland is calling!
This is the time, now or never!
Shall we be prisoners or free?

Sándor Petőfi: Nemzeti Dal
Pest, March 13, 1848

These stirring lines by the 1848 revolutionary poet Sándor Petőfi could be found in gimnázium textbooks prior to 1989. Even though the event was placed in the context of a logical progression towards a Marxist state, the nationalist sentiment of the poems and narrative remained. Linkages between the 1848 and 1956 Revolutions were forbidden, but the groundwork for doing so had already been laid by the state.[1] After 1989 this linkage was made explicit in textbooks and public commemorations. Important lessons regarding the nature of civil society and the role of the citizenry are embodied in these narratives. Students are presented with a portrayal of Imre Nagy and his fellow revolutionaries that include highlights of the heroic actions and supreme sacrifice they took on behalf of the nation. Though one can find political shadings reflective of center right or center left politics, the narratives overall provide a consensus about the role Nagy played in the Revolution that is in contrast to the tumultuous debate that engulfed the Parliament over the Imre Nagy Bill.

How will Nagy be remembered by the next generation in the context of the continuing battles over the history and memory of the Revolution? The stories found in these narratives are more than tales of national uplift. They are essential to the foundation of the Republic. An examination of school texts and curriculum used by gimnázium students may be useful in examining this critical question, because it is in the schools where state and community meet and the interpretations of public symbols are discussed and reconciled. Accordingly, in this chapter I will undertake a close examination of selected texts, curricula, and their interpretation by classroom teachers set in the context of the continued debates over Nagy and the Revolution.

The historian and teacher Gábor Gyapay claimed that post 1989 Hungary was beset with large numbers of textbooks that were just as bad as what had preceded them, as they simply reversed the heroes and villains.[2] Though the rapid transition that took place in Hungary was characterized by a surfacing of historical debate, it also heralded a process in which education overtook the slow results of historical debate and created its own perspective.[3] According to Mihály Pálinkás, the production manager of history textbooks at Tankönyvkiadó (the National Textbook Publishing House), in order to meet the demand for revised textbooks in fall 1989 the publishing house rewrote the chapters relevant to 1956 in Ágota Jóvérné Szirtes' History IV text. This text, like all others written prior to 1989, described 1956 as a counterrevolution and portrays Nagy and his confederates as traitors.[4] Pálinkás said that the book was "unsuccessful because they had simply replaced revolutionary for counterrevolutionary without bothering to rewrite any of the chapters that led up to the Revolution, and so history after 1945 did not make a great deal of sense."[5] Perhaps mirroring the confusion caused by the seemingly overnight shift regarding post-1945 Hungarian history, the next version of the text produced in 1990 ended with World War II.[6]

The Hungarian Education Act, 1993 established local control over the schools. Though there is a core curriculum mandated by the national government, schools are now allowed a greater flexibility over the choice of materials and texts in the implementation of the curriculum. Further, teachers themselves exercise a certain degree of independence as to how texts and materials are interpreted.[7] Unlike the earlier state-mandated curriculum used throughout the communist period, the *National Core Curriculum* provides a frame for working out detailed curriculum, which is left to planners at a local level.[8] It does mandate, however, that each student should "become acquainted with the characteristics of our national heritage and the traditional values of our national culture."[9] For example, under the social studies section dealing with objectives, fourth-year students are required to know stories about "model figures in Hungarian history . . . and events connected to our national holidays . . . ," that span from the Hungarian conquest of the Carpathian basin to the "heroes of the 1956 Revolution."[10] In the same section under Hungarian national symbols students are expected to know the national anthem, national holidays, and memorials including the significance of relics such as St. Steven's crown. The detailed objectives for the end of grade 10 stipulate that students know about the main events of the 1956 Revolution including the significance of October 23, 1956, the ÁVH, worker's councils, and Imre Nagy.[11] Péter Szebenyi, who acted as a consultant in the construction of this curriculum proudly stated, "This is a curriculum for a free society."[12]

In spite of this greater flexibility, textbook choice is conditioned by determining which text will best prepare a student for entry into a university. Until the 2006 school year, entry into one of Hungary's elite universities was based on a combination of the *érettségi* (school leaving exam), a university entry exam, and the student's grades. Lists ranking the various gimnáziums in Hungary are regularly published in newspapers and magazines such as the *Heti Világgazdaság* (Weekly World Economy) and prestige is placed in how many students are admitted into elite institutions such as the Economics University, Eötvös Loránd University and the other premier institutions.[13] Therefore a fair amount of pressure is placed on teachers and schools by the community to perform well on these exams. Illés Kocsis, a history teacher at the elite Radnóti Gimnázium in Szeged, asserted, "there are only eight or nine texts right now on which the *érettségi* is based."[14] Today the market is still dominated by the National Textbook Publishing house, but their preeminence has been challenged by other publishing houses such as Cégér Kiadó (Cégér Publishing) and Műszaki Könyvkiadó (Technical Book publishers).

Though more texts are now available on the market the critical factor remains how they address the questions posed by the *érettségi*.[15] Success on the exam remains important as since 2006 the university entry exams have been abandoned for a refined version of the school exam. Significant to this discussion, history remains one of the four required areas for testing ensuring that high school students wishing to gain entry into an institution of higher learning will have to be able to address key historical events outlined in the national curricular framework, including the 1956 Revolution and Imre Nagy.[16] The textbooks I review here are the ones brought to my attention by history educators in Budapest, Szeged, and Debrecen.

The stories found in textbooks generally agree on the trajectory of the events leading up to the 1956 Revolution and its demobilization. Differences can be found in the emphasis placed on various events. For example, in the chronological and highly detailed book by Konrád Salamon, emphasis is placed on the critique of the Stalinists by Nagy's associates citing Géza Losonczy's critique of Ernő Gerő's "meaningless politics."[17] Whereas Mihály Benkes' text approaches the Revolution using more of a broad sweep approach and connects the reader to Khrushchev's critique of Stalin at the 20th Party Congress and the fact that ". . . Rákosi had to go."[18] Another interesting difference between the two texts lies in their description of Rajk's funeral on October 6, 1956. Benkes states that the event "heated [the people's] emotions to the boiling point."[19] The Salamon text goes further, explaining that Rajk was only a symbolic representation of the Hungarian people's suffering at the hands of the Stalinists. Attention is placed on Rajk's association with the ÁVH and his unswerving loyalty to Stalin and Rákosi stating, "if poor Laci [Rajk] had seen this [the funeral], he would have started shooting at us."[20]

Imre Nagy is variously described as the communist who was "the most Hungarian" in the Salamon text and in the Benkes text as the communist who "tried to restore lawfulness."[21] Distinctions are also evident in regard to the unfolding of the events of October 23, 1956. Salamon highlights the fact that Nagy was originally against the student demonstrations and came to Parliament only when called by the party.[22] In another textbook by Ildikó Repárszky and Csaba Dupcsik, Nagy's initial reluctance to accept the demonstrations was legitimate, but asserts that Nagy wanted "payback" from the party as a vindication of his platform and defiance of party etiquette after his ouster in 1955.[23] The Benkes text simply explains that "at first Nagy didn't realize that this was a real uprising against the Stalinist dictatorship."[24]

The heroic nature of the War of Independence is emphasized in most texts with pictures of revolutionaries on top of captured or destroyed Soviet vehicles. Salamon stresses the fact that the Revolution was a countrywide event and includes pictures of civilians massacred by the ÁVH in the town of Mosonmagyaróvár on October 26, 1956.[25] Repárszky and Dupcsik provide more detail regarding the Kossuth Square fight in front of the Parliament on October 25, 1956, emphasizing the fact that the Soviets at first began shooting at snipers, but then turned their fire on the Hungarian crowd who were peacefully demonstrating. The Soviet action resulted in Hungarians returning the Soviet's fire with a result of between sixty to seventy Hungarian dead and one hundred fifty injured.[26] Salamon's text states that the armed forces started fighting on the square resulting in two hundred deaths and many injuries. Both texts agree that the ÁVH was blamed for initiating the fighting, further stoking Hungarian emotions against them. They also state that the massacre of Hungarians at Mosonmagyaróvár and Kossuth Square served to fuel the Revolution and highlighted the ineffectiveness of the Soviet response. It also made clear that a new response to the Revolution was needed from the Nagy government.[27]

The victory of the Revolution begins with the establishment of a new government between October 27 and 28 that recognizes the Revolution as a national and democratic movement.[28] Interestingly, the Salamon text spends more time examining the assault on the Party headquarters on October 30, 1956. The text separates the new government from the right wing militia under József Dudás and connects his activities to the assault on the headquarters.[29] Importantly, after the capture of the building the text describes the fate of those captured as a lynching. The Repárszky and Dupcsik text also informs the reader that the assault on the Communist headquarters was carried out by revolutionary groups who were not in accord with the Nagy government. Instead of being described as a lynching the executions are described as "unusual in the scale of people's justice."[30] Salamon further highlights the fact that one of Nagy's supporters, Imre Mező, was among those lynched.[31]

The Salamon and Benkes texts use October 30 to emphasize Nagy's role in the Revolution. According to Benkes, ". . . after negotiations with the Soviets . . . it seemed the events would take a fortunate turn . . . Nagy accepted the idea of a multiparty system . . . " The democratic aim of the Revolution had been fulfilled.[32] Salamon highlights Nagy's indecision, reiterating Nagy's belief that the uprising was a "counterrevolution." Nagy is only slowly convinced to change his political thinking and October 30 is marked both by Nagy's historic announcement and the attack on the Party headquarters.[33]

Another noticeable difference between the Benkes and Salamon texts can be found in their descriptions of the multi-party government after October 30. For example, the Benkes text reports that the establishment of the MSZMP (Hungarian Socialist Worker's Party) following the dissolution of the Stalinist MDP (Hungarian Worker's Party) ". . . was based on the democratic nationalist and socialist achievements of the Revolution." After noting Kádár's disappearance the narrative continues: "The War for National Independence united different people and different political factions . . . the Revolution remained mostly a left-wing socialist movement . . . because . . . Imre Nagy and his followers played a dominant role as the Revolution moved their original ideas further than what they had originally imagined." According to the text, the unification of the right wing was made possible under the leadership of Cardinal Mindszenty. His active anticommunism made him very popular despite his conservative political views.[34]

The Salamon text explains the new government and the reemergence of political factions after October 30 in this way. "Reliable political forces worked on peaceful development and tried to maintain a positive situation. First of all, Zoltán Tildy, the leader of the Independent Smallholders Party became the pivotal member of the new government." The radio address of Cardinal Mindszenty on November 3, 1956, is described as a call for national consensus and underscores Mindszenty's call for national unity and "democratic development based on private property . . . but limited by social interest."[35]

The political shading of the texts seems most evident at this point, utilizing relationship to Cardinal Mindszenty to indicate a viewpoint nearer to contemporary center right or center left politics. Mindszenty's radio address of November 3 can be interpreted differently. For example, the historians Charles Gati and György Litván note that while Mindszenty supported the Revolution he expressed reservations regarding the Nagy government. According to Litván, Mindszenty felt that Hungary should return to the political traditions "disrupted by 1945."[36] The Cardinal himself on the other hand, remembered that after his radio address "Zoltán Tildy had tears in his eyes . . . and thanked me on behalf of the Nagy government . . . for supporting . . . Hungary's policy of neutrality . . . and emphasizing the importance of unbiased new courts [in accord with Nagy's demands for procedural justice]."[37]

All texts point to the inability or unwillingness of the international community to react, leaving Hungary to face its fate against the Soviets alone. The result was inevitable and the stage was set for counterrevolution and the brutal retribution led by the Soviet-backed Kádár regime. The heroic role of István Bibó, Minister without Portfolio in the last Nagy government, who remained in the Parliament as the representative of the legitimate government is highlighted here. Students are reminded of his message to various embassies refuting the claims made by the counterrevolution that the Revolution was anti-Semitic or fascist.[38] In addition, the Repárszky and Dupcsik text briefly discusses the lasting impact of his political writings on the democratic opposition during the 1980s.[39] Bibó, though silenced by the Kádár regime, was rediscovered by younger dissident intellectuals in the mid 1970s.[40]

The texts go on to show that the worker's council's were helpless against the Soviets and the *pufajkások*, leading to the massacres at industrial towns like Salgótarján. The consequences of the counterrevolution are evaluated not just in terms of the imprisonments and executions, but by the mass exodus out of Hungary. The Repárszky and Dupcsik text includes a quote from János Kádár regarding the role of the political police [and his legitimacy], "Political police are very important . . . we have to tell them who has to be arrested . . . "[41] All of the texts highlight the trial of Nagy and his confederates and report his refusal to acknowledge the legitimacy of his verdict using selected passages from the trial transcript.

The texts under review all portray the Soviets as outsiders who exert their hegemony over the sovereign Hungarian nation in a way that foists the illegitimate government of János Kádár on the Hungarian people. For example, the Salamon text calls attention to the fact that when Kádár's speech announcing the establishment of the MSZMP was being played on November 1 he was already on his way to Moscow.[42] Kádár's November 4, 1956, address to Hungarians from the city of Szolnok clearly demonstrates what side he had chosen. Kádár entered Budapest on November 7 only under the heavy escort of Soviet military vehicles.

Differences among the texts exist primarily in their narrative approach. For example, the Benkes and the Repárszky and Dupcsik texts tend to use a more generalized approach that sets the Revolution in the context of Cold War politics and asks the students to explain and analyze the importance of key events. In the Repárszky and Dupcsik text, students are provided with excerpts from Nagy's speeches from October 23, 28, and November 1 and asked questions such as: "How did Nagy's language change during the course of the Revolution? Why did Nagy's political viewpoint change?" Another interesting exercise has students examine excerpts from Cardinal Mindszenty's November 3 radio address and asks, "What kind of social political system would he have liked? Why did he emphasize that this was a War of Independence and not a Revolution?"[43] In contrast, the Salamon text relies on a chronological approach that attempts to capture each detail of the event. This approach certainly provides a solid foundation of information regarding the Revolution, but one wonders if time is provided for students to approach the material critically. A review of Konrád Salamon's text appearing on the Association of Hungarian History Teacher's website claims that the lessons outlined cannot be taught in one session and more importantly, critical concepts such as Cold War, counterrevolution, and anti-Semitism are not explained well.[44] All of the textbooks reviewed here include primary sources, but the Repárszky and Dupcsik text utilizes longer selections that are accompanied with questions that encourage higher-level reasoning. Gábor Gyapay's text published in 2004 seems to combine the two approaches creating an eighty-seven-page narrative as opposed to the more typical length of approximately eighteen pages.[45] How do these accounts and approaches accord with preparation for the *érettségi*?

The *érettségi* is offered in two versions, a middle and raised level. Students choose which one they will take based on their aspirations in higher education. The raised level requires more sophisticated reasoning and expects the student to make broader connections to the Cold War. For example, a middle level study question from a guide prepared by the Nemzeti Tankönyvkiadó asks students to explain the reasons for the 1956 Revolution including the main events and retribution, whereas the raised level asks students to explain the importance of the Revolution in an international context utilizing examples that included the Suez Crisis and the Hungarian question in the United Nations.[46] One interesting review question has students examine pictures and memoirs of young people during the Revolution and then attempt to reconstruct their particular life situation in the context of the Revolution. Another exercise uses documents and addresses the ÁVH role surrounding the events at Köztársaság Square on October 25 and asks students to hypothesize how the lynching mood originated.[47] Exercises that require students to connect the present to the past also figure prominently. For example, students review the state security plans regarding Imre Nagy's funeral on June 16, 1989, and then are asked questions related to the political importance of the reburial and why the state security service was so alert to the event.[48] The Nemzeti Tankönyvkiadó review is centered on Hungary's history in the twentieth century studied in the twelfth year and approximately 84 pages out of 311 focuses on the two communist regimes and their demise.

A one-volume study guide printed by the Corvina publishing house provides a sense of the scope of the exam reviewing the history of the Carpathian basin from prehistoric times to the present. Twelve pages out of 340 are devoted to review of the relevant history and its consequences.[49] Perhaps out of necessity, the Corvina study guide emphasizes a broad sweep approach. For instance one exercise asks the student to identify and make connections between names, terms, and dates such as June 16, 1989, October 23, 1989, popular uprising, and Imre Pozsgay.[50] Students certainly need to know some detail regarding the 1956 Revolution and its relation to regime change in 1989. On the 2007 "raised level" exam five points out of forty-four in the short answer portion of the exam were allocated to the student demands issued from the Budapest Technical University October 22–23, 1956, and their relationship to social and political life of the time. One out of the ten choices for the thematic questions required students to understand the negotiations between the opposition parties and the communist regime along with the significance of Nagy's funeral. These were set in the context of the crisis of the Socialist system. Although a student could select thematic questions that emphasized competence in earlier historical eras, the contemporary history of Hungary and 1956 could not entirely be avoided.[51]

From this brief overview it seems that the texts and exam preparation materials, with minor exceptions, are in accord. On one hand there is agreement regarding the meaning of the Revolution and its promise of democracy. But at the same time this portrayal that highlights Kádár's villainy may not accord with the understandings of teachers trained as historians prior to the change. As the history teacher Géza Závodszky claimed, "we moved old stuff into a new building . . . we can't empty our heads overnight." According to Závodszky, the hope expressed in the Internationale where workers are called to join our forces "so we can erase the past" was fulfilled in the Soviet Union, "the distortion of Marxism did much to distort the teaching of history in Hungary."[52] Sentiments echo István Bibó's critique of Marxism as practiced within the Soviet orbit in which he explains that by reducing all phenomena to "shallow economic motives . . . the [Marxist] saves himself the trouble of more intensive reflection."[53]

Leo Zacharia who teaches history at Tóth Árpád Gimnázium in Debrecen and graduated from the university pre-1989 explained that "[1956] is difficult because teachers feel unsure what to teach . . . the political scene is so divided that it is not easy to please everyone."[54] Illés Kocsis claims that though he never belonged to a political party, he felt that the communist period was too often disparaged without its positive aspects being revealed, pointing to the rebuilding of Budapest after World War II in only five years as an example.[55] Similar sentiments were expressed by István Farkas from the Ságvári Gimnázium located in Szeged who stated that Nagy can really only be understood in contrast to the Rákosi period. "Students have a hard time coming close to Nagy because they didn't experience the Stalinist period." He likened the Hungarians relief of living under the Kádár regime to a man needing water and once having found it, not realizing there was champagne to be had as well. Perhaps reflecting János M. Rainer's observation that the ". . . tragic story [of 1956] became the success story of *Kádárizmus* . . . ," which became paradigmatic both inside and outside Hungary, Farkas asserted that " . . . only 400 families were actually affected by the terror after the Revolution. Most Hungarians noticed the improvement in living standards." This pragmatic approach extended to his own circumstances: "I don't like dictatorships, but I had no choice, I had to compromise to survive," echoing a sentiment expressed by many educators and professionals I interviewed.[56]

The importance of teaching the history of the Revolution in the classroom, however, has strong advocates. László Miklósi, the President of the Association of Hungarian History Teachers, advocates learning the topic well [1956 and its aftermath] and then "being brave enough to fully examine it with students."[57] Andrea Kökény of Deák Ferenc Gimnázium in Szeged started university in 1988 and claimed that her professors stopped teaching about contemporary history when they arrived at the end of World War II. "The events of 1989 were really confusing to me; it was strange to me that they [the government] would proclaim the Republic on October 23, 1989, as these events were in contradiction to what I had been taught in secondary school." At the time "I did not know about the symbolic meaning [of these events] and I became more alert after the changes . . . Now that I am teaching . . . I am learning about Nagy and the 1956 Revolution with my students."[58]

At the same time, teachers expressed reservations about holding open conversations with their students when examining a controversial issue. According to Tamás Kovács from the Kölcsey Gimnázium in Budapest, "you don't dare have an opinion . . . Parent letters tend to moderate what teachers teach in the schools." He complained that students hear what they think instead of reaching a deliberative conclusion based on multiple perspectives.[59] Textbooks can be used as a way to get around this problem. In an earlier interview in 1998 with Illés Kocsis he explained that he preferred the detailed chrono-logical approach found in the Salamon text as it provided a more useful re-view for students taking the *érettségi* and the university entrance exams. Teachers at the Móra Ferenc Gimnázium in Kiskunfélegyháza agreed, stating that students needed to "learn from the texts" and asserted that the questions on the exam remained "neutral."[60] Béla Jazimicky of Deák Ferenc Gimánz-ium disagreed with this assessment explaining that "the hour by hour ac-counting of events is too complicated and obscures the aims of the Revolu-tion and the changes that took place afterwards . . . [this] approach is not useful to students."[61] He prefers texts that take a broader approach such as the Benkes text.

Most of the teachers utilize other materials in the classroom in addition to the text. For example, both Kökény and Farkas utilize the Salamon text as a point of departure for discussion of the larger issues surrounding the Revolu-tion. Films such as *Tükör-Cserepek: Magyarország—1956* (The Cracked Mirror: Hungary—1956) provide students with a pictorial compilation of im-ages from the Revolution that invites the viewer to create their own narrative and interpretation.[62] Kökény, who also teaches literature to the bi-lingual stu-dents, investigates authoritarianism through the use of books such as *Lord of the Flies* and *Animal Farm*. The Association of Hungarian History Teachers actively promotes the use of primary and alternative source materials through their annual meetings and special events. For example, a special viewing of the documentary *Forró ősz a Hidegháborúban—Magyarország 1956-ban* (A Fiery Autumn in the Cold War—Hungary in 1956) was shown for teachers the week prior to the fiftieth anniversary commemorations of the Revolu-tion.[63] The documentary examines the event from a local, regional, and global perspective, and is in accord with Rainer's suggestions as to how to approach the event with secondary students.[64] Like textbooks, these materials are ex-pensive, but with access to libraries and the Internet it is possible to gain ac-cess to primary source materials such as newspapers of the period through web sites such as the one from the Széchényi National Library, the collections located in university libraries, or institutions such as the Open Society Archives.

Complaints abounded regarding young people's lack of interest in twentieth-century history, but perhaps part of this lack of interest stems from a lack of substantive engagement with material. How interesting is a debate in which one engages only passively?[65] Reflective of the issues raised during the 1996 parliamentary debate over Nagy's status as a martyr, the teachers pointed out the contested nature of Nagy as a politician and a man from Moscow. Pres-sure from parents regarding the teaching of controversial ideas continues to play a role in teaching since 1998 when I conducted my initial interviews.

History teacher, László Kiss blames this in part on the attitudes of some teachers who continue the tradition of rote learning in which students learn from the limited source of a text or the word of the teacher. He sees a real danger in the number of students that can neither read maps nor understand how to analyze primary source documents, skills necessary for critical thinking and for informed debate.[66] At the same time the pressure of time is intense, as teachers need to prepare students for an exam whose scope spans the ancient to the contemporary periods. This makes for selective coverage, even for narratives considered essential to the national drama. Kiss weighs in on this issue as well, proposing that more time should be spent on substantive issues of contemporary history instead of what he sees as an overemphasis on earlier periods such as Medieval Hungary. Instead of avoiding bitter issues such as the Holocaust and the role of the ÁVH in Hungarian society, students should be able to confront this history with the wide array of resources that are available to them. This seems to be the approach Gábor Gyapay has taken with his textbook that offers the most in-depth examination of the Revolution and surrounding events than any of the other texts examined. On the other hand the suggestions made by Kiss would have to be reflected in similar revisions to the *érettségi*. These are substantive problems, given that the Revolution represents a pivotal moment in Hungarian history both regionally and globally. Critical thinking can be seen as politically dangerous in the context of the debate over the Revolution and Nagy, perhaps similar to the inclusion of more confrontational figures in American History textbooks such as Malcolm X in the narrative of the American Civil Rights movement taught in American secondary schools. The desire of those involved with history education in Hungary to have a voice in this debate may explain why yhe Association of Hungarian History Teachers constitutes one of the largest nongovernmental organizations in Hungary.

For the most part the texts reviewed provide a consensus view of the Revolution and Imre Nagy reflecting both the First Act of Parliament, 1990 and the Imre Nagy Bill, 1996, and certainly could not be anything else in this context. The shadings are subtle and come to the surface most forcefully as the Benkes and Salamon texts evaluate the role of Cardinal Mindszenty, Zoltán Tildy, and the last phase of the Nagy government. Reflective of the Antall government who wanted to subdue Nagy's role in the Revolution, the Salamon text highlights politicians such as Tildy who formed the core of the coalition and later multiparty government established on October 30, 1956. The Benkes text portrays Nagy and his government in full control as they move to consolidate power after October 30, very much in keeping with a narrative that highlights the Revolution and its goals rooted in social democracy, critical to the legitimizing story forwarded by the center left. The

Repárszky and Dupcsik text does more to promote critical thinking by including questions that assist the learner to analyze and critically assess the
primary source documents included in the text. This type of analysis was certainly expected on the 2007 raised level exam.

Imre Nagy's death is regarded by the majority of teachers I interviewed as
the supreme act of patriotism, shaded only by caveats found in the texts that
make him a man from Moscow, or as a follower of events. Yet, István Farkas
claimed that Nagy was more of a misguided politician who acted out of self-
interest rather than patriotism. For him Kádár was more of a legitimate expression of the Hungarian people. "Most people had a feeling that freedom
was born after 1956 . . . The feeling of freedom and economic security that
Kádár provided made the discussion of 1956 uncomfortable."[67] For Farkas,
naming perpetrators of the terror serves only to stir up old animosities rather
than focusing on fostering economic progress initiated by Kádár's modernization programs. This was in contrast to Illés Kocsis who though like Farkas
found Nagy's Stalinist past problematic, had no sympathy with Kádár. He explained, "my mother and father were both peasants and anticommunists . . .
They never accepted the communists as having a legitimate program for the
peasantry . . . The Revolution shaped Nagy . . . and had a transforming effect
on a number of Hungarians who exchanged red for the tricolor." The Communists, including Kádár, had no legitimate symbols, as they embraced a system foreign to the Hungarian nation. "Petőfi and Kossuth were heroes in that
they led the 1848 Revolution . . . Nagy is different, he was shaped by the Revolution and then died a martyr's death."[68]

Not surprisingly, the teachers' sentiments about Nagy reflect many of the
arguments presented during the debate over the Memorial Bill in 1996 and the
various public reservations regarding Nagy as an official martyr of the nation.
As we have already examined, there is a certain nostalgia among some Hungarians for life under Kádár, in part premised by what is remembered as an
assured standard of living.[69] Given the contested nature of Nagy's symbolic
status and in some cases of the Revolution itself, avoidance may be prefer-
able in the institutional context of a school. And yet, the event is paramount
in the context of the civil society established after 1989. The First Act of Parliament declares that the 1956 Revolution like the 1848 Revolution is foun-
dational to the Hungarian Republic.[70] This is certainly reflected both in textbooks and on the *érettségi*. And so, a paradox is presented to the students by
the contest that continues in the public realm, in contrast to a consensus regarding the Revolution and its actors that are provided in the materials students use to understand the event.

The continuing contest over the history of the Revolution and Nagy can be
viewed as a continuation of working through the trauma of the past, a process

thwarted by the demobilization and fostered by the establishment of the Republic. The historian Dominick LaCapra argues that this always involves orientation towards others. Collective memory is essential to the polity and its sense of identity; and how that identity is negotiated with regard to past trauma. Memory is located in the contested discourse about the past.[71] In this sense the sociologist Maurice Halbwach's observations regarding generational memory might be useful. Halbwach's observation of generational memory applies to the current collection of memories regarding the Revolution and Nagy found in film and narratives, where they help feed the current debate. How might these memories be reinterpreted once the current political actors retire from the scene and the need for political legitimacy no longer rests with their relationship to the Revolution and its actors?[72] The historian Barry Schwartz has illustrated Abraham Lincoln's changing status in the American consciousness through the use of a cartoon from a 1912 edition of the *Chicago Daily Tribune*. In 1858 he is portrayed as being overshadowed by politicians such as Sumner and Seward. In 1865 he occupies the foreground and by 1912 he stands alone. Public memory can change over time as long as it is sustained by popular interpretation. In this sense the traces of the past that remain in present are fluid.[73]

The factional portrayal of Nagy is very much like the cartoon. His reemergence on the political stage in 1989 was useful to many in the bid to unseat the communists. After the Republic had been assured the Antall government wanted to place him in the background only to be thwarted in their attempt by the Imre Nagy Bill of 1996. Whereas the portrayals of Nagy found in the textbooks seem to stabilize his image portraying him neither alone nor in the background, but in the company of his confederates. His martyrdom assured by the heroic stand he takes at his trial.

In the dramatic film entitled *A Temetetlen Halott* (The Unburied Man), director Márta Mészáros portrayed the death of Imre Nagy as a redemptive sacrifice. In her version of the story, Nagy repudiated and separated himself from his former colleagues at the end of the trial. Mészáros depicted Nagy in an *Ecce homo* posture, standing alone, abandoned by his friends.[74] In the trial transcript, by contrast, Nagy's final words repudiated his accusers, but maintained his staunch allegiance to communism and the working class.[75]

The film set off a storm of controversy among families whose loved ones were part of Nagy's inner circle. Defense Minister Pál Maléter and Press Secretary Miklós Gimes had both been executed with Nagy. In a letter to Mészáros published in *Népszabadság*, the Maléter and Gimes families complained that these were the people who remained faithful to Nagy and through their shared ordeal "belonged to each other." According to them Mészáros's portrayal of Nagy was unbelievable.[76]

And yet, the film is compelling, precisely because it leaves out many of the complications that informed Nagy's life. At its conclusion, two young girls walk to Plot 301 to leave flowers at Nagy's grave, in a reminder to the audience of the events that helped topple the communists. Mészáros thus represented Nagy as the embodiment of the republican spirit revealed at his funeral in 1989. A depiction of Nagy as a more contested figure might have broken with this reification and therefore may not have been as accessible to the public. And indeed, over 150,000 Hungarians saw the picture in the theatres.

According to Márta Mészáros it is the political use of Imre Nagy by both the right and left wing factions that underlie the historical distortion of his character. Mészáros claims when she approached the former FIDESZ Secretary Attila Várhegyi to discuss her film project she was told, "Nagy is not our hero." Her attempts to interest the Socialists with her project were equally unsuccessful. Financial support outside Hungary from Poland and Slovakia are what made the film possible. The lack of enthusiasm for the film underline the importance the two largest parties in Hungary have in controlling the portrayal of Imre Nagy and the 1956 Revolution. The remedy for this kind of manipulation according to Mészáros is to tell the truth [about Nagy] in a popular language.[77]

The current contest between political parties has continued unabated, with the participants ceaselessly supplicating specters from the past in their bid to dethrone their opposition. One wonders if in spite of this bitter feuding that an unintended consequence of the post-1989 textbook revision will be the formation of a consensus interpretation in some ways similar to the Mészáros presentation of Nagy, especially as those closest to the Revolution and its consequences fade from the contemporary political theater of the Republic.

NOTES

1. See my discussion in chapter 5.

2. Gábor Gyapay, "Some Current Issues in Hungarian History Teaching," *History Teaching in Central and Eastern European Countries*, 2 (April–June, 1996): 39–40.

3. See: Péter Szebenyi, "In the Crossfire of Debates, History Teaching – The Volcano of Hungarian Schooling," *Studies in Educational Evaluation*, 18 (1992): 108 and Ottó Szabolcs, "Történelemtanítás tegnap és ma (History teaching yesterday and today)," *Történelem Metodikai Műhely Tanulmányok* (History method workshop), László Molnár, ed. (Budapest: Tárogató Kiadó, 1996), 28.

4. See chapter 5.

5. Mihály Pálinkás, interview by author, March 20, 1998.

6. Ágota Jóvérné Szirtes, Péter Sipos, *Történelem Gimnáziumok IV Osztály* (History IV) (Budapest: Tankönyvkiadó, 1990).

7. Act LXXX of 1993 on Public Education of the Republic of Hungary, 45–46, 54.

8. Hungary, Ministry of Culture and Education, *National Core Curriculum*, 1996, 15.

9. *National Core Curriculum*, 20.

10. *National Core Curriculum*, 103.

11. *National Core Curriculum*, 129.

12. Péter Szebenyi, interview by author, February 9, 1998.

13. Through the 1990s only 10–15% of Hungary's gimnázium graduates attended an institution of higher education each year in Hungary.

14. Illés Kocsis, interview by author, February 24, 1998.

15. This was a point underscored by the history teacher Tamás Kovács at Kölcsey Gimnázium in Budapest, interview by author, October 27, 2006.

16. The other three required subject areas are Hungarian literature and grammar, math, and a foreign language. See: The Ministry of Education's website www.ohm.gov.hu.

17. Konrád Salamon, *Történelem IV* (Budapest: Nemzeti Tankönyvkiadó, 1996), 195.

18. Mihály Benkes, et al., *Történelem IV, 1914–1994* (Budapest: Cégér Kiadó, 1996), 323–24.

19. Benkes, 324.

20. Salamon, 196.

21. Salamon, 192 and Benkes, 322, respectively.

22. Salamon, 196–97.

23. Ildikó Repárszky and Csaba Dupcsik, *Történelem IV* (Budapest: Műszaki Könyvkiadó, 2005), 202.

24. Benkes, 327.

25. Salamon, 198. See also: Csaba Békés et al. ed., *The 1956 Hungarian Revolution: A History in Documents* (Budapest: Central European University Press, 2002), 199.

26. Repárszky and Dupcsik, 204.

27. See: György Litván, ed., *The Hungarian Revolution of 1956: Reform, Revolt, and Repression, 1953–1963* (London: Longman Group Ltd., 1996), 69–70 and Charles Gati, *Failed Illusions: Moscow, Washington, Budapest, and the 1956 Hungarian Revolt* (Stanford: Stanford University Press, 2006), 161–62.

28. Salamon, 200 and Repárszky and Dupcsik, 204.

29. Salamon, 202.

30. Repárszky and Dubcsik, 204.

31. Salamon, 202.

32. Benkes, 328–29.

33. Salamon, 199–201.

34. Benkes, 330–31.

35. Salamon, 203–4.

36. György Litván ed., *The Hungarian Revolution of 1956*, 125. Charles Gati asserts that Mindszenty echoed Radio Free Europe's line that endorsed the Revolution without fully backing the Nagy government (*Failed Illusions*, 197).

37. József Mindszenty, *Emlékirataim* (My Memoirs) (Budapest: Az Apostoli Szentszék Könyvkiadó, 1989), 426.

38. For example see Salamon, 205 and Repárszky and Dubcsik, 213. Bibó was a member of the Petőfi Party (Peasant's Party) that had been included in the last government on November 3, 1956.

39. According to the political scientist Rudolf L. Tőkés, Bibó's death in 1979 and the subsequent reexamination of his writings was a seminal moment in creating a more cohesive opposition to the regime in *Hungary's Negotiated Revolution: Economic Reform, Social Change, and Political Succession* (Cambridge: Cambridge University Press, 1996) 184–86.

40. Sándor Szilágyi, one of the founder's of the samizdat publication Beszélő viewed Bibó as "the symbol of intellectual resistance," "Postscript" in István Bibó, *Democracy, Revolution, Self-Determination: Selected Writings*, Károly Nagy ed., András Boros-Kazai trans. (New York: Columbia University Press, 1991), 541, 543.

41. Repárszky and Dubcsik, 214.

42. Salamon, 203.

43. Repárszky and Dubcsik, 205 and 206, respectively.

44. Twelve teachers reviewed this textbook. See: László Miklósi et al., "Tankönyvbírálatok, Konrád Salamon Történelem IV., Szakvélemény (Textbook review, Expert opinion)," Junie 30, 1998, http://www.tte.hu/?page=dok&id=38&print=1.

45. Gábor Gyapay, *Történelem IV* (Budapest: Corvinus Kiadó Kft., 2004), 137–224. The millennial scope of the *érettségi* may account for the more common eighteen-page approach.

46. József Kaposi, Márta Szabó, Miklós Száray, *Feladat-gyűjtemény az új történelem írásbeli érettségihez* (Collection of exercises for the new written érettségi), 12 évfolyam (Budapest: Nemzeti Tankönyvkiadó, 2005) 104.

47. *Feladat-gyűjtemény*, 201.

48. *Feladat-gyűjtemény*, 233.

49. Csaba Hornyák, András Kálmán, Edit Kulcsár, Ibolya Mózer, *Új Érettségi: Történelem Tételek* (History themes for the new érettségi) (Budapest: Corvina Kiadó Kft., 2005).

50. *Új Érettségi*, 304.

51. Történelem Emelt Szintű Irásbeli Vizsga 2007, Május 9, 8:00 I–II. See: Oktatási Minisztérium web site: http://www.okm.gov.hu/index_erettsegi_2007.php. (http//193.225.13.214/érettségi2007/e_tort_07maj-fl.pdf.)

52. Géza Závodszky, "A történészek demokráciája vagy a demokrácia története? – A tananyagszerkesztés néhány dilemmája a rendszerváltozás után (1993) (Democracy of historians or the history of democracy? — A few dilemma of curriculum building after the regime change)," *Civil történelem: A Történelemtanárok Egyletének 15 Éve* (Civil History: 15 years of the Association of Hungarian History Teachers) (Budapest: Felelős kiadó, 2005), 95, 99.

53. Bibó, "Reflections on the Social Development of Europe," *Democracy, Revolution, Self-Determination*, 520.

54. Leo Zacharia, interview by author, October 31, 2006.

55. Illés Kocsis, interview by author, February 17, 1998.

56. János M. Rainer, "Magyarország és a világ – 1956 (2001) (Hungary and the world)," *Civil történelem*, 156 and István Farkas, interview by author, February 3, 1998.

57. László Miklósi, interview by author, October 19, 2006. This point was also made in an earlier interview that I had with Professor Judit Pihurik, Director of History Pedagogy at Szeged University who directs her students to the ever increasing bibliography regarding 1956, interview by author, April 2, 1998. Interestingly, Miklósi told me that the Association of Hungarian History Teachers is the largest NGO in Hungary.

58. Andrea Kökény, interview by author, February 9, 1998.

59. Tamás Kovács, interview by author, October 27, 2006.

60. Éva Rostáné Földényi and Józsefné Kelemen, interview by author, January 28, 1998.

61. Béla Jazimicky, interview by author, April 2, 1998.

62. *Tükörcserepek: Magyarország—1956* (The Cracked Mirror: Hungary—1956). 1996. Produced by Gábor Vitéz. Budapest: 1956 Institute. Hungarian Film Institute. Videocassette.

63. *Forró ősz a Hidegháborúban—Magyarország 1956-ban* (A Fiery Autumn in the Cold War—Hungary in 1956). 2006. Produced by Réka Sárközy. 2006. Budapest: 1956 Institute. DVD.

64. Rainer, "Magyarország és a világ—1956," 153–57.

65. Gábor Gyapay was much admired as a history teacher for making the subject come alive. Very much in keeping with what Roy Rosenzweig and David Thelen found in their investigation of history teaching in the United States, reporting that admired teachers were those "who made them [the students] participants instead of spectators" in *The Presence of the Past: Popular Uses of History in American Life* (New York: Columbia University Press, 1998), 110.

66. László Kiss, "Trident, Trikolór, Trianon (A történelemtanítás átalakításának szükségességéről) (the importance of changing how to teach history)," *Magyar Narancs Online*, April 26, 2007 http://www.mancs.hu/index.php?gcPage=/public/hirek/hir.php&id=14660.

67. István Farkas, interview by author, February 3, 1998.

68. Illés Kocsis, interview by author, February 24, 1998.

69. For example, the historian György Litván addresses this issue in his reflections regarding the significance of June 16 for Hungarians in *Népszabadság*, June 16, 2005.

70. Found in: Lee W. Congdon and Béla K. Király, ed., *The Ideas of the Hungarian Revolution, Suppressed and Victorious, 1956–1999* (New York: Columbia University Press, 2002), 636–37.

71. Dominick LaCapra, "Revisiting the Historian's Debate: Mourning and Genocide," *History and Memory*, 9, 1/2 (Fall, 1997): 80–84, 104–6.

72. See: Maurice Halbwachs, *On Collective Memory*, trans. and ed., Lewis A. Coser (Chicago: University of Chicago Press, 1992) especially, "The Legendary Topography of the Gospels in the Holy Land," 194, 231–35.

73. Barry Schwartz, *Abraham Lincoln and the Forge of National Memory* (Chicago: The University of Chicago Press, 2000), 260, 302–3.

74. Márta Mészáros, *A Temetetlen Halott*, Budapest Film KFT., 2004 and *Beszélő Online*, http://www.beselo.hu, http://beszelo.c3.hu/archivum/index.htm (November, 2004).

75. Nagy spoke these final words to the court, "The Hungarian people and the International working class will acquit me of the allegations set against me and as a result I have to sacrifice my life." János M. Rainer, *Nagy Imre 1953–1958: Politikai Életrajz II* (Imre Nagy a Political Biography) (Budapest: 1956-os Intézet, 1999), 430–31.

76. Nyílt levél Mészáros Mártának (letter to Márta Mészáros) *Népszabadság*, January 25, 2005, *Népszabadság Online:* http://www.nol.hu/cikk/349100 and György Litván, *Népszabadság*, June 16, 2005, p. 5.

77. See: *Beszélő Online*, http://www.beszelo.hu, http://beszelo.c3.hu/archivum/index.htm (November, 2004).

Chapter Nine

Epilogue: Restless Heroes and the Continued Debate over History and Memory

> As for the Hungarian people . . . It is not their task to initiate a new uprising . . . however, it is their task to honor and safeguard—against slander, forgetting, and fading—the banner of their Revolution, which is also the banner of a freer mankind.
>
> —István Bibó, "The Hungarian Revolution
> of 1956: Scandal and Hope (1957)"[1]

A beautiful morning marked the October 23, 2006, flag-raising ceremony at the Hungarian Parliament commemorating the fiftieth anniversary of Hungary's historic Revolution. Astonishingly, Hungarian citizens and many visitors were denied access to the public ceremony taking place at a location central to the memory of the event.[2] Guards manning barricades told people that they could watch the event on television. Being denied access to the commemoration enraged some and disheartened many.

Later that day, the very moving ceremony commemorating Imre Nagy and his fellow martyrs at Plot 301 was marred by a noticeable absence of the major opposition party FIDESZ. FIDESZ had earlier announced that they would boycott the official government commemorations. A bitter fight between the Socialist and FIDESZ coalitions had unfolded in September after revelations that the Socialist Party had lied about the state of the economy in order to secure a second term in the Parliament. A series of attempts to force the Prime Minister to resign had led to this standoff and politicians from both coalitions utilized the commemorations as platforms to strengthen their positions. October 23 unfolded in stark contrast to the commemorations the day before. Among the programs on October 22 had been an illumination of the Parliament in red, white, and green, accompanied by a reading of the Petőfi verse, a dramatic rendition of the *Marseillaise* by the French chanteuse Edith Piaf, and a host of other period songs one could hear as they strolled along the Buda side of the Danube.

Demonstrations and violence marked the afternoon of October 23 and were met head-on by the police. One such demonstration was driven towards Astoria trapping some of those who attended the FIDESZ rally in a police cordon. The confrontation ended with the police breaking up the demonstration only in the early hours of the next morning.[3]

The missing ingredient of mass participation on this great occasion could be found only at the Astoria, where close to 100,000 Hungarians gathered for the commemoration organized by FIDESZ. The Socialist's strategy of keeping noisy protestors away from the opening ceremony at Parliament backfired and seemed only to strengthen the legitimacy of the FIDESZ event for many in the crowd. But how well did the intense politicking that marked the day accord with Hungarians who had stayed away from the chaos?

The fiftieth anniversary commemorations betrayed deep divisions within the polity rather than a sense of national solidarity. How had this come to pass? I had the privilege of observing much of what transpired between the opposing camps during the summer and fall of 2006. Though the immediate answers lie in the current political turmoil sparked by the Socialist revelations about the condition of the economy, a deeper answer must include the history of the bitter suppression of the Revolution, the co-optation of much of Hungarian society by the government, and the bitter divisions spawned by the contested interpretations of this event and Hungary's twentieth-century past. The Revolution remains a fulcrum from which all parties derive their legitimacy, but it is the stories that are created from the event that provide the variety of interpretations that stoke debate. What is Nagy's place in this debate? This study concludes with the bitter politics of the fiftieth anniversary commemorations and the uneasy visitants they conjure.

Discussions of Imre Nagy can easily melt into an evaluation of the communist past. According to President László Sólyom, "It's up to the youth to create a holiday on October 23 like that on March 15 . . . we have almost everything for that . . . even if we do not have symbolic individuals like Petőfi and Kossuth . . ."[4] László Sólyom's comments seem to eliminate a place for Nagy among Hungary's heroes when contrasted with the revolutionaries of 1848. Though the statue of Imre Nagy that gazes intently on Kossuth Square and the Parliament is in no danger of being removed, the remarks reflect an uneasiness that some within the polity continue to feel about Nagy and many of his confederates who remained loyal to the International Worker's movement until their last moments at the gibbet. The revolutionaries of 1848 present much less controversy, as they are portrayed as remaining steadfast to the ideals of the liberal revolution until the end.

The events and players of 1848 have been highlighted by Hungarian governments since the establishment of the Dual Monarchy in 1867. Even Rákosi's People's Republic included the heroic drama replete with Petőfi's Verse in secondary school textbooks, albeit with a Stalinist interpretation tagged on at the end. In this light 1848 provides a certain consensus that legitimizes the actions of its heroes. The historical actors of 1956, however, are "interwoven in the past and present."[5] This concern with politicized memory was acknowledged by the Socialist Prime Minister Ferenc Gyurcsány during the course of the commemorations when he stated, ". . . the Revolution of 1956 was about freedom . . . 2006 is about democracy . . . the question is about what kind of democracy . . ."[6]

Political actors on the left and right are regularly consigned to oblivion only to be later restored to the political community.[7] Most recently, the head from the body of János Kádár was stolen from his grave in the National Cemetery. A spray-painted message on the Worker's Movement Pantheon asserted that the remains of Kádár and his colleagues could not rest in sacred ground.[8] The cemetery also contains the remains of such notables as Lajos Kossuth, Governor of the Republic in 1849.[9] What is the legitimate story of the new Republic? Is the period between 1948 and 1989 an aberration, and if so, what parts of the twentieth century are worthy of being included in the national story?

The first four national elections in Hungary after 1989 were characterized by a shifting between center right/center left coalitions. The electorate continued to take vengeance on those in power, blaming them for a lagging economy that left many feeling abandoned to the fortunes of the free market.[10] The economic stabilization plan put into effect by the Socialists in 1995 resulted in a 10% cut in earnings.[11] The austerity measures were largely deemed necessary for European integration, but FIDESZ was able to build on public dissatisfaction with the economy to forward its vision of civic Hungary. The areas made prosperous by the transition, primarily in the Transdanubia west of the Danube, responded to what they considered was a message that promoted economic liberalism with conservative values.[12]

The nationalist agenda that had characterized the Antall government proved to be another rich source of voters who had turned away from the platform of social democracy promoted by the Socialist/SZDSZ coalition. As Viktor Orbán proudly proclaimed at the counter commemoration on October 23, 2006, "Hungary saved Europe from communism . . . many in the West viewed socialism as an exciting experiment . . . this misleading idea was unveiled by the 1956 Hungarian Revolution."[13] Nagy fits uncomfortably in this formulation and although Orbán's speech at Nagy's funeral had fueled his rise and that of FIDESZ in 1989, Nagy is often kept at a distance.[14] FIDESZ came to power in 1998 in coalition with the Smallholders, MDF, and the nationalist right wing Hungarian Justice and Life Party (MIÉP) led by István Csurka that had gained over 5% of the vote, ensuring that mixed feelings would continue regarding Nagy and the Revolution.[15]

The strong nationalist sentiment expressed by József Antall was epitomized by the reburial of Miklós Horthy. In spite of it not being an official state ceremony, the event underscored Antall's determination to highlight Horthy's anti-bolshevism and legitimize a broad swath of Hungarian history that had been damned by both Communist regimes. The funeral was attended not only by government officials, but also skinheads and members of MIÉP. Csurka, who had been part of the MDF, viewed their agenda as a failure and proposed that Hungary's real problems were caused by outsiders, a cabal that included Jews, Communists, and other outsiders, ultimately leading to a break with the MDF.[16] His message appealed to a sizeable minority who felt left out of the opportunities gained by the advent of a free market economy.[17] Though many within FIDESZ were wary of this brand of populism, it was trumpeted by their coalition partners the Smallholders. The issue came to a head with the movement of the crown of St. Steven from the National Museum to the Parliament on New Year's Day 2000 and served to harden the ideological lines between the two coalitions. Both the Socialists and Free Democrats boycotted the ceremony.[18] In a move that was meant to celebrate the one thousand years of Hungary and provide a source of national inspiration, József Torgyán, chairman of the Smallholders Party, suggested that the constitution be modified so that the crown would once again embody the symbolic unity of the nation.[19] Bálint Magyar, chairman of the Free Democrats, strongly objected, worrying that the crown's move would set off a constitutional debate and reopen old wounds.[20]

The nature of these wounds was clear to all and amplified by MIÉP who had decided to attempt to rehabilitate the memory of László Bárdossy, Hungary's Prime Minister from 1941 to 1942. Bárdossy had been tried and executed as a war criminal on January 9, 1946. Forty-four years later, on the anniversary of his execution, a well-attended memorial mass was said for him in St. Steven's Basilica.[21] Later, in November 2000, Csurka filed a brief with the Hungarian Supreme Court on behalf of MIÉP to grant Bárdossy a retrial. Csurka asserted that trials conducted by the People's Courts in Hungary after World War II were trials of the victors. "For us it is not just the rehabilitation of an unlawfully convicted politician, but the true evaluation of an historical era."[22]

Tamás Fricz claims that it was FIDESZ's strategy to bring hidden disagreements to the surface in order to formulate clear positions and to keep them from intensifying later on.[23] Yet just the opposite happened. MIÉP's agenda provided the Socialist coalition with ammunition to claim that part of the FIDESZ program was a purposeful historical distortion that legitimized the politics that had brought Hungary into coalition with the Axis powers and genocide. At the same time, their accusations echoed Communist charges launched against the Smallholder government (1945–1948). FIDESZ countered by reminding the public of the Communist use of former fascist Arrow Cross members in the ÁVH and then linking this story to revelations regarding Prime Minister Ferenc Gyurcsány's residence that revealed Communist complicity, both passive and active, in the odious politics of the 1940s.[24]

Gyurcsány's home once belonged to Antal Apró, a high-ranking functionary under both Rákosi and Kádár. As Apró rose in the ranks he became the beneficiary of property that had been confiscated from a Jewish family in 1944.[25] FIDESZ parliamentarian and former revolutionary Mária Wittner utilized this connection to damn the Socialists and justify her decision not to participate in the fiftieth anniversary commemorations stating, "Under no circumstances do I want to join the memory of the victims of Antal Apró and the victorious celebration of the heirs of Antal Apró . . . I am not going to stab my comrades who were hanged in the back . . . there will be no separate remembrance . . . We the living and the dead will remember together . . . Our hangmen can celebrate separately if they wish."[26] Her comments uncannily echoed the sentiments expressed in 1997 by rival SZDSZ PM and former revolutionary Imre Mécs, reflecting the then uneasy relationship within the Socialist coalition. These tactics were akin to 1989 when the reform communists were unable to disconnect themselves from the suppression of the Revolution.

The historian Zoltán Ripp suggests that from the perspective of November 4, it is possible to portray the Revolution selectively as a War of National Liberation where focus is placed on the heroism of the streets and as an uprising against communism. This also served the needs of those distancing themselves from Nagy and his fellow communist reformers.[27]

According to journalist Ildikó Hankó, "We will need many decades to understand that the true heroes were not those thinking within reform [Imre Nagy and his confederates], but the young ones whose natural instinct was for freedom."[28] For some within the spectrum of the center right coalition it remained galling that former members of Kádár's regime were still actively engaged in politics and desired what they considered a completion of the goals of the Revolution that included purging communists from government.[29] The question of lustration had been raised in 1989 and in response to the demand for a more radical regime change József Antall replied, "[you] should have fomented Revolution."[30] If Nagy's gradual acceptance of the Revolution and continued loyalty to communism make him problematic for some, who then can be considered a hero?

Stories of heroism during the Revolution abound, but the actors in them, like Nagy, present their own complications. For example, Péter Mansfeld who was only eighteen years old when he was hanged in 1959 is commonly portrayed as emblematic of the unforgiving terror following the second Soviet invasion. The public at large learned about Mansfeld's fate only in 1989, causing outrage among many that one so young had fallen victim to the terror. He was fifteen when he fought with the Revolutionaries at Széna Square ferrying weapons, food, and acting as a liaison between the command and the fighters.[31] Mansfeld and other children who fought in the Revolution are called *szent suhanc*, the holy adolescents. He was recently honored with a statue in Budapest and memorialized on November 4, 2006.[32]

Mansfeld was first arrested in 1957 not for his revolutionary activities, but for auto theft. According to historian László Eörsi of the 1956 Institute it was in prison when Mansfeld's feelings against the regime were solidified. He was arrested again in February 1958 following his participation in a gang attack against a police officer for the purpose of obtaining the officer's weapons and ID to carry out robberies.[33] Instead of charging Mansfeld and his gang with the assault they were charged with conspiring to ferment counterrevolution. The connection between the Revolution and the assault was made during the trial when he was coerced into stating that, "The goal of the Counterrevolution was to overthrow the Revolutionary government of 1945."[34] Mansfeld's story is tragic and certainly representative of the Kádár regime's determination to provide tutelage to the working class who shouldered a great deal of the fighting. In this way he became an ideal hero. On the other hand, his story is complicated by his delinquency. Paradoxically, it was the state that fortified his heroic image in which Mansfeld's activities in 1958 were connected to 1956 and he was tried and executed as a counterrevolutionary.[35]

Another revolutionary hero that typifies the heroism of youth is Ilona Tóth also known as the Hungary's Jeanne d'Arc.[36] Tóth was a medical student who tended to the wounded of both sides during the Revolution and helped prepare pamphlets after the second Soviet invasion. She was arrested on November 16, 1956. She is presented as the selfless embodiment of the revolutionary whose deeply religious convictions reveal the righteousness of the Hungarian cause. After her arrest she was charged with the brutal murder of István Kollár whom she believed was an informer. She supposedly murdered him with the use of chloroform, asphyxiation, the injection of air, and stabbing. According to László Eörsi, Tóth may have panicked in the chaos of the demobilization.[37] She confessed to all of the accusations however, and was sentenced to die. According to one story, at her mother's last visit before her execution in June 1957 she reportedly said, "I will die as a brave Hungarian soldier . . . the charges aren't true . . . they only want to besmirch the holy Revolution." The journalist Ildikó Hankó claims that Tóth's confession was extracted by torture, reminding her readers that Cardinal Mindszenty's confession had also been extracted by the same means, and that Tóth went to her death proclaiming "long live freedom and Hungary."[38]

Tóth's case became wrapped up in the partisan politics of post-1989 when her relatives brought her case to the Supreme Court in 1990 for reconsideration. The court ruled that though the murder was related to the uprising, as a doctor she remained culpable for the crime. The family was shocked, as many of those revolutionaries caught in the terror had been exonerated and honored as martyrs in Plot 301. Mária Wittner and the Political Prisoners Association (POFOSZ) pressed the case with the Ministry of Justice and seemed to be making progress until the Socialist ascension to power in 1994. It was only in 2000 that the Parliament passed a law nullifying the decisions made in the show trials.[39] At the dedication of a bust to Ilona Tóth, Ibolya Dávid, Minister of Justice from the MDF, echoed the moral imperative that was made by Tibor Méray at Nagy's graveside, in 1989. Dávid asked, "Why did she have to die?" The ones who can answer this question are not here today. She continued, "I am thinking of those who take advantage of the chance for legal oblivion that comes with the passage of time . . . they are responsible for these deeds."[40]

Tóth's story certainly accords with the gray areas associated with Revolutions and war where questions of morality and law get blurred. But in the context of politics, Ilona Tóth's story as told in *Magyar Demokrata* creates an ideal type martyr without the complexity and confusion that followed the Revolution. For example, in spite of István Bibó's call for non-cooperation on November 4th, how realistic was his call in the context of the summary justice being meted out by the Soviets and their Hungarian allies?[41] Bibó had claimed that the Soviet-backed government was illegitimate, and perhaps in the mind of Tóth and her colleagues they were acting legitimately under the circumstances. What was viewed as a politically motivated attempt to thwart justice for Tóth by the Socialists all but ensured that the center right MDF would champion her case.

Very few would contest the heroic status of either Mansfeld or Tóth. In many ways they act out of inexperience, a necessary ingredient for a revolution fought for ideals against overwhelming odds. Nagy is different in that as a sixty-year-old he acts deliberatively, knowing full well what the consequences of failure could portend for himself and his comrades. In the cases of all three the politicized stories forwarded by the competing factions utilize their personages to create dichotomies of good and evil with which to bludgeon their opponents.

In many ways this is understandable, as the demand for justice is inexorably linked to the Republic that was the foundation of the 1848 and 1956 Revolutions, and the negotiated regime change of 1989. While democracy was assured, the accompanying expectation for justice by those aggrieved by the various communist regimes was not. In the absence of substantive legal proceedings against those who were responsible for the onerous crimes perpetrated by the Kádár regime, there was no mechanism to reexamine grievances in a way that permitted some kind of national atonement and forgiveness.[42] Perhaps it is for this reason that the selected memories of the tragic stories embodied by the likes of Tóth and Mansfeld continue to be called upon to do battle once again.[43]

The debate over 1956 continued unabated and intensified during the 2002 election when the Socialists gained a narrow victory. It has been argued that problems with the economy and the resurrection of divisive memories from Hungary's divisive past contributed to their defeat.[44] The potency of the debate was demonstrated in spring 2002 when FIDESZ revealed that the Socialist candidate for Prime Minister had been a member of Hungary's secret service during the 1970s. The charges continued to dog him even after his election with calls for his resignation based on his lack of candor.[45] Following fast upon these charges were countercharges leveled at the new chairman of FIDESZ, Zoltán Pokorni, that his parents had collaborated with the Kádár regime in the wake of the failed Revolution. Pokorni resigned within a week of these charges being leveled against him.[46]

Imre Nagy's graveside memorial at Plot 301, June 16, 2006, foreshadowed the divisive political climate that would manifest itself in full later that fall. Among those attending the memorial were President László Sólyom, Katalin Szili, from the MSZP and chairperson of the Parliament, and Mária Wittner. Szili gave a short speech in which she attached her party to Nagy claiming that he was ". . . our predecessor and role model . . . he united the country and remained faithful to his beliefs to the end . . . his greatest love was for his country."[47] Wittner rhetorically asked at Plot 301, "Is this what we really wanted? No!" In spite of László Sólyom's participation at the ceremony that included laying a wreath, Wittner remained uncomfortable with what she saw as false professions of unity and announced that the fiftieth anniversary commemorations of the Revolution could not take place with the perpetrators.[48] The connection between the Socialist Party and the former Communist regime was simply too close for some.[49]

Simplification of the heroes and history of the 1956 Revolution in the service of political grandstanding only helped poison the political atmosphere prior to 2006. In this light the possibility of reconciling diverse memories of the Revolution and historical research is remote.[50] In response to my question regarding

Mária Wittner's statement that a unified commemoration was impossible, fellow FIDESZ MP János Horváth who had been a member of Nagy's government replied that he was saddened by the comments and hoped that differences could yet be put aside for the sake of the momentous national occasion.[51] And yet at the time of Nagy's memorial Viktor Orbán had remained silent and FIDESZ did not organize a memorial for the occasion, giving the impression that Nagy embodied the ideas only for the center left parties.[52]

In the wake of the unprecedented Socialist victory in spring 2006 that accorded them a second term, questions about the economy took center stage as the Socialist/SZDSZ coalition unrolled an agenda that proposed severe cutbacks in health and education to the chagrin of the public.[53] The election like the one in 2002 was close in both rounds of voting.[54] The opposition seethed over what they viewed was a purposeful subversion of democracy made plain by the withholding of critical information regarding Hungary's economic health during the first and second rounds of voting. Discussions and problems regarding the fiftieth anniversary commemorations were placed in the background as Hungarians discussed and debated the economic program forwarded by the majority.

On Saturday September 16, 2006, a stunned nation listened to the broadcast of a leaked tape that captured Prime Minister Ferenc Gyurcsány admitting in a closed door session that his party had lied about the state of the Hungarian economy. The effect was immediate. Demonstrators primarily from the center right opposition parties gathered the next day at Kossuth Square, and the demonstrations continued day and night through the evening of October 22. FIDESZ responded to the Prime Minister's announcement by insisting that he resign because of his lack of veracity with the public.[55] The size of the crowd at Kossuth Square ebbed and flowed, and swelled to the size of tens of thousands at major events sponsored by FIDESZ that included speakers and music.

Protestors moved from Kossuth Square to the headquarters of the national television on Monday September 18, 2006, and took up in the downstairs foyer. They were ultimately driven out, but not before they set several cars on fire and damaging the building.[56] The violence and vandalism was apparently the work of an extreme right wing faction associated with a soccer club, although a FIDESZ representative was spotted among the crowd. Viktor Orbán disavowed the use of violence and quickly distanced himself and his party from the incident at the television station and other instances of violence in the streets that occurred that week. But the Socialists quickly countered that because of the FIDESZ support for the demonstrations in front of the Parliament they were in fact encouraging the more extremist right wing elements that had attached themselves to the demonstration. Indeed, some demonstrators carried flags emblazoned with the Royal Coat of Arms, and the red and silver Árpád flag that had been incorporated into the fascist Arrow Cross flags at the end of World War II. Some even voiced their demand for the restoration of the borders of the *Királyság* (Kingdom) before its dismemberment after World War I.[57]

Neither Gyurcsány nor Orbán were willing to back down and both jockeyed for political advantage. The countrywide elections for local governments on October 1 provided the opposition with an opportunity to gauge dissatisfaction with the Socialist coalition and their economic program. During the run up to the elections Orbán and other FIDESZ leaders energized the base underlining the importance of the elections. The mayor of Debrecen Lajos Kósa called for Gyucsány to step down, "The government can not ask for sacrifice from the people if they can not let go of the leaders who are responsible for the current situation." He suggested that mayors and local leaders be given the power to veto governmental budget proposals and concluded by encouraging a strong voter turnout to "help Hungarians defend their towns and cities against the Prime Minister." At the same rally Viktor Orbán hoped that if the Socialists lost they would be forced to give up the Gyurcsány package.[58]

The rhetoric became even more heated as Election Day approached. At a rally in mid-September Orbán stated, "We need every single vote so we could begin moving against the government . . . Once they have the results of the Revolution [election] . . . they [the opposition in Parliament] can stand up to the government in a radical deliberate way . . . the foundation to stand up against the government must be laid by the people." Gyurcsány pounced, "Orbán is questioning the legitimacy of the government . . . we can have a debate about everything, government decisions, promises. . . . But to promote radical resistance . . . steps over the line . . . Today the President of FIDESZ crossed over the Rubicon."[59] If Gyurcsány's proposed cutbacks to Hungarian's social security had enraged the populace, his revelations on September 16 sealed the deal and the Socialists took a beating at the polls.[60] Gyurcsány all but ignored calls for his resignation and his coalition remained firm in their promotion for austerity. He instead requested a vote of confidence from the Parliament on October 2, 2006.

Orbán responded to Gyurcsány by demanding that the Socialists dismiss Gyurcsány from office within seventy-two hours. Orbán dismissed Gyurcsány's request for a vote of confidence saying that this was "an old trick," what was really needed was a vote of censure.[61] The vote was a foregone conclusion for the center left coalition, 207–165, with twelve abstentions. The vote was followed by an apology of sorts from the Prime Minister. He apologized that " . . . they [the Socialists] had tried to avoid simple answers . . . they did not speak honestly with the people." Gyurcsány continued by apologizing for his use of "harsh and rude language" that many found offensive. He also defended himself against the accusations that the government had cheated and knowingly mislead the people in connection with the national elections the previous spring. He then launched into a frontal attack against Orbán stating, ". . . the debate in Parliament is an attempt by the minority to attack the constitution . . . their goal is to force early elections . . . and [once in power] rewrite the constitution to Viktor Orbán's taste."[62] It was in this atmosphere that FIDESZ spokesman Péter Szijjártó announced that they would not participate in any of the planned commemorations in which the Prime Minister was scheduled to speak. FIDESZ would only attend ceremonies where the President would speak as he represented a symbol of national unity. The final blow came with the announcement that FIDESZ would hold a separate commemoration on October 23.[63]

The demonstrations continued right up to the weekend that the official state commemorations were to begin. Initially the demonstrators had been told that they would have to clear the square by midnight Friday, October 20. At the last minute the authorities changed their minds and instead erected a barricade that cut off the demonstrator's sight line to the area where the ceremonies would take place.[64] In response, demonstrators threatened to use their amplifiers to drown out the commemorations taking place on the other side of the barricade. Then, early in the morning of October 23, the police used the pretext of a security search to ensure the safety of the foreign delegation attending the ceremonies that day, and cleared the demonstrators off the square.[65] The square was sealed off from the public with a fence manned by the police. A series of noisy but small demonstrations ensued later that morning resulting in the police expanding the security zone around the Parliament.

Commemorations did take place, but with the public in most cases kept at a distance for fear of violent disruption. The exclusive nature of the official celebrations was a sharp contrast to the mass participation that was the mark of the actual Revolution, and a photograph of the Prime Minister performing *kegyelet* at the new monument to the Revolution during the dedication ceremony seemed to heighten this fact.[66] Even more bizarre were a series of performances at the Parliament that took place with no audience. During the performances a television camera panned an empty Kossuth Square.[67]

This pattern continued throughout the next two weeks and concluded on the evening of November 4. The final event of the commemorations that took place on Heroes Square was the wreathing of the tomb of the Unknown Soldier in honor of those revolutionaries who had died fighting for their country. Prior to the ceremony the public was told via loudspeaker to leave as the official commemoration was about to begin. The Prime Minister, his guests, and a military honor guard alone in the square conveyed a message far different from the message that briefly informed the Hungarian polity on June 16, 1989.

Where did everybody go on October 23? A counter commemoration was sponsored by FIDESZ and KDNP at Astoria, the site of bitter fighting during the Revolution. A crowd of over 100,000 showed up, and included many families with children. The speeches were fiery in their denunciation of the Gyurcsány and the Socialist coalition. FIDESZ and the Christian Democrats proposed that a referendum in which education, pensions, health care, and what they identified as democratic guarantees should be presented to the Hungarian people. Orbán proclaimed, "This [the referendum] will seal the fate of the government based on lies." He explained that by lying about the economy during the spring elections they had "cheated us . . . they took away the right of free elections . . . the right that was achieved by the heirs of 1956." The impassioned speech hearkened back to the tactics FIDESZ and SZDSZ had used to push the communists out of power in 1989. He concluded, "1956 was a miracle in its birth, short life and death . . . it happened in a country tortured twice by the greatest lie of the twentieth century, Socialism!"[68] The speech concluded with thunderous applause by an enthusiastic audience unaware that the police were driving a violent demonstration in their direction.

A group of several thousand noisy demonstrators confronted the police on Károly körút, which is part of the inner ring of Pest and not far from Astoria. The violence was reminiscent of clashes that had characterized the week of September 18, except this time the police were much more aggressive in their use of tear gas, water canons, and rubber bullets. Orbán had again distanced himself from the violence and instructed those attending the commemoration to do so as well. The demonstrators cast themselves as inheritors of the Revolution and were not to be quelled. Their nationalist banners pointed to the recidivist politics of the extreme right wing, and yet there was also a certain feeling of anarchy to the event. At one point several young men commandeered a Russian tank that had been on display and drove through the streets adding to the unreality of the scene.[69] The riot ultimately wound up near Erzsébet Bridge with the police and demonstrators doing battle until the early hours of October 24. Accusations abounded that the police had trapped innocents in their cordon, including some of those who attended the FIDESZ event at Astoria only a few blocks away.[70] There was an investigation of Budapest's chief of police regarding his responsibility in the wake of charges that included overzealousness and mishandling of security. On October 31 it was announced on the Kossuth Rádió that conversations regarding security on October 23 were classified as a state secret.

The somberness of Heroes Square on November 4 with its monuments draped in black bunting was further intensified by the rain and mist so characteristic of the season. But further down from the square on Andrássy Street the bleakness was made even more eerie by a candlelit procession sponsored by FIDESZ. As tens of thousands of candle-holding marchers set off, some began singing the Székely hymn that is traditionally sung on St. Steven's Day, creating a certain ambiguity regarding their political motives.[71] It seemed at first glance that the large scale attendance at the FIDESZ events of October 23 and November 4 had legitimized their platform.

Denying the public the opportunity to participate in the state commemorations certainly played into their opponents hands. But what of the many who had remained at home? Demonstrators began calling the protests Hungary's second Revolution and utilized the state's official commemorations as platforms from which to launch their attacks on the Prime Minister and the Socialist coalition in general. Police manning cordons and barricades were mocked with calls of "ÁVH!" The lack of police response on the evening of the riot in front of MTV headquarters was more than compensated for in the following weeks and especially on October 23–24. The demonstrations that turned violent had a staged feel and produced at least temporarily the desired result of presenting the state as the aggressor interested in stifling dissent. Yet what FIDESZ might have gained by Gyurcsány's revelations seemed to be somewhat thwarted by a public disgruntled by the violence. Many Hungarians were horrified to see a building that had been beautifully restored after the Revolution being damaged. Disillusionment with Gyurcsány and the lack of veracity regarding the health of the Hungarian economy didn't necessarily translate into sympathy with aspects of the right wing agenda that promoted restoration of Hungary's pre-Trianon borders. This was very much in evidence during many of the demonstrations. The political crisis seemed only to further divide or estrange Hungarians from the politics being played out. The end result blunted what had been planned as a celebration of the nation and the fruits of the Revolution. What was clear was that the political drama had left a sense of bitterness whose legacies were yet to be determined.

At a conference held at the Italian Institute of Culture in Budapest on September 28, 2006, Jenő Fónay provided an account of the fighting at Széna Square, his relationship with Péter Mansfeld, and his time in prison. Fónay's anticommunist views are well known and he wrote passionately regarding the Socialist appropriation of Imre Nagy prior to the parliamentary debate over the Memory Bill. And yet, at the conference he underscored the connection between Imre Nagy and the revolutionaries, echoing Ottó Sándorffy's assertions that the two cannot be separated.[72] He was among many former revolutionaries who accepted honors from the Hungarian government and on October 22 shook hands in the Parliament with both the President László Sólyom and Prime Minister Ferenc Gyucsány. This act of reconciliation was not followed by all present, but indicated the possibility that the commemorations signified.[73]

When stripped of the myths forwarded by factional politics, the story of Imre Nagy and the Revolution becomes a heroic story because the actors of the drama are human. And in spite of their foibles they still do battle against insurmountable odds. János M. Rainer believes that the Revolution of 1956 can be understood from two points of view. One perspective highlights the national tragedy that is reinforced by the funeral of Imre Nagy, while the other promotes October 23 as a day in which to celebrate the bravery of youth and as a holiday of freedom. Rainer believes that ultimately a future [generation] will join the two approaches to 1956. In this way, 1956 will be understood in the way the 1848 Revolution is in which the steps of the National Museum (March 15, 1848) are connected to the gallows of Arad (October 6, 1849).[74]

Sándor Márai claimed that when he crossed the border into what would become a lifetime exile he felt fear for the first time, a fear of the unknown. For him the authoritarian state that was being created before his eyes was predictable in its suppression of creativity and the penchant for sameness that dulled the wits. Time is a critical factor in the development of democracy, and the political dialogue that includes central issues regarding the nature of the state is part of this process. The process is not necessarily predictable and uneasily formulated, because the many contingencies that play a role in the development of the state are unique in context. At a personal level, Márai knew this "for the first time in my life—I really felt fear. I realized I was free."[75]

This study has argued that the attempt to create Hungarian solidarity comes from memorial practices fused to a desire for democracy in competition with strands of desire represented by those who demand the restoration of the borders of the kingdom, or those who actively promoted the authoritarian regimes of Rákosi and Kádár. The tradition of 1848 is fused to 1956. As Charles Gati reminds us, the revolt of the mind laid the groundwork for this linkage, ultimately represented by the student demands and later in the establishment of the Republic.[76] It was this linkage that provided the legitimacy the opposition needed in its bid to topple the communists in 1989, and symbolized by the funeral of Imre Nagy. Nagy had demanded procedure within the context of a one-party state and only reluctantly joined with the Revolution to proclaim the establishment of a sovereign republic. Importantly, however, and in spite of his allegiance to the International Workers, he remained steadfast in his assertion that the multiparty Republic was legitimate. In this sense the tradition of 1956 was very definitely part of the contemporary state.

The negotiated nature of the regime change left many questions unanswered. Would the demand for procedural law include justice for those victimized under the communists? The funeral of Imre Nagy explicitly recognized the injustices done to him and his confederates, but failed to recognize the consequences of state suppression in the present and to face the past with some sort of process that could bring reconciliation. In the context of politics, those feeling aggrieved continue to call upon the departed to bring justice and legitimacy to their cause. But memory is selective in this process, and only the traces of memory that accord with the story proposed by the various factions comes to the fore. Suppression of memory is critical as its uncovering by the opposition in the debates over Nagy and the Revolution are the forces that stimulate the debate over history and memory.

In conversations with teachers many complained of strong disinterest on the part of their students in regard to the Revolution and Imre Nagy.[77] But again, I was struck with the difference between students and teachers who were actively engaged in the discussion of history and its connection to the present. At Néri Szent Fülöp Általános Iskola teachers, students, and their parents transformed the second floor of the school into a living museum. Parents and teachers had provided artifacts from the Revolution and the period creating displays that covered political, social, and economic life in Hungary during the mid-1950s. One was directly engaged in the period with toys, kitchen artifacts, clothed mannequins, and an interesting assortment of photos, posters, flags, uniforms, and other relics that included a tank tread. The narrative was created and presented collaboratively and it was clear that there was a general feeling of pride in its creation. In an interesting conversation that I had with a class of history students at Kölcsey Gimnázium in Budapest, they complained of the politicization of the commemoration on October 23. Many felt that an opportunity to learn more about the event had been lost in the political theater of the streets. Several felt that the anniversary deserved more solemnity. It seemed to them that the importance of the national celebration had been squandered by the adults. Though my work does not constitute a comprehensive study, it does indicate the efficacy of direct engagement with students and the study of history and politics. What kind of narrative will these students create regarding the history of the Revolution and its relationship to contemporary Hungary?

The past remains unsettled and unsettling to many of the actors on the contemporary political stage in Hungary. At times it seems like disequilibrium within the polity. But these arguments rooted in history are probably necessary. Many of those active in politics since 1945 have experience in both the authoritarian and democratic systems. It could be argued that the complicated dialogue created by competing narratives represents an attempt to come to terms with a past that included compromise, co-optation, and the search for absolution.

The macabre desecration of Kádár's tomb seems like the fulfillment of an earlier myth told to me by a student on my first visit to Hungary in 1992, in which the ashes of Mátyás Rákosi were removed from his tomb and placed on an ash can outside the cemetery where he was buried. This deliberate act was certainly meant to shock and underscores the bitterness revealed during various parts of the fiftieth anniversary commemorations. It is hard to know what the political price will be for this unleashing of the furies.

What is Nagy's place in this context? His story is not made easy as it is complicated by his association with the Stalinists that reveals him to be more an opportunist than loyal servant of the people. His ideas about land reform were popular, but the police state that he helped create was not. The challenge he laid down to his opponents that included a demand for procedure was outpaced by the Revolution and he remained true to his belief in communism to the end. It is his transformation and devotion to the Revolution that are the stuff of real patriotism. The story of the Revolution and the contemporary state cannot be told without him. There probably is a need for heroes in the pedagogy of the state as they provide clear exemplars of the ideal citizen. But what about the complexity and uncertainty that seem to possess most mortals? The story of Imre Nagy is compelling because it reveals human foibles, the unpredictability of life, and finally a sense of purpose that takes him beyond everyday experience, a story that has all the ingredients needed for an investigation and debate about the development of civil society in Hungary.[78]

NOTES

1. Found in: István Bibó, *Democracy, Revolution, Self-Determination: Selected Writings*, Károly Nagy, ed., András Boros-Kazai, trans. (New York: Columbia University Press, 1991), 352.

2. For example see "Köszönet a szabadság hőseinek, 1956–2006 (Thank you to the heroes of freedom)," *Népszabadság*, October 21, 2006, 10. The events began on October 21 and continued through November 4.

3. The official commemoration at the statue to the Revolution on the site where the statue erected to Stalin had been pulled down on the evening of October 23, 1956, by students and workers was marked by a small but angry demonstration. *Népszabadság*, October 24, 2006, 2.

4. From a speech given at the State Opera House as part of the national commemoration of the fiftieth anniversary of the 1956 Revolution, Zsolt Gréczy, "Zárt Kapuk mögött, méltósággal, Biztonsági okok miatt az állami vezetők többsége lemondta részvételét az esti ünnepségeken (Behind closed doors with dignity, due to security reasons the majority of the state leaders excused themselves from the evening celebrations)," *Népszabadság*, October 24, 2007, 2.

5. "When past and present remain interwoven, there is no clear dichotomy between history and memory." Saul Friedlander, "A Conflict of Memories? The New German Debates about the Final Solution," Leo Baeck Memorial Lecture 31 (Leo Baeck Institute: New York, 1988), 18.

6. "Egyetlen '56 többféle üzenettel, Barroso, Fischer, Sólyom, Gyurcsány és Orbán a Magyar forradalomról (There is a single 56 with different messages)," *Népszabadság*, October 24, 2007, 3.

7. For example, Imre Nagy, László Rajk, and József Antall. The political scientist Katherine Verdery asserts, ". . . dead bodies are uncommonly lively in the former socialist bloc . . . the vastness of the transformations there . . . make bodies worth fighting over . . ." and comments regarding the "political work" of dead bodies, in *The Political Lives of Dead Bodies: Reburial and Postsocialist Change* (New York: Columbia University Press, 1999), 52 and 127, respectively.

8. The message was very probably addressed to all of the communist remains, not just Kádár, who is buried in a separate grave.

9. "A sírrongálók magukkal vitték Kádár János csontjait (Tomb desecrators took János Kádár's bones)," May 2, 2007, *Népszabadság Online* http://www.nol.hu.

10. For example see chapter 7 and MDF's reversal of fortune.

11. Barnabás Rácz, "Regional Voting Trends in Hungarian National Elections 1985–2002, *East European Quarterly*, 37, 4 (Winter, 2003): 449.

12. Tamás Fricz, "The Orbán Government: An Experiment in Regime Stabilization: The First Two Years (1998–2000)," *The Ideas of the Hungarian Revolution,* Lee W. Congdon and Béla K. Király, ed., *Suppressed and Victorious, 1956–1999* (New York: Columbia University Press, 2002), 398–401.

13. "Egyetlen '56 többféle üzenettel," *Népszabadság*, 3.

14. It should be noted that not all within FIDESZ are inclined to take this stance.

15. The Socialists had won the largest percentage of voters, but FIDESZ cobbled together the stronger coalition. Rácz, "Regional Voting Trends," 450–51.

16. The charge that connected Jews to the Communist accession to power is an old one. An important rationalization for anti-Semitism during the Horthy period was the connection between Jews and the Hungarian Soviet Revolution. The historian Charles Gati points to private conversations during the 1950s in which connections were made between Stalinist leaders and their Jewish origins. Interestingly, he claims that close to 75% of those intellectuals that promoted an anti-Stalinist platform prior to the Revolution also had Jewish backgrounds. Gati doesn't buy into either argument, claiming that Hungarians in general, including Hungarian Jews, did little to promote or denounce Stalinism out of self-preservation. See: Vera Ránki, *The Politics of Inclusion and Exclusion: Jews and nationalism in Hungary* (New York: Holmes & Meier, 1999), 206–8 and Charles Gati, *Failed Illusions: Moscow, Washington, Budapest, and the 1956 Hungarian Revolt* (Stanford: Stanford University Press, 2006), 133–34, respectively.

17. The historian István Rév points out charges by the right wing that the Communists had agreed to the transition in exchange for economic gain in his fine work, *Retroactive Justice: Prehistory of Post Communism* (Stanford: Stanford University

Press, 2005), 310–11. See also: Robert M. Bigler, "Back in Europe and Adjusting to the New Realities of the 1990's in Hungary," *East European Quarterly*, 30, 2 (Summer, 1996): 222–24.

18. Fricz, "The Orbán Government," 404–5, 415–16.

19. Endre Babus, "A Szent Korona rehabilitálása? (Is it the rehabilitation of the Holy Crown?)," *Heti Világgazdaság*, 37 (September 18, 1999): 107–8.

20. *Magyar Hírlap*, January 3, 2000.

21. *Népszava*, January 10, 2000.

22. Tamás Mászáros, "Jobbra Átérékelés (Re-evaluation to the right)," *168 óra*, 13, 4 (January 25, 2001): 10–11. Bárdossy's trial was conducted under the auspices of the Nuremberg Tribunal in accord with the armistice. Karl P. Benziger, "The Trial of László Bárdossy: The Second World War and Factional Politics in Hungary," *Journal of Contemporary History*, 40, 3 (July, 2005): 472–74, 477.

23. Fricz, "The Orbán Government," 416.

24. For example, Sándor Márai, *Memoir of Hungary, 1944–1948* (Budapest: Corvina, 1996, 2000), 212–13. This is also emphasized in a joke told to me by several Hungarian friends. An uncle encourages his nephew who plays the violin to join the Communist Party shortly after the establishment of the People's Republic. When the nephew returns from the interview his uncle asks if he got in. The nephew replies that he didn't and when asked why, he replies, "they asked me if I had ever played for the Arrow Cross [Hungarian fascists], to which I replied yes." The uncle exclaimed, "Why did you not deny that?" To which the nephew replies, "I couldn't, because they all were sitting there."

25. Ferenc Gyurcsány is married to Apró's granddaughter. "Vendégségben Apróéknál: A Sebestyén család már soha nem kaphatja vissza villáját (Visiting with the Aprós: The Sebestyén family will never be able to get their villa back)," *Magyar Nemzet Online*, May 24, 2007, http://www.mno.hu/print.mno?type=3&id=412735&rvt=2&t=undefined.

26. Péter Tarics, "Együtt emlékezünk, Wittner Mária: Példát kellene vennünk a lengyelekről (We will remember together, we should follow the Polish example)," *Magyar Demokrata*, 10, 2 (October 12, 2006): 92.

27. Zoltán Ripp claims that this approach can easily be connected to the hero cult of the *Pesti Srác* (young street fighters of Pest) whose memory can be constructed in contrast to the communist reformers, in "Problémák, hiányok és nézetkülönbségek 1956 történetírásában (Problems, absence and differences of viewpoints in the writing of history of 1956)," *Múltunk*, 51, 4 (2006): 106, 108.

28. Ildikó Hankó, "A Magyar Jeanne d'Arc, Te is tudod, hogy a vád hamis, csak a szent forradalmat akarják bemocskolni," (You know, too, that that accusation is fake, they just want to besmirch the holy Revolution) *Magyar Demokrata*, 10, 2 (October 12, 2006): 66.

29. A policy of lustration had not been enacted in 1989. According to Beverly A. James in her fine work, a verbal agreement had been reached at the roundtable talks that ensured there would be no retaliatory justice of this kind, in *Imagining Post Communism: Visual Narratives of Hungary's 1956 Revolution* (College Station: Texas A&M University Press, 2005), 107.

30. András Bozóki, "The Hungarian Roundtable Talks of 1989 in a Central European Comparison," *The Ideas of the Hungarian Revolution*, 252.

31. For example, György Litván, ed., The Hungarian Revolution of 1956: Reform, Revolt, and Repression 1953–1963 (London: Longman, 1996), 142, Attila Szakolczai, "Repression and Restoration, 1956–1963," *The Ideas of the Hungarian Revolution*, 179, 674, and László Eörsi, *The Hungarian Revolution of 1956: Myths and Realities*, trans. Mario D. Fenyo (New York: Columbia University Press, 2006), 163.

32. "Mansfeld Péter szobránál (At the Péter Mansfeld statue)," *Magyar Demokrata*, 10, 44 (November 2, 2006): 4.

33. Mansfeld's motives were more complicated and included breaking his brother-in-law, who had fought in the Revolution, out of prison and taking revenge for the execution of János Szabó who had led the revolutionaries at Széna Square. László Eörsi, "A széna téri felkelők fegyveres ellenállása (The Armed Resistance of the Széna Square Group)," *Rubicon*, 9 (2006): 35.

34. Mansfeld refused to be cowed by his interrogators and defended his friends claiming only he had counterrevolutionary motives in mind. László Eörsi, "Mansfeld Péter És Kultusza (Peter Mansfeld and his Cult)," *Népszbadság*, October 22, 2002, www.rev.hu/portal/page/portal/rev/tanulmanyok/1956/mansfeld.

35. László Eörsi, "Péter Mansfeld."

36. A title cast by Gyula Obersovszky who stood trial with Tóth. See Berverly A. James fine work on semiotics in post-1989 Hungary, *Imagining Post Communism,* 87.

37. László Eörsi, "Tóth Ilona, valóság és mitosz (Ilona Tóth, truth and myth)," 1956–os Magyar Forradalom, történetének Dokumentációs és Kutatóintézete Közalapítvány, http://www.rev.hu/portal/page/portal/rev/tanulmanyok/toth_ilona/eorsi_beszelo.

38. Hankó, "A Magyar Jeanne d'Árc," 67–68. Beverly James underscores the Christian symbolism connected to the Tóth legend in *Imagining Post Communism*, 91.

39. László Eörsi, "Tóth Ilona, valóság és mitosz (Ilona Tóth, truth and myth)," 1956–os Magyar Forradalom történetének Dokumentációs és Kutatóintézete Közalapítvány, http://www.rev.hu/portal/page/portal/rev/tanulmanyok/toth_ilona/eorsi_beszelo.

40. James, *Imagining Post Communism*, 108. See also chapters 2 and 6.

41. See: István Bibó, "For Freedom and Truth Proclamation," November 4, 1956, in Bibó, *Democracy, Revolution, Self Determination, Selected Writings*, 325–26.

42. According to the political scientist Andrew Arato, "Legality is always heavily challenged by demands of substantive justice by innocent victims." In the absence of an effective legal process, he points to the effectiveness of the South African Truth and Reconciliation model that established a history of human rights violations in exchange for amnesty in the aftermath of apartheid in his essay, "The Roundtables, Democratic Institutions and the Problem of Justice," *The Roundtable Talks of 1989: The Genesis of Hungarian Democracy*, András Bozóki, ed. (Budapest: Central European University Press, 2002), 229, 232–33.

43. See Jay Winter's discussion of the Abel Gance film *J'accuse* when Jean Diaz conjures the dead to prevent the outbreak of another world war in his work *Sites of*

Memory, Sites of Mourning: The Great War in European Cultural History (Cambridge: Cambridge University Press, 1995), 17.

44. Barnabás Rácz also thinks that Socialists were successful in presenting an image of a Social Democratic Party akin those found in the West. The margin of victory was razor thin with center left receiving 49.80% and center right receiving 46.19% of the vote. See: Rácz, "Regional Voting Trends in Hungarian National Elections, 1985–2002," 452–55.

45. For example see the synopsis in *168 óra*, June 27, 2002.

46. *Magyar Hírlap*, July 4, 2002.

47. "Nagy Imre emlékezek (Imre Nagy's memory)," *Népszava*, June 17, 2006, 3.

48. Zsolt Grécy, "Nagy Imre csak a balodalé? (Does Imre Nagy belong only to the left?)," *Népszabadság*, June 17, 2006, 3 and Zsolt Grécy, "Két ünnepre készül a jobboldal? (Does the right wing prepare for two celebrations?)," *Népszabadság*, June 16, 2006, 3.

49. FIDESZ MP László Kövér played on an old Hungarian saying in 1998, "You can't turn a communist dog into democratic bacon." See: György B. Nagy, "Gyurcsány harmadszor is bizalmat kapott (Gyurcsány receives a vote of confidence for a third time)," *Népszabadság*, October 7, 2006, 2.

50. See: Éva Standeisky, "56-os kérdések (Questions about 56)," *Múltunk*, 51, 4 (2006): 117 and Ripp, "Problémák," 109.

51. János Horváth, Interview by author, September 12, 2006.

52. Grécy, "Nagy Imre csak a baloldalé?"

53. For example, the proposed reduction of hospital beds, closing of hospitals, introduction of co-pays for medical visits, and the introduction of tuition in higher education. See: "Miniszteri programmorzsák,: Megkezdődtek a bizottsági meghallgatások-Slágertémák, hatósági energiaár (Ministerial program crumbs: Committee hearings began-Most popular subjects co-pay, centrally regulated energy pricing)," *Népszabadság*, June 7, 2006, 1–2.

54. In the first round FIDESZ polled 42.16% of the vote as opposed to the Socialist majority off 43.30%. The other two parties polling over 5% were the SZDSZ 6.29% and MDF 5.03%. See: "Négypárti parlament! (Four Party Parliament)," *Népszabadság Online*, April 9, 2006, http://www.nol.hu/cikk/400127 and Csaba Lukács, "Még négy nehéz év (Four more hard years)," *Magyar Nemzet Online*, April 24, 2006, http://www.mno.hu/print.mno?type=3&id=350393&rvt=114&t=undefined.

55. President Sólyom seemed to support the opposition's position saying, "There was nothing new in the content of [Gyurcsány's speech]" and claimed that the false promises made by the Socialists had created a moral crisis. As the President however, he could not request his resignation. "Morális válság Magyarországon (Moral crisis in Hungary)," *Népszabadság*, September 19, 2006, 2.

56. After the crowd was driven away from the building they attacked a monument commemorating the Soviet liberation of Budapest. "Megtámadták az MTV-t, az ellenzék sem ura a helyzetnek-Mi lesz ma (They attacked the MTV, even the opposition parties can not control the situation, what will happen today)?" *Népszava*, Septmeber 19, 2006, 1–2 and Összecsapás a tévé előtt (Riot in front of the television station)," *Népszabadság*, September 19, 2006, 1.

57. For example see: Antónia Rádi, "Ria, ria, Hungária (football slogan that rhymes with Hungary)," Heti Vilaggazdaság, 28, 38 (September 22, 2006): 10–11 and in regard to the sighting of the FIDESZ representative *Népszava*, September 19, 2006, 1. These symbols were ever present throughout the demonstrations and were available at small stands set up along the periphery of Kossuth Square.

58. Dávid Trencséni, "Vakhit (Blind belief)," *168 óra*, 18, 36 (September 7, 2006): 10–11.

59. "Orbán radikális fellépést ígér (Orbán is promising a radical platform)," *Népszabadság*, September 14, 2006, 2.

60. The FIDESZ victory at the mayoral and county level was decisive. Though SZDSZ/MSZP and MSZP candidates won mayoralties in four of Hungary's major cities, Budapest, Szeged, Miskolc, and Pécs, FIDESZ won decisive county majorities in all but Budapest and Heves county. See: *Népszava*, October 2, 2006, 1–2.

61. See: "Gyurcsány Ferenc bizalmi szavazást kér (Gyurcsány requests a vote of confidence)," and Ildikó Csuhaj, "Orbán Viktor 72 órás ultimátomot adott (Viktor Orbán issues a 72 hour ultimatum)," both in *Népszabadság*, October 3, 2006, 3.

62. "Folytathatja munkáját a kormány (The government can continue with its work)," *Népszava*, October 7, 2006, 3 and György B. Nagy, "Gyurcsány harmadszor is bizalmat kapott (Gyurcsány received a vote of confidence for a third time)," *Népszabadság*, October 7, 2006, 2.

63. Ildikó Csuhaj, "FIDESZ-Gyurcsány ne szólaljon meg az 56-os megemlékezéseken (Gyurcsány should not speak at the 56 commemorations)," *Népszabadság*, October 12, 2006, 2.

64. The demonstrators had the legal right to be on the square until October 25, so the government had to negotiate with them. The police ordered them off the square, but renewed negotiations led to an arrangement in which the demonstrators agreed to a police cordon and to maintain order. Later it was reported that they could stay with no restriction. See: "Feltételekkel maradhatnak a tüntetők (The demonstrators can stay with restrictions)," *Népszabadság*, October 19, 2006, 2 and Maradhatnak a Kossuth tériek (The Kossuth Square demonstrators can stay)," *Magyar Nemzet*, October 21, 2006, 5.

65. "Vízágyú, könnygáz és gumilövedék az utcákon (Water cannons, tear gas, rubber bullets on the street)," *Népszava*, October 24, 2006, 11.

66. For example see Gábor Kertész' picture of Gyurcsány on page 3 of *Népszava*, October 24, 2006.

67. Fireworks that took place later in the evening could only be viewed on the public television, see: Zsolt Gréczy, "Zárt kapuk mögött, méltósággal (Behind closed doors with dignity)," *Népszabadság*, October 24, 2006, 2.

68. "Refomnépszavazást kezdeményez a Fidesz (FIDESZ will initiate a reform referendum)," *Magyar Nemzet Online*, October 24, 2007, http:/www.mno.hu/print .mno?type=2&id=380010&rvt=2&t=undefined.

69. See the Árpád Kurucz photo and "Az erőszak dúlt az utcán (Violence in the streets)," *Népszabadság*, October 24, 2006, 4 and "Vízágyú (Water cannon)," *Népszava*, October 24, 2006, 11.

70. Dávid Trecséni, "Ünnep az utcán (Holiday in the streets)," *168 óra*, 28, 43 (26 October, 2006): 10. Népszava reported that the day began and ended the same way with the police dispersing demonstrators. In the middle of Orbán's speech it was learned that the police were dispersing the riot on Károly ring and some tried to leave, but were unable to do so because of the size of the crowd. "Tízezrek az Astoriánál (Tens of thousands at Astoria)," *Népszava*, October 24, 2006, pages 1 and 9, respectively. According to László Rab some thought that the crowd had been provoked but the nature of the crowd definitely changed around seven in the evening when a barricade was erected and some within the crowd appeared with baseball bats and masks. The location of the rally certainly made it hard for some at the rally trying to leave in "Csapdába csalt nagygyűlés (Entrapped Rally)," *Népszabadság*, October 24, 2006, 6. According to HetiVálasz the police were supposed to protect the FIDESZ rally from the other group, in "Erőszakspirál (Spiral of violence)," 6, 43 (October 26, 2006): 4.

71. The hymn has connections to Horthy's Christian National coalition, see chapter 2. The quiet march began with Beethoven's *Egmont Overture* and ended with the National Anthem. The organizers and volunteers ensured that no violence would come to the marchers. See: Ildikó Csuhaj, "Gerlóczy utca: FIDESZ-megálló (Gerlóczy Street: FIDESZ [bus] stop)," and Tamás Bárkay, "Szolid menet gyászzenével (Quiet march with somber music)," *Népszabadság*, November 6, 2006, 3.

72. "1956 and Hungary: The Memory of Eyewitnesses in Search of Freedom and Democracy," Conference, Italian Institute of Culture, Budapest, September 28–29, 2006.

73. "Kitüntetések az évfordulón (Honors on the anniversary)," *Népszabadság*, October 22, 2006, 7.

74. János M. Rainer, "56-os kérdések (questions of 56)," *Múltunk*, 51, 4 (2006): 97.

75. Márai, *Memoir of Hungary*, 397.

76. Gati, *Failed Illusions*, 131, 143.

77. Éva Standeisky echoed these sentiments in her article commenting that the "youth find it [56] a boring theme," associating it with an older generation, politics, and the media. She sees little chance of getting them interested engaging the present with the past in "56-os kérdések," 119.

78. As I was in the process of completing the manuscript it came to my attention that Katalin Jánosi, Nagy's granddaughter, has invited the members of all of the major political factions to the Nagy villa to participate in a common prayer followed by quiet talk on June 15, 2007. Though Viktor Orbán will not attend he will send a representative, PM László Kövér, in his stead. Only the KDNP will not attend the event. One wonders if this represents the beginning of some kind of reconciliation with the past for those in the political spectrum. See: "Nagy Imre unokája közös imára hívja a pártelnököket (Imre Nagy's granddaughter is inviting the Party chairs for a common prayer)," *Népszabadság Online*, June 8, 2007 online@nepszabadsag.hu, June 14, 2007, "Nem imádkozik Gyurcsánnyal és Kókával Orbán és Semjén (Orbán and Semjén will not pray with Gyurcsány and Kóka)," *Magyar Nemzet Online*, June 2, 2007, http://www.mno.hu/print.mno?type=3&id=414113&rvt=2&t=undefined, June 14, 2007.

Appendix A

THE NATIONAL VERSE SÁNDOR PETŒFI: NEMZETI DAL PEST, MARCH 13, 1848[1]

Petőfi's National Verse is a stirring call to arms written in the first days of the Hungarian rebellion against the Hapsburg monarchy. The first two verses provide an example of the sentiment exuded in the poem.

> Talpra Magyar, hi a haza!
> Itt az idő, most vagy soha!
> Rabok legyünk, vagy szabadok?
> Ez a kérdés, válasszatok!
> A magyarok istenére esküszünk,
> Esküszünk, hogy rabok tovább nem leszünk!

> Rise Hungarians, the homeland is calling!
> This is the time, now or never!
> Shall we be prisoners or free?
> This is the question to choose!
> We swear to the Hungarian God,
> We will not be held prisoners anymore!

> Rabok voltunk mostanáig,
> Kárhozottak ősapaink.
> Kik szabadon éltek-haltak,
> Szolgaföldben nem nyughatnak.
> A magyarok istenére esküszünk,
> Esküszünk, hogy rabok tovább nem leszünk!

We have been prisoners, damned.
Our ancestors who lived and died freely,
Can not rest in the earth of servants.
We swear to the Hungarian God.
We will not be held prisoners anymore.

NOTE

1. *Petőfi, Sándor Összes költeményei, II kötet* (The Collected Poems of Sándor Petőfi) (Budapest: Szépirodalmi könyvkiadó, 1978) 331.

Appendix B

THE HUNGARIAN NATIONAL ANTHEM FERENC KÖLCSEY: HIMNUSZ CSEKE, JANUARY 22, 1823

At official national celebrations in Hungary, only the first verse is sung. The Himnusz recounts the glories of the Hungarian past, but then places the misfortunes of Hungary in stark contrast that include the occupation and devastation by the Mongols and the Turks. The then current occupation by the Hapsburgs was obliquely referred to by the castles that had been destroyed by the Hapsburgs after the unsuccessful Rakóczi Rebellion, 1704–1711. The Himnusz finishes with a plea for God's mercy on the nation.

Isten, áldd meg a magyart jó kedvvel, bőséggel,
Nyújts feléje védő kart, ha küzd ellenséggel.
Balsors akit régen tép, hozz rá vig esztendőt,
Megbünhödte már e nép a múltat s jövendőt.

God bless the Hungarian with happiness, wealth,
Extend a protecting arm towards them, when they fight with the enemy.
Misfortune has punished them for a long time,
This nation has been penalized for the past and future.

Appendix C

MAJOR POLITICAL PARTIES[†]

MSZMP (Hungarian Socialist Workers Party) was established on October 30, 1956 to replace the **MDP** (Hungarian Workers Party) branded as illegitimate by the Revolutionaries and the Nagy government.

MSZP (Hungarian Socialist Party) was established in October 1989 and represented the triumph of the reform faction within the MSZMP to break with the communists and their desire to create a Party more in accord with democratic socialists in Europe.

In opposition in 1989:

FIDESZ (Alliance of Young Democrats) was created in March 1988 by students from Law and Economic departments from universities across Hungary to oppose the hegemony of KISZ (League of Communist Youth). Initially interested in educational reforms that would foster political change their agenda developed into a robust demand for a democratic state.

FKgP (Independent Smallholders Party) was the governing party of Hungary following their sweeping victory over the communists in fall 1945. As recounted in chapter three the Party was co-opted and destroyed by the communists, returning to the political scene only in 1988. Their democratic agenda included strong nationalist sentiments. Their origins as a Peasant's Party provided them with a rural base.

KDNP (Christian Democratic Party) was one of the historic parties having roots that go back to the early twentieth century that was persecuted and then marginalized by the communists. They forwarded a conservative Christian democratic agenda for Hungary.

MDF (Hungarian Democratic Forum) was founded in September 1987. They were a coalition of thinkers and politicians that included reform communists, populists, and nationalists. They strongly forwarded the establishment of a multiparty state and emerged as the most powerful coalition party in 1989.

SZDSZ (Alliance of Free Democrats) began as an underground movement focusing on human rights. They maintained a strong connection with Solidarity in Poland and the Charter 77 group in Prague. Organized in the spring of 1988 as the Free Initiative Network that included veterans of the 1956 Revolution, environmentalists, and economic reform they established themselves as a Party in November of that same year.

NOTE

† Please note that I am providing brief descriptions of the parties described in this chapter and chapter 7. For a full account of the Parties involved in the negotiations consult the sources I have used for this appendix in full. See: András Bozóki, "Democracy Across the Negotiating Table," *The New Hungarian Quarterly*, 33 (Spring, 1992): 59, Rudolf L. Tőkés, *Hungary's Negotiated Revolution: Economic Reform, Social Change, and Political Succession* (Cambridge: Cambridge University Press, 1996) 308–314, 374, András Bozóki and Gergely Karácsony, "The Making of a Political Elite: Participants in the Hungarian Roundtable Talks of 1989,"*The Roundtable Talks of 1989: The Genesis of Hungarian Democracy*, András Bozoki, ed. (Budapest: Central European University Press, 2002) 72–74, 77–78, 82–92, and Imre Pozsgay, *1989: Politikus-pálya a pártállamban és rendszerváltásban* (Political career in the party state and in the regime change) (Budapest: Püski Kiadó Kft., 1993) 186.

Bibliography

There are many reasons for the political changes that swept dramatically over Hungary in 1989 and led to establishment of the Republic of that same year. The changes that led to the dissolution of the Soviet empire certainly hastened the disintegration of communism inside Hungary. Linked inexorably to this story of political transition are the stories from the past that included Imre Nagy and the 1956 Revolution.

The study of the negotiations that established the Republic of Hungary have been well told, for example: András Bozóki, ed., *The Roundtable Talks of 1989: The Genesis of Hungarian Democracy* (Budapest: Central European University Press, 2002), Rudolph L. Tőkés, *Hungary's Negotiated Revolution: Economic Reform, Social Change, and Political Succession* (Cambridge: Cambridge University Press, 1996), and Béla K. Király and András Bozóki ed., *Lawful Revolution in Hungary, 1989–1994* (New York: Columbia University Press, 1995). Likewise excellent accounts of the history of the 1956 Revolution abound in essay and document collections such as: Csaba Békés, Malcolm Byrne, and János M. Rainer, ed., *The 1956 Hungarian Revolution: A History in Documents* (Budapest Central European University Press, 2002), Zoltán Ripp, *Ötvenhat októbere és a hatalom: A Magyar Dolgozók Pártja vezető testületeinek dokumentumai 1956, október 24–október 28* (October '56 and the power: The documents of the Hungarian Worker's Party Leadership) (Budapest: Napvilág kiadó, 1997), and György Litván, ed., *The Hungarian Revolution of 1956: Reform, Revolt, and Repression* (London: Longman, 1996) among others. The Hungarian Revolution set in an international context has been well revealed in Johanna C. Granville, *The First Domino: International Decision Making During the Hungarian Crisis of 1956* (College Station: Texas A & M Press, 2004) and Ignác Romsics, ed., *20th Century Hungary and the Great Powers* (New York: Columbia University Press, 1995).

The recent publication of Nagy's diaries and letters written while he was imprisoned in Snagov, Romania found in István Vida, ed., *Nagy Imre Snagovi jegyzetek: Gondolatok, emlékezések 1956–1957* (Notes from Snagov: Thoughts, memories) (Budapest: Gondolat Kiadó-Nagy Imre Alapítvány, 2006) provides an invaluable resource to scholars and helps further illuminate Nagy's thoughts regarding the Revolution and his confrontation with the Stalinist faction of the Hungarian Communist Party found in his published compilation of essays entitled, *On Communism: In Defense of the New Course* (London: Thames and Hudson, 1957). János M. Rainer's two volume biography of Imre Nagy remains unsurpassed in its detailed examination of Nagy's life, *Nagy Imre: Politikai Életrajz, I*, 1896–1953 (Imre Nagy: A Political Biography 1896–1953, I) (Budapest: 1956-os Intézet, 1986) and *Nagy Imre 1953–1958, II* (Budapest: 1956-os Intézet, 1999). Alajos Dornbach's fine work entitled *The Secret Trial of Imre Nagy* (Westport: Praeger, 1994) provides essential documents and details the process of juridical murder carried out by the state against Nagy, further underscoring the importance placed on damning Nagy and his associates outlined in the official White Paper offered by the Kádár regime.

Several fine biographies of Nagy's nemesis János Kádár have been published recently. In addition to Tibor Huszár's magnificent two volume biography entitled, *Kádár János: Politikai Életrajz* (János Kádár: A Political Biography) (Budapest: Szabad Tér-Kossuth, 2001, 2003), *Kádár: A hatalom évei, 1956–1989* (Kádár: The years in power, 1956–1989) (Budapest: Corvina Kiadó kft., 2006) provides deep insight into Kádár's thoughts and actions based on a wide array of documentary evidence. Likewise Roger Gough's single volume *A Good Comrade: János Kádár, Communism and Hungary* (London: I.B. Tauris, 2006) gives us an excellent account of Kádár's rise to power in the treacherous waters of communist politics. Both authors examine Kádár's relationship to Nagy and his motives regarding Nagy's demise. Importantly, they shed more light regarding Kádár's compromise with the Hungarian people following his brutal five-year terror.

The historian István Rév's insightful monograph, *Retroactive Justice: Prehistory of Post-Communism* (Stanford: Stanford University Press, 2005), is closer to my study and investigates many of the deceased actors of the later half of the twentieth century whose phantoms continue to haunt the present as a way of understanding how history has been written to accommodate or deny their impact over time. A wonderful review of the Revolution and the significance of its ideas can be found in Lee W. Congdon and Béla K. Király ed., *The Ideas of the Hungarian Revolution, Suppressed and Victorious 1956–1999* (New York: Columbia University Press, 2002). What follows is a selected list of secondary and primary sources that informed this study:

BOOKS, ARTICLES, AND CHAPTERS

A Magyar Nyelv Értelmező Szótára (Etymological dictionary of the Hungarian language). Edited by the Nyelvtudományi Intézet. Budapest: Akadémia Kiadó, 1987.

Agócs, S. "The Collapse of Communist Ideology in Hungary." *East European Quarterly*, 27 (1992): 190.

Anderson, Benedict, *Imagined Communities: Reflections on the Origin and Spread of Nationalism*. New York: Verso, 1991.

Arato, Andrew. "The Roundtables, Democratic Institutions and the Problem of Justice." Pp. 229, 232–23 in *The Roundtable Talks of 1989: The Genesis of Hungarian Democracy*, edited by András Bozóki. Budapest: Central European Press, 2002.

Auge, Marc. *Oblivion*. Translated by M. de Jager. Minneapolis: University of Minnesota Press, 2004.

Barany, George. "Epilogue, 1985–1990." P. 401 in *A History of Hungary*, edited by Peter F. Sugar, Péter Hanák, and Tibor Frank. Bloomington: Indiana University Press, 1994.

Békés, Csaba. "Back to Europe: The International Background of the Political Transition in Hungary, 1988–1990." Pp. 242–45 in *The Roundtable Talks of 1989: The Genesis of Hungarian Democracy*, edited by András Bozóki. Budapest: Central European University Press, 2002.

Benziger, Karl P. "The Funeral of Imre Nagy: Contested History and the Power of Memory Culture." *History and Memory* 12, 2 (Fall/Winter, 2000): 152–53.

———. "Imre Nagy, Martyr of the Nation: Contested History and Social Cohesion." *East European Quarterly*, 36, 2 (June, 2002): 171–90.

———, "The Trial of László Bárdossy: The Second World War and Factional Politics in Contemporary Hungary." *Journal of Contemporary History* 40, 3 (July, 2005): 467–68, 477.

Berecz, János. *Counter Revolution in Hungary: Words and Weapons*. Budapest: Akadémia Kiadó, 1986.

Bibó, István. *Democracy, Revolution, Self-Determination: Selected Writings*. Edited by Károly Nagy and Translated by András Boros-Kazai. New York: Columbia University Press, 1991.

Bigler, Robert M. "Back in Europe and Adjusting to the New Realities of the 1990's in Hungary." *East European Quarterly*, 30, 2 (Summer, 1996): 222–24.

Bodnar, John. "Public Memory in an American City: Commemoration in Cleveland." P. 75 in *Commemorations: The Politics of National Memory*, edited by John R. Gillis. Princeton: Princeton University Press, 1994.

Borhi, László. "Soviet Expansionism or American Imperialism?" In *Twentieth Century Hungary and the Great Powers* edited by Ignác Romsics. New York: Columbia University Press, 1995.

———. *Hungary in the Cold War 1945–1956: Between the United States and the Soviet Union*. Budapest: Central European University Press, 2004.

Bozóki, András. "Hungary's Road to Systematic Change: The Opposition Roundtable." Pp. 80, 85–87 in *Lawful Revolution in Hungary, 1989–1994* edited by Béla K. Király and András Bozóki. New York: Columbia University Press, 1995.

———. "The Hungarian Roundtable Talks of 1989 in a Central European Comparison." P. 252 in *The Roundtable Talks of 1989: The Genesis of Hungarian Democracy*, edited by András Bozóki. Budapest: Central European University Press, 2002.

Bozóki, András and Karácsony, Gergely. "The Making of a Political Elite: Participants in the Hungarian Roundtable Talks of 1989." Pp. 192–93 in *The Roundtable Talks of 1989: The Genesis of Hungarian Democracy* edited by András Bozóki. Budapest: Central European University Press, 2002.

Braham, Randolph L. "An Assault on Hungarian Memory: Hungarian Nationalists and the Holocaust." *East European Quarterly*, 33, 4 (Winter, 1999): 411, 416.

Burcur, Maria. "Birth of a Nation: Commemorations of December 1, 1918, and National Identity in Twentieth Century Romania." P. 289 in *Staging the Past: The*

Politics of Commemoration in Hapsburg Central Europe, 1848 to the Present, edited by Maria Burcur and Nancy M. Wingfield. West Lafayette, Indiana: Purdue University Press, 2001.

Cohen, Stephen F. *Bukharin and the Bolshevik Revolution: A Political Biography 1888–1938*. New York: Alfred A. Knopf, 1973.

Cooper, L. and Kinesei, A. *Hungarians in Transition*. New York: McFarland and Co., Inc., 1993.

Csicsery-Rónay, István. "Csillagos órak: a kommunisták kétszeres veresége" (Starry hours: the double defeat of the communists). P. 120 in *Tiltott történelmünk 1945–1947* (Our forbidden history) edited by János Horvath. Budapest: Századvég Kiadó.

Deák, István. *The Lawful Revolution: Louis Kossuth and the Hungarians 1848–1849*. New York: Columbia University Press, 1979.

———. "A Fatal Compromise? The Debate Over Collaboration and Resistance in Hungary." P. 48 in *The Politics of Retribution in Europe: World War II and its Aftermath* edited by István Deák, Jan T. Gross, Tony Judt. Princeton: Princeton University Press, 2000.

Deme, László. "Liberal Nationalism in Hungary, 1988–1990." *East European Quarterly*, 32, 1 (Spring, 1998): 63–64.

Dienstag, Joshua Foa. "The Pozsgay Affair: Historical Memory and Political Legitimacy." *History and Memory*, 8, 1 (Spring/Summer, 1996): 57, 61.

Dudziak, Mary L. *Cold War Civil Rights: Race and the Image of American Democracy*. Princeton: Princeton University Press, 2000.

Durkheim, Emile. *The Elementary Forms of the Religious Life*. Translated by Joseph Ward Swain. New York: The Free Press, 1965.

Ekiert, Grzegorz. *The State Against Society: Political Crises and Their Aftermath in East Central Europe*. Princeton: Princeton University Press, 1996.

Ember, Judit. *Menedékjog* (Right of Asylum). Budapest: Szabadtér Kiadó, 1989.

Eörsi, László. "A széna téri felkelők fegyveres ellenállása" (The Armed Resistance of the Széna Square Group). *Rubicon*, 9 (2006): 35.

Faludy, George. *My Happy Days in Hell*, 6th ed. Trans. Kathleen Szász. Budapest: Forever Kiadó, 2002.

Fehér, Ferenc and Heller, Ágnes. *Hungary 1956 Revisited: The Message of a Revolution, A Quarter of a Century Later*. London: Allen and Unwin, 1983.

Feitl, István. "Szembesülés: Az MDP vezetői és a XX Kongresszus" (Facing [the facts]: The Leaders of the Hungarian Worker's Party and the 20th Congress). *Múltunk*, 51, 2 (2006): 224, 226.

Felkay, Andrew. "Hungary and the Soviet Union in the Kádár Era." Pp. 274, 276, 279 in *20th Century Hungary and the Great Powers* edited by Ignác Romsics. New York: Columbia University Press, 1995.

Ferge, Zsuzsa. *A Society in the Making*. New York: M. E. Sharpe Inc., 1979.

Foucault, Michel. *Discipline and Punish*. New York: Vintage Books, 1977.

Freifeld, Alice. *Nationalism and the Crowd in Liberal Hungary, 1848–1914*. Baltimore: The Johns Hopkins University Press, 2000.

———. "The Cult of March 15: Sustaining the Hungarian Myth of Revolution, 1849–1999." Pp. 264–76 in *Staging the Past: The Politics of Commemoration in Hapsburg Central Europe, 1848 to the Present*, edited by Maria Burcur and Nancy M. Wingfield. West Lafayette, Indiana: Purdue University Press, 2001.

Fricz, Tamás. "The Orbán Government: An Experiment in Regime Stabilization: The First Two Years (1998–2000)." Pp. 398–401, 404–5, 415–16 in *The Ideas of the Hungarian Revolution, Suppressed and Victorious, 1956–1999*, edited by Lee W. Congdon and Béla K. Király. New York: Columbia University Press, 2002.

Friedlander, Saul, "A Conflict of Memories? The New German Debates About the Final Solution," Leo Baeck Memorial Lecture 31. New York: Leo Baeck Institute, 1988.

———. *Memory, History, and the Extermination of the Jews in Europe*. Bloomington: Indiana University Press, 1993.

———. *The Years of Extermination: Nazi Germany and the Jews, 1939–1945*. New York: Harper Collins Publishers, 2007.

Gati, Charles. *Hungary and the Soviet Bloc*. Durham: Duke University Press, 1986.

———. "From Liberation to Revolution, 1945–1956." Pp. 352, 369, 371–72, 378 in *A History of Hungary* edited by Péter F. Sugar, Peter Hanák, Tibor Frank. Bloomington: Indiana University Press, 1994.

———. *Failed Illusions: Moscow, Washington, Budapest, and the Hungarian Revolt*. Stanford: Stanford University Press, 2006.

Geertz, Cliffod. *Local Knowledge: Further Essays in Interpretive Anthropology*. New York: Basic Books, 1983.

Gerő, András. *Modern Hungarian Society in the Making: The Unfinished Experience*. Budapest: Central European University Press, 1995.

Glatz, Ferenc. "Multiparty System in Hungary, 1989–1994." P. 22 in *Lawful Revolution in Hungary, 1989–1994*, edited by Béla K. Király and András Bozóki. New York: Columbia University Press, 1995.

Granville, Johanna C. "Tito and the Nagy Affair." *East European Quarterly*, 32, 1 (Spring, 1998): 41.

Gyapay, Gábor. "Some Current Issues in Hungarian History Teaching." *History Teaching in Central and East European Countries*, 2 (April–June, 1996): 39–40.

Györkei, Jenő. "A Spanyolországi Rajk-Ügy" (The Rajk case from Spain). *Múltunk* 41, 40 (1996): 150–51, 159.

Hajdú, Tibor. "The Party did Everything For You." *The Hungarian Quarterly* 37 (Spring, 1996): 86.

Hajdú, Tibor, Nagy, Zsuzsa L. "Revolution, Counterrevolution, Consolidation." Pp. 308–12 in *A History of Hungary* edited by Peter F. Sugar, Péter Hanák, Tibor Frank. Bloomington: Indiana University Press, 1994.

Halbwachs, Maurice. *On Collective Memory*. Translated and edited by Lewis A. Coser. Chicago: Chicago University Press, 1992.

Hanák, Péter, "A nemzeti identitás konstrukciója" (The structure of national identity). *Európai Szemle*, 3. (October, 1997): 66–67.

Hegedűs, András, B. *A Történelem és a Hatalom Igézetében* (Within the Facination of History and Power). Budapest: Kossuth Kiadó, 1988.

"History, Democracy, and Citizenship: The Debate over Citizenship and Patriotism." Organization of American Historians, 2004. http://www.oah.org/reports/tradhist .html

Hodos, George H. *Show Trials: Stalinist Purges in Eastern Europe, 1948–1954*. New York: Praeger, 1987.

Horváth, Miklós. "Soviet Aggression Against Hungary in 1956." Pp. 70–76, 80, 85, 87 in *The Ideas of the Hungarian Revolution, Suppressed and Victorious 1956–1999*. Lee W. Congdon and Béla K. Király ed. New York: Columbia University Press, 2002.

Hubai, László. "A korlátozott polgári demokrácia politikai rendszere Magyarországon: 1945–1947" (The political system of the limited civic democracy in Hungary). P. 59 in *Tiltott történelmünk, 1945–1947* (Our prohibited history, 1945–1947) edited by János Horváth. Budapest: Századvég Kiadó, 2006.

Hutton, Patrick J. "Sigmund Freud and Maurice Halbwachs: The Problem of Memory in Historical Psychology." *The History Teacher* 27, 2 (February, 1994): 149–50.

James, Beverly A. *Imagining Post Communism: Visual Narratives of Hungary's 1956 Revolution*. College Station: Texas A & M University Press, 2005.

Jarausch, Konrad H. *The Rush to German Unity*. Oxford: Oxford University Press, 1994.

Jeszenszky, Géza. "Hungary through World War I and the end of the Dual Monarchy." P. 270 in *A History of Hungary* edited by Peter F. Sugar, Péter Hanák, Tibor Frank. Bloomington: Indiana University Press, 1994.

Jonás, Paul. "The Hungarian Economy in Transition." Pp. 478–79 in *The First War Between Socialist States: The Hungarian Revolution and Its Impact* edited by Béla K. Király, Barbara Lotze, and Nándor Dreisziger. New York: Brooklyn College Press, 1984.

Joseph, Peniel E., "Waiting for the Midnight Hour: Reconceptualizing the Heroic Period of the Civil Rights Movement," *Souls* (Spring, 2000): 8.

Kadarkay, Árpád. *George Lukács: Life, Thought, and Politics*. Cambridge: Basil Blackwell Inc., 1991.

Kenez, Peter. *Hungary from the Nazis to the Soviets: The Establishment of the Communist Regime in Hungary, 1944–1948*. Cambridge: Cambridge University Press, 2006.

Király, Béla K. "The Hungarian Revolution and Soviet Readiness to Wage War Against Socialist States." Pp. 3–6, 8, 14–16, 18–23, 28–30 in *The First War Between Socialist States: The Hungarian Revolution of 1956 And Its Impact* Béla K. Király et. al., ed. New York: Brooklyn College Press, 1984.

——. "Soviet Aggression against Hungary in 1956." Pp. 67–69 in *The First War Between Socialist States: The Hungarian Revolution of 1956 And Its Impact* Béla K. Király ed. New York: Brooklyn College Press, 1984.

——. "An Abortive and the First Real War." Pp. 53 in *The Ideas of the Hungarian Revolution Suppressed and Victorious, 1956–1999*. Lee W. Congdon and Béla K. Király ed. New York: Columbia University Press, 2002.

Kis, János. *Politics in Hungary: For a Democratic Alternative*. New York: Columbia University Press, 1989.

———. "Between Reform and Revolution: Three Hypotheses About the Nature of Regime Change." Pp. 41, 45 in *Lawful Revolution in Hungary, 1989–1994*, edited by Béla K. Király and András Bozóki. New York: Columbia University Press, 1995.

Kornai, János. "The Dilemmas of Hungarian Economic Policy." P. 338 in *Lawful Revolution in Hungary, 1989–1994*, edited by Béla K. Király and András Bozóki. New York: Columbia University Press, 1995.

Kovács, Nóra. "Kopjafas: The anthropological deconstruction of Hungarian grave posts as national monuments." Master's Thesis: Central European University, 1997.

Kramer, Mark. "The Soviet Union and the 1956 Crisis in Hungary and Poland: Reassessments and New Findings." *Journal of Contemporary History*, 33, 3 (April, 1998): 169, 172–74, 182–83, 185, 207.

Krassó, György. "The Memory of the Dead." *Survey*, 28, 2 (Summer, 1984): 135, 151.

Kunt, Ernő, *Temetők az Aggteleki-karszt falvaiban* (Village Cemeteries in the Aggtelek-karszt region). Debrecen: Alföldi Nyomda, 1978.

La Capra, Dominick, "Revisiting the Historian's Debate: Mourning and Genocide." *History and Memory* 9, 1/2 (Fall, 1997): 80–84, 104–6.

La Feber, Walter. *America, Russia, and the Cold War, 1945–2000*. Boston: McGraw Hill, 2002.

Laquer, Walter. *Europe in Our Time*. New York: Penguin Books, 1992.

Lemert, Charles. *Durkheim's Ghosts: Cultural Logics and Social Things*. Cambridge: Cambridge University Press, 2006.

Lipsett, Seymour Martin. *First New Nation*. New York: W.W. Norton and Company, 1960.

Lomax, Bill. *Hungarian Worker's Councils in 1956*. New York: Columbia University Press, 1990.

Ludanyi, Andrew. "Programmed Amnesia and Rude Awakening." Pp. 318, 321–24 in *20th Century Hungary and the Great Powers* edited by Ignác Romsics. New York: Columbia University Press, 1995.

Lukacs, John. *Budapest 1900*. New York: Grove Weidenfeld, 1988.

Lukes, Igor. "The Rudolf Slánsk? Affair." *Slavic Review* 58, 1 (Spring, 1999): 166–72.

Macartney, C.A. *October Fifteenth*. Edinburgh: The Edinburgh University Press, 1961.

Maier, Charles S. *The Unmasterable Past, History, Holocaust, and German National Identity*. Cambridge: Harvard University Press, 1988.

———, "Immoral Equivalence: Revisiting the Nazi Past for the Kohl Era." Pp. 38–39, 42 in *Reworking the Past: Hitler, The Holocaust, and the Historian's Debate*, edited by Peter Baldwin. Boston: Beacon Press, 1990.

Márai, Sándor. *Memoir of Hungary, 1944–1948*. Translated by Albert Tezla. Budapest: Corvina, 2000.

Masát, Ádám. "Beyond the One-party System: The Debate on "The Party Law." P.151, 153 in *The Roundtable Talks of 1989: The Genesis of Hungarian Democracy*, edited by András Bozóki. Budapest: Central European University Press, 2002.

Mason, John. Hungary's Battle for Memory." *History Today* 50, 3 (March, 2000): 28–34.

Mindszenty, József Cardinal. *Memoirs*. Translated by Richard and Clara Winston. New York: Macmillan Publishing Co., 1974.

Mink, András. "Keresztény Politikai Pártok és az 1956-os Forradalom" (Christian Political Parties and the 1956 Revolution). Pp.151–52 in *Pártok 1956: Válogatás 1956-os pártvezetők visszaemlékezéseiből* (Selection from the memories of 1956 Leaders), Zsuzsanna Kőrösi and Péter Pál Tóth, ed. Budapest: 1956-os Intézet, 1997.

Murányi, Gábor. "Második helyben futás/Törvények Nagy Imréről" (Running in place for a second time/Bills about Imre Nagy). *Heti Világgazdaság*, 12 (March, 1996): 94, 96.

Nash, Gary B., Crabtree, Carlotte, Dunn, Ross E. *History on Trial: Culture Wars and the Teaching of the Past*. New York: Alfred K. Knopf, 1997.

Némethné Dikán, Nóra, Szabó, Róbert, Vida, István. "Egyetemisták és főiskolások Követelései: 1956 Októberében" (The demands of the University and College Students in October 1956). *Múltunk*, 48, 4 (2003): 282, 289–90.

Olick, Jeffrey K. and Robbins, Joyce. "Social Memory Studies: From 'Collective Memory' to the Historical Sociology of Mnemonic Practices." *Annual Review of Sociology* 24 (1998): 109.

Pető, Andrea. *Rajk Júlia*. Budapest: Balassi Kiadó, 2001.

Pozsgay, Imre. *1989: Politikus-pálya a pártállamban és a rendszerváltásban* (1989: A politician's career in the Party-state and transition). Budapest: Püski Kiadó Kft., 1993.

Rabinbach, Anson, "The Jewish Question in the German Question." Pp. 21–25 in Reworking the Past: Hitler, The Holocaust, and the Historian's Debate, edited by Peter Baldwin. Boston: Beacon Press, 1990.

Rácz, Barnabás. "Regional Voting Trends in Hungarian National Elections 1985–2002." *East European Quarterly*, 37, 4 (Winter, 2003): 446, 449–55.

Rainer, János M. "A Progress of Ideas: The Hungarian Revolution of 1956." Pp. 16, 20–21, 24–27 in *The Ideas of the Hungarian Revolution, Suppressed and Victorious 1956–1999*. Lee W. Congdon, Béla K. Király ed. New York: Columbia University Press, 2002.

———. "Regime Change and the Tradition of 1956." P. 219 in *The Roundtable Talks of 1989: The Genesis of Hungarian Democracy*, edited by András Bozóki. Budapest: Central European University Press, 2002.

———. "Magyarország és a világ-1956 (2001)" (Hungary and the World-1956). Pp. 153–57 in *Civil történelem: A Történelemtanárok Egyletének 15 Éve* (Civil history: 15 Years of the Association of Hungarian History Teachers). Budapest: Történelemtanárok Egylete, 2005.

———. "56-os kérdések" (Questions about 56). *Múltunk*, 51, 4 (2006): 97.

Ránki, Vera. *The Politics of Inclusion and Exclusion: Jews and Nationalism in Hungary*. New York: Holmes and Meier, 1999.

Rév, István. "Covering History." Getty Conference, "Memory, History, Narrative: A Comparative Inquiry into the Representation of Crisis. Hamburg, Germany, July 3–5, 1977.

———. "Parallel Autopsies." *Representations* 49. (Winter, 1995): 22, 31.

Ripp, Zoltán. "Unity and Division: The Opposition Roundtable and Its Relationship to the Communist Party." Pp. 13–14, 25–26, 30–33 in *The Roundtable Talks of 1989: The Genesis of Hungarian Democracy*, edited by András Bozóki. Budapest: Central European University Press, 2002.

———. "Problémák, hiányok és nézetkülönbségek 1956 történetírásában" (Problems, absence and differences of viewpoints in the writing of history of 1956). *Múltunk*, 51, 4 (2006): 106, 108–9.

Romsics, Ignác. "The First Four Years of Democratic Transformation." Pp. 315, 344–45 in *The Ideas of the Hungarian Revolution, Suppressed and Victorious 1956–1999*, edited by Lee W. Congdon and Béla K. Király. New York: Columbia University Press, 2002.

Rosenzweig, Roy, Thelen, David. *The Presence of the Past: Popular Uses of History in American Life*. New York: Columbia University Press, 1998.

Rothschild, Joseph. *Return to Diversity: A Political History of East Central Europe Since World War II, 2d ed.* Oxford: Oxford University Press, 1993.

Sakmyster, Thomas. *Admiral on Horseback: Miklós Horthy, 1918–1944*. Boulder: East European Monographs, 1994.

Sánta, Ilona, ed. *Politikus-Pályák* (Political Careers). Budapest: Kossuth Könyvkiadó, 1984.

Schöpflin, George. *Politics in Eastern Europe*. Oxford: Blackwell Publishers, 1993.

Schwartz, Barry. *Abraham Lincoln and the Forge of National Memory*. Chicago: University of Chicago Press, 2000.

Shawcross, William. *Crime and Compromise: János Kádár and the Politics of Hungary Since Revolution*. New York: E. P. Dutton and Co., 1974.

Somogyi, Éva, "The Age of Neoabsolutism, 1849–1867." P. 251 in *A History of Hungary*, edited by Peter F. Sugar, Péter Hanák, Tibor Frank. Bloomington: Indiana University Press, 1994.

Sophocles. *Antigone*. Edited by David Greene and Richard Latimore. Chicago: University Press of Chicago, 1960.

Standeisky, Éva. "56-os kérdések" (Questions about 56). *Múltunk*, 51, 4 (2006): 117, 119.

Stark, Tamás. *Hungarian Jews during the Holocaust and after the Second World War, 1939–1949: A Statistical Review*. Boulder: East European Monographs, 2000.

Stumpf, Iván. "Evolution of Political Parties and the 1990 Parliamentary Elections." P. 110 in *Lawful Revolution in Hungary, 1990–94*, edited by Béla K. Király and András Bozóki. New York: Columbia University Press, 1995.

Szabolcs, Ottó. "Történelemtanítás tegnap és ma" (History teaching yesterday and today). P. 28 in *Történelem Metodikai Műhely Tanulmányok* (History method workshop), edited by László Molnár. Budapest: Tárogató Kiadó, 1996.

Szakács, Sándor. "From 'Goulash Communism' to Breakdown." Pp. 195–97, 200–202, 205–7, 209, 211 in *The Ideas of the Hungarian Revolution, Suppressed and Victorious, 1956–1999* edited by Lee W. Congdon and Béla K. Király. New York: Columbia University Press, 2002.

Szakolczai, Attila. "Repression and Restoration, 1956–1963." Pp. 170–72, 179, 185–86, 204 in *The Ideas of the Hungarian Revolution, Suppressed and Victorious 1956–1999*. New York: Columbia University Press, 2002.

Szamuely, László. "The Costs of Transformation in Central and Eastern Europe." *The Hungarian Quarterly*, 37 (Winter, 1996): 67.

Szász, Béla. *Volunteers for the Gallows*. New York: W.W. Norton and Company, Inc., 1971.

Szebenyi, Péter. "Crossfire of Debates, History Teaching-The Volcano of Hungarian Schooling." *Studies in Education Evaluation*, 18 (1992): 102.

Szelényi, Szonja, Szelényi, Iván, and Poster, Winifred R. "Interests and Symbols in Post-Communist Political Culture: The Case of Hungary." *American Sociological Review*, 61, 3 (June, 1996): 469–72, 475.

Szilágyi, Zsófia. "For Hungarians, Memories of 1956 Lose Significance." *Transition*, 23, 2 (November 15, 1996): 38–39.

Szőke, Domonkos. "1945 szabad választás-szabad választás?" (1945 free elections-free elections?). Pp. 26, 40–42 in *Tiltott történelmünk 1945–1947* (Our prohibited history) edited by János Horváth. Budapest: Századvég Kiadó, 2006.

Temetési Szertartáskönyv (Funeral liturgy of the Hungarian Catholic Church). Budapest: Az Apostoli Szentszék Könyvkiadója, 1982.

Tilkovsky, Loránd. "The Late Interwar Years and World War II." P. 341 in *A History of Hungary* edited by Péter F. Sugar, Peter Hanák, Tibor Frank. Bloomington: Indiana University Press, 1994.

Tóka, Gábor. "Parties and their Voters in 1990 and 1994." Pp. 142–43 in *Lawful Revolution in Hungary, 1989–1994*, edited by Béla K. Király and András Bozóki. New York: Columbia University Press, 1995.

Turner, Victor Witter. *The Ritual Process: Structure and Anti-Structure*. New York: Aldine De Gruyter, 1969.

Tyson, Timothy B., *Radio Free Dixie: Robert F. Williams and the Roots of Black Power*. Chapel Hill: University of North Carolina Press, 1999.

Ungvári, Miklós. "Culture and Crisis: The Pains of Transition." P. 285 in *Lawful Revolution in Hungary, 1989–1994*, edited by Béla K. Király and András Bozóki. New York: Columbia University Press, 1995.

Ungváry, Krisztián. *Battle for Budapest: 100 Days in World War II*. Translated by Ladislaus Löb. London: I.B. Tauris and Co. Ltd., 2005.

Verdery, Katherine. *The Political Lives of Dead Bodies: Reburial and Post socialist Change*. New York: Columbia University Press, 1999.

Völgyes, Iván. "Never Again '56: Cooptation, Privatization, and Terror in Hungarian Society since the Revolution." Pp. 521–25 in *The First War Between Socialist States: The Hungarian Revolution and its Impact* edited by Béla K. Király, Barbara Lotze, and Nándor Dreisziger. New York: Brooklyn College Press, 1984.

Winter, Jay. *Sites of Memory, Sites of Mourning: The Great War in European Cultural History*. Cambridge: Cambridge University Press, 1995.

Young, James E. "Between History and Memory: The Uncanny Voices of Historian and Survivor." *History and Memory*, 9, 1/2 (Fall:1997): 50–51, 56–57.

Závodszky, Géza. "A történészek deomokráciája vagy a demokrácia története? A tananyagszerkesztés néhány dilemmája a rendszerváltozás utan (1993)" (Democracy of historians or the history of democracy?—A few dilemmas of curriculum building after the regime change). Pp. 95, 99 in *Civil történelem: A Történelemtanárok Egyletének 15 Éve* (Civil history: 15 Years of the Association of Hungarian History Teachers). Budapest: Történelemtanárok Egylete, 2005.

Zinner, Paul E. "Revolution in Hungary: Reflections on the Vicissitudes of a Totalitarian System." *The Journal of Politics*, 21, 1 (February, 1959): 21, 29.

COLLECTIONS OF PRIMARY SOURCES
AND GOVERNMENT DOCUMENTS

A Compendium of Declassified Documents and Chronology of Events. Edited by Csaba Békés and Malcom Byrne. Political Transition in Hungary 1989–1990 International Conference. Budapest, Hungary, 1999. National Security Archive/Cold War History Research Center/1956 Institute.

Act LXXX of 1993 on Public Education of the Republic of Hungary.

Az Országgyűlés tavaszi ülésszakának 41. Ülésnapja 1996 (Minutes of Parliament, June 3–4, 11, 1996).

Fehér Könyv: A Magyar Köztársaság és demokrácia elleni összeesküvés okmányai, Harmadik kiadás (White Book: The documents of the conspiracy against the Hungarian Republic and Democracy, Third edition). Budapest: A Szikra Irodalmi és Lapkiadó vállalat, 1947.

Foreign Relations of the United States, 1944, III, The British Commonwealth and Europe. Washington: United States Printing Office.

Hegedűs, András, B. and, Rainer, János, M., ed. *A Petőfi Kör vitái: hiteles jegyzőkönyvek alapján, Két közgazdasági vita I* (The debates of the Petőfi Circle based on the minutes: Two debates on the economy, vol. I). Győr: Kelenföld Kiadó-ELTE, 1989.

Hegedűs, András B., ed. *A Petőfi Kör vitái: hiteles jegyzőkönyvek alapján: Gazdasági vezetés, Műszaki fejlesztés, Kertmagyarország? V* (The debates of the Petőfi Circle based on the minutes: Leadership in the economy, Technical development, Garden Hungary,? vol. V). Budapest: 1956-os Intézet, 1994.

Hungary, Ministry of Culture and Education. National Core Curriculum. 1996.

Iakovlev, A. N., ed. *Molotov, Malenkov, Kaganovich. 1957. Stenogramma iiun'skogo plenuma TsK I drugie dokumenty Molotov, Malenkov, Kaganovich. 1957* (Stenographic Report of the June Plenum of the Central Committee of the Communist Party of the Soviet Union and Other Documents). Moscow: Mezhdunarodnyi fond "Demokratiia," Guverovskii institute voiny, revoliustsii i mira, Stenfordskii universitet, 1998 (Moscow: International Fund "Democracy," and the Hoover Institute of War, Revolution and Peace, 1998) 158–61, 477, 535.

Kenedi, János. Kis Állambiztonsági olvasókönyv, I, II (Little State Security Textbook). Budapest: Magvető Kiadó, 1996.

Koltai, Ferenc, ed. *László Rajk and his Accomplices Before the People's Court.* Budapest: Budapest Printing Press, 1949.

Szigethy, Gábor, ed. *Jelenidőben:1956 Október 23* (Present tense: 1956 October 23). Budapest: Holnap Kiadó, 2003.

White Book: Information Bureau of the Council of Ministers of the Hungarian People's Republic, vol. 5, The Counterrevolutionary Conspiracy of Imre Nagy and His Accomplices. Budapest.

TEXTBOOKS AND CURRICULUM MATERIALS

Almási, János. *Történelem az Általános Gimnáziumok IV osztálya számára* (History for Gimnáziums IV). Budapest: Tankönyvkiadó, 1965.

Balogh, Endre and Mann, Miklós. *Történelem IV* (History IV). Budapest: Tankönyvkiadó, 1982.

———. *Történelem az Általános Gimnáziumok IV osztálya számára* (History for Gimnáziums IV). Budapest: Tankönyvkiadó, 1974.

Balogh, Sándor, et. al. *A Magyar népi demokrácia története, 1944–1962* (The history of the Hungarian People's Democracy). Budapest: Kossuth Tankönyvkiadó, 1978.

Benkes, Mihály. *Történelem IV, 1914–1994* (History IV, 1914–1994). Budapest: Cégér Kiadó, 1996.

Gyapay, Gábor. *Történelem IV* (History IV). Budapest: Corvinus Kiadó Kft., 2004.

Hornyák, Csaba, Kálmán, András, Kulcsár, Edit, and Mózer, Ibolya. *Új Érettségi: Történelem Tételek* (History Themes for the New School Leaving Exam). Budapest: Corvina Kiadó Kft., 2005.

Jóvérné Szirtes, Ágota. *Történelem IV Dolgozók Középiskola részére* (History IV for Worker's Secondary School). Budapest: Tankönyvkiadó, 1987.

Jóvérné Szirtes, Ágota, and Sipos, Péter. *Történelem Gimnáziumok IV Osztály* (History for Gimnáziums IV). Budapest: Tankönyvkiadó, 1990.

Kaposi, József, Szabó, Márta, and Száray, Miklós. *Feladat-gyűjtemény az új történelem irásbeli érettségihez, 12 évfolyam* (Collection of exercises for the new written school leaving exam, 12th year). Budapest: Nemzeti Tankönyvkiadó, 2005.

Repárszky, Ildikó and Dupcsik, Csaba. *Történelem IV* (History IV). Budapest: Műszaki Könyvkiadó, 2005.

Salamon, Konrád. *Történelem IV a Középiskolák számára* (History IV for Secondary Schools). Budapest: Nemzeti Tankönyvkiadó, 1996.

Spira, Györgyi. *A Magyar Nép Története, II Rész, 1526–1849* (The History of the Hungarian People, II, 1526–1849), Ideiglenes Tankönyv (Temporary Textbook). Budapest: Tankönyvkiadó, 1951.

Szamuely, et. al. *Történelem Általános Gimnázium IV* (History for Gimnáziums IV). Budapest: Tankönyvkiadó, 1961.

Unger, Mátyás. *Történelem –Az Általános Gimnáziumok III* (History for Gimnáziums III). Budapest: Tankönyvkiadó, 1964.

Vidor, Pálné et. al. *Irodalmi Szöveggyűjtemény III* (Collection of Literature). Budapest: Tankönyvkiadó, 1970.

Závodszky, Géza. *Történelem III, Gimnázium* (History for Gimnáziums III). Budapest: Tankönyvkiadó, 1980.

NEWSPAPERS, MAGAZINES, AND POPULAR JOURNALS

"A Szovjetunió Kommunista Pártjának XX Kongresszusa után" (After the 20th Congress of the Soviet Union's Communist Party). *Társadalmi Szemle*, 11, 3 (March, 1956): 16–20.

"A Pártélet további Demokratizálásának Utjai" (Further avenues to Democratizing the Party Life). *Társadalmi Szemle*, 11, 5 (May, 1956): 5–6.

Babus, Endre. "A Szent Korona rehabilitálása?" (Is it the rehabilitation of the Holy Crown?). *Heti Világgazdaság*, 37 (18 September 1999): 107–8.

Bozsik, József. "Hagyjanak békén, mondja Dudás" ("Leave me in peace," says Dudás). *Heti Magyarország*, 44 (October 29, 1993): 7.

Csuhaj, Ildikó, "Orbán Viktor 72 órás ultimátumot adott" (Viktor Orbán issues a 72 hour ultimatum). *Népszabadság*. 3 October 2006, 3.

———. "FIDESZ-Gyurcsány ne szólaljon meg az 56-os megemlékezéseken" (Gyurcsány should not speak at the 56 commemorations). *Népszabadság*. 12 October 2006, 2.

Fónay, Jénő. "Nagy Imre emberi nagyságat sértő törvény születhet" (A bill may be born that would hurt Imre Nagy's greatness). *Új Magyarország*. 18 May 1996, 4.

Fontaine, Andre. "Törvényesség, létbiztonság, reális távlat mindenkinek (Lawfulness, Security, A Realistic Future for Everybody): Kádár János interjúja a Parizsi LeMonde-nak" (János Kádár's interview for *LeMonde*). *Magyarország*, 23 (February, 1964): 4.

Göncöl, György, "Bandung és a békes együttlétezés elve" (Bandung and the Theory of Peaceful Coexistance). *Társadalmi Szemle*, 10, 5 (May, 1955): 95, 97.

Gréczy, Zsolt. "Két ünnepre készül a jobboldal?" (Does the right wing prepare for two celebrations?). *Népszabadság*. 16 June, 2006, 3.

———. "Nagy Imre csak a balodalé?" (Does Imre Nagy belong only to the left?). *Népszabadság*. 17 June 2006, 3.

———. "Zárt kapuk mögött, méltósággal, Biztonsági okok miatt az állami vezetők többsége lemondta részvételét az esti ünnepségeken" (Behind closed doors with dignity, due to security reasons the majority of the state leaders excused themselves from the evening celebrations). *Népszabadság*. 24 October 2007, 2.

Gyertyán, Ervin. "A temetés elé" (Before the funeral). *Népszava*. 5 October, 1956, 4.

Halda, Aliz. "Halda Aliz levelezése Gimes Miklós sirhelyének helyszínéről" (Aliz Halda's correspondence about the location of Miklós Gimes' gravesite). *Beszélő*, 24 (1988).

Hankó, Ildikó. "A Magyar Jeanne d'Arc, Te is tudod, hogy a vád hamis, csak a szent forradalmat akarják bemocskolni" (The Hungarian Jeanne d'Arc, You know too, that the accusation is fake, they just want to besmirch the holy revolution). *Magyar Demokrata*, 10, 2 (12 October 2006): 66.

Jobbágyi, Gábor. "56'Vérontó sortüzei" (Bloody Massacres of '56). *Heti Magyarország*, 43 (October 23, 1993): 6.

Kamm, Henry. "The Funeral of Imre Nagy." *New York Times*. 17 June, 1989, 6.

Kaufman, Michael T. "Forgotten in a Weedy Cemetery." *The Herald Tribune*. 28–29 June 1986.

Kornis, Mihály. "Kádár" (Magyar Dráma). *Beszélő*, 3 (May, 1996): 86, 89, 91.

Kövér, Béla. "301-es parcella Köztemető" (The Public Cemetery's Plot 301). *Magyar Nemzet*. 3 May 1989, 21.

Mászáros, Tamás. "Jobbra átérékelés" (Re-evaluation to the right). *168 óra*, 13, 4 (January 25, 2001): 10–11.

Patkó, Imre. "A Nép Rendőrsége" (A Police of the People). *Szabad Nép*. 15 August, 1947, 3.

———. "Az MKP Listavezetői Nagy Imre" (Imre Nagy from the top of the MKP list). *Szabad Nép*. 27 August, 1947, 3.

Pintér, Dezső. "Miniszterelnöki mérleg 16 hónap után" (Review of the Prime Minister after 16 months). *Magyar Hirlap*. 28 October 1988.

Schmidt, Maria. "Miért kell a kormánypártoknak Nagy Imre?/Miért nem támogatják a Szabad Demokraták az MSZP indítványát" (Why do the governing parties need Imre Nagy? Why the Free Democrats do not support the MSZP proposal?). *Népszabadság*. 4 June 1996, 10.

Szalai, József, "A Szocialista Törvényesség megszilárdításának néhány kérdése (A few questions about the strengthening of Socialist lawfulness)." *Társadalmi Szemle*, 11, 7 (July, 1956): 32–33.

Tarics, Péter. "Együtt emlékezünk, Wittner Mária: Példát kellene vennünk a lengyelekről" (Maria Wittner, "We will remember together, we should follow the Polish example"). *Magyar Demokrata*, 10, 2 (12 October 2006): 92–93.

Timmer, József. "Temetünk" (We Bury). *Népszava*. 7 October, 1956, 1.

Trencséni, Dávid. "Vakhit" (Blind belief). *168 óra*, 18, 36 (7 September 2006): 10–11.

———. "Ünnep az utcán" (Holiday in the streets). *168 óra*, 28, 43 (26 October 2006): 10.

Virág kedvelő (Flower lover). "Nap Története" (Story of the Day). *Demokrata* (1988).

TRANSCRIPTS

Hungarian Monitoring Service (MTI). "The Ceremony Begins." 19 June 1989.

Kossuth Rádió Transcript. "168 Hours," 4:00 P.M. 8 October 1988.

Kossuth Rádió Transcript. "Végtisztesség" (Final honor). 16 June 1989.

Kossuth Rádió Transcript. Esti Magazin (Evening Magazine), 6:30 P.M. 15 June 1989.

Radio Free Europe Transcript. Béla Lipták. "Searching for the Grave of Imre Nagy." *Wall Street Journal*, 15 October 1985.

FILM AND VIDEO

A temetés (The funeral). (16 June, 1989). Produced by Ferenc Székely. Budapest: Nyitott Szem (Open Eye) Különkiadás, 1989. Videocassette.

Egri Csillagok (Stars over Eger). Directed by Zoltán Várkonyi. Budapest: MOKÉP, Zrt., 1968. DVD.

Forró ősz a hidegháborúban-Magyarország 1956-ban (A Fiery Autumn in the Cold War-Hungary in 1956). Produced by Réka Sárközy. Budapest: 1956 Institute, 2006. DVD.

June 16, 1988. Budapest: Black Box, 1988. Vdeocassette.

June 16, 1989. Produced by Dér-Pesty. Budapest: Black Box, 1989. Videocassette.

Nagy Imre Élete és halhatatlansága (Imre Nagy's life and immortality). Produced by Róbert Bokor. Budapest: Hungarian Television, 1996. Videocassette.

Szegénylegények (The Roundup). Directed by Miklós Jancsó. Budapest: MOKÉP, Rt., 1965.

Tükörcserepek Magyarország-1956 (Cracked Mirror, Hungary 1956). Produced by Gábor Vitéz. Budapest: 1956 Institute/Hungarian Film Institute, 1996. Videocassette.

Index

About the Author

Karl Benziger is an associate professor of history and secondary education at Rhode Island College. Previously he taught social studies in New York City and was a co-founder of an interdisciplinary mini-school at South Shore High School in Brooklyn through an American Forum project funded by the Rockefeller Foundation. His association with Hungary was fostered through several Fulbright Teaching scholarships and a Civic Education Project grant funded through the Soros Foundation. In addition to several studies regarding history and memory in Hungary, he has worked with professors, social studies teachers, and students in Hungary and the United States developing global United States, American Studies, and World History curriculum. He is currently working on a project that examines the convergence of domestic and foreign policy in the United States 1956–1965. Whenever possible, he enjoys playing music and rediscovering the world anew with his family. He makes his home in Rhode Island with his wife Klara and two children Emese and George.

"Batthány Eternal Light Monument" (credit photo to James Ulrich)

"Imre Nagy Statue" (credit photo to James Ulrich)

"Imre Nagy gravesite, Plot 301" (credit author)

"Unknown freedom fighter gravesite, Plot 301" (credit author)

"Heroes Square" (credit photo to James Ulrich).

"Demonstration in the streets near Parliament, October 23, 2006" MTI Fotó, Zsolt Szigetváry.